SOCIETY FOR NEW TESTAMENT STUDIES

MONOGRAPH SERIES

General Editor: G. N. Stanton

66

STUDIES ON THE TESTAMENT OF JOB

Studies on the Testament of Job

edited by
MICHAEL A. KNIBB and
PIETER W. VAN DER HORST

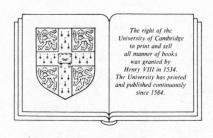

*The right of the
University of Cambridge
to print and sell
all manner of books
was granted by
Henry VIII in 1534.
The University has printed
and published continuously
since 1584.*

CAMBRIDGE UNIVERSITY PRESS

CAMBRIDGE
NEW YORK   PORT CHESTER
MELBOURNE   SYDNEY

Published by the Press Syndicate of the University of Cambridge
The Pitt Building, Trumpington Street, Cambridge CB2 1RP
40 West 20th Street, New York, NY 10011, USA
10 Stamford Road, Oakleigh, Melbourne 3166, Australia

First published 1989

Printed in Great Britain at the University Press, Cambridge

British Library cataloguing in publication data

Studies on the Testament of Job
1. Bible, O.T. Job – Critical studies
I. Knibb, Michael A.   II. Horst, Pieter
Willem van der   III. Society for New
Testament Studies   IV. Series
223'.106

Library of Congress cataloguing in publication data

Studies on the Testament of Job / edited by Michael A. Knibb and
Pieter W. van der Horst.
     p.   cm. – (Society for New Testament Studies monograph series
66)
Includes indexes.
ISBN 0 521 37216–X
1. Testament of Job – Criticism, interpretation, etc.   I. Knibb,
Michael A. (Michael Anthony), 1938–   .   II. Horst, Pieter Willem
van der.   III. Series: Monograph series (Society for New Testament
Studies) : 66.
BS1830.T17S78   1989
229'.914 – dc20   89-31416   CIP

ISBN 0 521 37216 X

C

6 0 0 3 5 6 7 6 0 3

WG

CONTENTS

v

ABBREVIATIONS

ALGHJ	Arbeiten zur Literatur und Geschichte des hellenistischen Judentums
BZNW	Beihefte zur Zeitschrift für die Neutestamentliche Wissenschaft
CB	Coniectanea Biblica
CBQ	*Catholic Biblical Quarterly*
CRINT	Compendia Rerum Iudaicarum ad Novum Testamentum
EncJud	*Encyclopaedia Judaica*
EWNT	*Exegetisches Wörterbuch zum Neuen Testament*
FRLANT	Forschungen zur Religion und Literatur des Alten und Neuen Testaments
GGA	*Göttingische Gelehrte Anzeigen*
HUCA	*Hebrew Union College Annual*
IDB	*Interpreter's Dictionary of the Bible*
JEH	*Journal of Ecclesiastical History*
JJS	*Journal of Jewish Studies*
JQR	*Jewish Quarterly Review*
JSHRZ	Jüdische Schriften aus hellenistisch-römischer Zeit
JüdLex	*Jüdisches Lexikon*
MGWJ	*Monatsschrift für Geschichte und Wissenschaft des Judentums*
NedThT	*Nederlands Theologisch Tijdschrift*
NovTest	Novum Testamentum
PsVTG	Pseudepigrapha Veteris Testamenti Graece
RAC	*Reallexikon für Antike und Christentum*
RB	*Revue Biblique*
RGG	*Die Religion in Geschichte und Gegenwart*
StUNT	Studien zur Umwelt des Neuen Testaments
Suppl Nov Test	Supplements to *Novum Testamentum*

SVTP	Studia in Veteris Testamenti Pseudepigrapha
ThR	*Theologische Revue*
ThSt B	*Theologische Studien*
TLZ	*Theologische Literaturzeitung*
TRE	*Theologische Realenzyklopädie*
TSt	Texts and Studies
TU	Texte und Untersuchungen
TWNT	*Theologisches Wörterbuch zum Neuen Testament*
UNT	Untersuchungen zum Neuen Testament
VT	*Vetus Testamentum*
WMANT	Wissenschaftliche Monographien zum Alten und Neuen Testament
WUNT	Wissenschaftliche Untersuchungen zum Neuen Testament
ZAW	*Zeitschrift für die Alttestamentliche Wissenschaft*
ZNW	*Zeitschrift für die Neutestamentliche Wissenschaft*

1

INTRODUCTION[1]

Pieter W. van der Horst and Michael A. Knibb

The SNTS Seminar on Early Jewish Writings and the New Testament took as its subject for 1986 and 1987 the Testament of Job (hereafter T. Job). This testament is one of the less familiar writings among the pseudepigrapha, but deserves — for reasons indicated below — to be more widely known. Since the five papers read at the two meetings cover between them several of the most important issues that arise in the study of T. Job it seemed desirable to the conveners of the Seminar (Knibb and Van der Horst) that they should be published as a group rather than scattered amongst different journals. The volume will, it is hoped, provide a comprehensive introduction to the study of this writing and serve to make it more accessible to scholars. Matters of a bibliographical, text-critical, literary-critical, exegetical and theological nature are all discussed in this volume, and the contributors include the two scholars who have most recently produced translations of and commentaries on this work.

During the sessions of the Seminar it became increasingly clear that T. Job sheds light on several aspects of ancient Judaism and early Christianity. In the first place, it is a fascinating example of early post-biblical haggada which deserves to be studied closely for its haggadic procedures and as such invites comparison with other writings of a similar midrashic nature. Secondly, T. Job is of interest from the view-point of the history of religions, for example in its image of Satan, its magical aspects and its ecstaticism. Thirdly, it sheds light on the Jewish background of the early Christian phenomenon of glossolalia ('the language of the angels'). Fourthly, T. Job has proved to be of impor-tance for women's studies in the field of early Judaism in view of the

---

[1] The first draft of this introduction was written by P. W. van der Horst. For details of the publications referred to in the introduction, see Spittler's bibliography at the end of chapter 2.

remarkable images of women in this treatise. And finally, the writing provides the background to the striking fact that the only time Job is mentioned in the New Testament, in James 5.11, it is solely his endurance that is mentioned. Most of these matters are dealt with extensively in this volume.

Chapter 2, by Professor Russell P. Spittler of Fuller Theological Seminary in Pasadena (California), contains a very valuable and complete history of research on and interpretation of T. Job, accompanied by an exhaustive bibliography from the beginnings up to 1987. Research can only be done fruitfully when the results of previous investigations can be consulted. Hence surveys of research and bibliographies are invaluable tools that may prevent the scholar from falling into pitfalls that can be avoided when the work of one's predecessors in the field is known. In this respect the bibliographies of Delling, Charlesworth and Schürer–Vermes–Miller–Goodman are so helpful. But it should be said that they are far from being complete, and for that reason the very detailed survey with accompanying bibliography by Spittler serves a real need and forms an important basis for further research.

During the last two decades two new editions of T. Job have seen the light of day, the first by Sebastian Brock in 1967, the second by Robert Kraft with three collaborators (of whom one was Spittler) in 1974. Both these editions are based on Greek manuscripts, of which there are only four, dating from the eleventh to the sixteenth century. Brock took as the basis of his edition the oldest manuscript, P; Kraft edited the sometimes widely differing text of S (fourteenth century) and V (thirteenth century). (The sixteenth-century manuscript is only a transcript of P.) For about twenty years, however, it has been known that there existed fragments of a Coptic papyrus containing a translation of T. Job. This papyrus is of a much earlier date than the oldest Greek manuscript, sc. of the fifth century, and the importance of this early version should not be underrated, however fragmentary the papyrus may be. The fact that its text is often shorter and sometimes longer than the Greek manuscripts causes intriguing and complicated problems for the textual critic of T. Job. Its speedy publication is a real desideratum after all these years (it has been in Cologne since as long ago as 1964). Hence it is of real importance that Dr Heinz J. Thissen and Dr Cornelia Römer, both researchers at the Papyrologische Abteilung of the Institut für Altertumskunde in

Cologne, present in this volume their preliminary report on the papyrus. After some preparatory work by M. Weber, they have recently taken over from him the task of editing this important textual witness. The edition, which they hope to be able to publish in 1989, will include a German translation and notes. In this volume Römer discusses the papyrological/codicological aspects, whereas Thissen presents his findings concerning the linguistic classification of the text. Both tend to date the text, on different grounds, to the early part of the fifth century. The implications of the nature of this textual witness, briefly discussed by them, are still to be spelt out in full, but will certainly make scholars rack their brains.

Chapter 4 is by Berndt Schaller, Professor of Ancient Judaism and New Testament Exegesis at the University of Göttingen. He is well known especially for his excellent German translation of T. Job (in JSHRZ) with its copious annotations and its well-balanced introduction, and is one of the best experts in the study of T. Job. Schaller presents a thorough criticism of the literary-critical methods of several of his predecessors and makes a new attempt to prove that the author of T. Job has consciously endeavoured to rewrite the traditions and sources at his disposal according to a uniform compositional concept. This is demonstrated in a detailed analysis of the four blocks of material Schaller has marked out, in which he points out the numerous cross-references between these blocks by means of catchword-links ('Stichwortverknüpfungen') and other redactional devices. So there is no reason to speak of interpolations or later additions, for all parts of the text in its present form have gone through the hands of the final author/redactor.

In view of this convincing analysis of the author's procedure, the material and conceptual discrepancies if not contradictions within T. Job become the more conspicuous and sometimes even enigmatic. There is much in this writing that cannot be reduced to a common ideological denominator. As far as there is such a common denominator at all, Schaller describes it with the words of 1 Tim. 4.7–8: 'Train yourself in godliness. For while bodily training is of little value, godliness is of value in every way, as it holds promise for the present life and also for the life to come.' Schaller emphasizes that our writing is not a theological treatise but 'a product of the ancient art of story-telling that aims at having an edifying effect upon the various fields of religious life'.

Whereas Schaller points out the author's efforts to unify, albeit superficially, the different strands of tradition, Pieter W. van der Horst, Senior Lecturer in New Testament and Early Jewish Studies at the University of Utrecht, stresses in his contribution the phenomenon of contradiction or disharmony within T. Job, especially with regard to the images of women. He argues that the images presented of women are diametrically opposed. On the one hand, Job's first wife is depicted certainly as a loyal and loving wife and mother, but also as a creature that is easily and continually led astray, does not have any spiritual insight and is characterized by a complete lack of awareness of where God or Satan are at work. On the other hand there are Job's daughters (from his second wife, Dinah, Jacob's daughter), who play such a leading and prominent role in the eight final chapters as to reduce Job and his sons to the status of super-numerary actors. They are spiritually highly gifted, have insight into heavenly realities, and speak the language of the angels. The depiction of the daughters creates a real reversal of roles in the story. The chapters on Job's daughters, so van der Horst contends, derive from a source other than those on Job's wife, and probably had their origin in an ecstatic-mystical group in which women played a or the leading role, a most unusual phenomenon in early Judaism.

In the final chapter, Dr Cees Haas, minister of the Reformed Church in Vlaardingen (the Netherlands), examines the theme of Job's perseverance in T. Job (which is the only quality for which Job is mentioned in the New Testament at all – James 5.11). He discusses all the passages in which *hypomonē*, *karteria* and *makrothymia* (and the related verbs) occur and tries to mark off their respective semantic fields and to indicate the overlappings. In contradistinction to the biblical book of Job, so it appears, the hero of T. Job is convinced that as a reward for his suffering and perseverance he will receive from God eternal bliss in heaven. This conviction turns out to have its origin in Hellenistic Jewish literature, especially the martyrological writings, and to have influenced heavily the New Testament and early Christian martyria.

This concise survey of the contents of this volume will make clear, the editors hope, that important steps forward have been made in the study of this fascinating pseudepigraphon. However, all the con-tributors are aware that these steps are only first steps, no more than a modest beginning of the research that has still to be done. For it is not to be denied that the study of T. Job is still in its infancy. Apart from the need to update the bibliography continually, let us try to give only a rough sketch of the tasks ahead of us. First and foremost is the need to have a full edition of all the Coptic fragments of T. Job, a desideratum that will, it is hoped, be fulfilled by the time this book appears. The publication of this Sahidic version may indicate that a completely new edition of the Greek text will be required. It may turn out to be impossible to reconstruct an 'Urtext' because of the too great divergencies between the respective textual witnesses (comparable to the situation in, for example, the *Hekhalot*-literature or the Greek *Physiologus*). Perhaps the edition of a synopsis will be the only way to do justice to the complexity of the textual tradition. A fresh study of the relationships between the various recensions will consequently be of paramount importance.

Only after more light has been shed on the problem of the original form of the text, if ever there was any such form, may problems of literary unity or non-unity be more satisfactorily solved. Also the problem of the sources, so boldly dealt with by Nicholls, has to be studied in a more refined way along the lines indicated by Schaller. This will require much sophistication and caution. As to conflicting images, not only those of women, but also the picture(s) of Satan must be studied, since, apart from the fact of his much-aggrandized role as compared to the biblical book (both MT and LXX), the images of Satan in the different parts of T. Job do not seem to be wholly reconcilable. With regard to the figure of Job himself, there is certainly a need for a full-scale study of the development of his image in all post-biblical literature, in other 'intertestamental' writings, in both Targumim, in the Midrashim and the haggadic portions of the Talmudim (e.g. *Bava Bathra* 15a–16b), and also in early Christian literature which may have been influenced by Jewish haggada (*pace* Ginzberg). There is no doubt that T. Job played an important part in the development of Job-Haggada, and its place in that development needs closer scrutiny.

Further, the problem of the origin and function of the various hymns or hymnic portions requires further study. Also the language of T. Job deserves closer analysis, for example as to the question whether the language of the longer recension/version is less Semitic than the shorter one or not. Now that the study of ancient magic is coming more to the forefront again, the magical elements in T. Job, especially in the closing chapters (46–53), should be studied anew, for they may shed fresh light on certain aspects of early Jewish magic. Another desideratum is an investigation of the purpose of the (final) author, especially of the target-group he had in mind. Contradictory solutions have been proposed for the problem of whom the author aimed at. A refined analysis on the basis of a new critical edition of the text(s) may bring this problem closer to a solution that will be acceptable to many scholars. Last but not least, when (some of) these preliminary studies have been done, the final task of students of T. Job will be to write a comprehensive commentary on this work, in which the results of previous research, as far as they have stood up to the test of criticism, are synthesized and remaining problems are, it is hoped, brought nearer to a solution. This task will demand much courage and require a mastery of several areas. But, if done with critical acumen, the final result will earn the commentator the gratitude of the scholarly world.

The editors would like to thank Mrs Katrina Larkin for kindly compiling the indexes. They would also like to thank Professor M. de Jonge of Leiden for advice and help.

2

THE TESTAMENT OF JOB: A HISTORY OF RESEARCH AND INTERPRETATION

Russell P. Spittler
Fuller Theological Seminary

For much of the modern period, the Testament of Job (T. Job) has been one of the lesser-known pseudepigraphic products of early Judaism. Approximately the length of the NT book of Romans, T. Job celebrates the virtue of patience (ὑπομονή) through a folkloristic elaboration of the biblical story of Job that may be compared in its method of treatment with the elaboration of incidents in the lives of the patriarchs by the author of the Testaments of the Twelve Patriarchs.

Early use

Ancient references

Among eight lists (ranging from the fourth to the fourteenth centuries) distinguishing biblical from non-canonical books,[1] only the sixth-century Gelasian Decree (5.6.4) mentions a 'Liber qui appellatur Testamentum Job, apocryphus'.[2] The same Decree (5.8.6), interestingly enough, proscribes 'Phylacteria': according to T. Job 47.11, it was by one such φυλακτήριον that Job was cured of his illness. M. R. James records the suggestion that T. Job 20.7−9 served as Tertullian's source for a reference to Job's worm-ridden illness (*De patientia* 14.5, *c*. AD 200−203),[3] and the same tradition appears in

---

[1] A.-M. Denis, *Introduction aux pseudépigraphes grecs d'Ancien Testament*, SVTP 1 (Leiden, E. J. Brill, 1970), XI−XVI.

[2] E. von Dobschütz, *Das Decretum Gelasium*, TU 38/4 (Leipzig, J. C. Hinrichs, 1912), 306.

[3] *The Lost Apocrypha of the OT* (London, SPCK, 1920), 93 n. 1. M. Delcor (independently?) noticed the same connection: 'Le Testament de Job, la prière de Nabonide et les traditions targoumiques', in S. Wagner (ed.), *Bibel und Qumran*, H. Bardtke Festschrift (Berlin, Evangelische Haupt-Bibelgesellschaft, 1968), 60−1.

the Visio Pauli as well as the Aboth de Rabbi Nathan.[4] The book, it seems, was as little used in ancient times as in the modern era.

Ancient versions

Until the query of Denis can be settled by evidence — 'une version latine est peut-être visée par Décret gélasien, [5.]6.4'[5] — one must say that T. Job is known in only two ancient versions, one of those as yet unpublished.

Coptic

When in 1968 M. Philonenko published his French translation, he brought to the attention of the academic world the existence of an incomplete fifth-century Coptic papyrus of T. Job.[6] Designated P. Köln 3221 and as yet unpublished, the MS is to appear 'sous peu sous le n° 4 dans l'édition des papyrus coptes de Cologne'.[7] The publication process was at first in the hands of Dr Manfred Weber of the University of Cologne, who gave access to the original text to B. Schaller for use in his preparation of the German translation of T. Job.[8] In late 1986, the editing of P. Köln 3221 was transferred to Dr Cornelia Römer and Dr Heinz J. Thissen of the same university (see their report below, pp. 33–45). As is clear from Philonenko's few remarks, 'ces exemples montrent que le codex de Cologne permettra de mieux établir le texte du Testament de Job'.[9]

---

[4] S. Schechter (ed.), *Aboth de Rabbi Nathan* (New York, Philipp Feldheim, 1945); ET, A. Cohen, *The Minor Tractates of the Talmud* (2 vols., London, Soncino, 1965), I, i–ix, 1–210; and J. Goldin, *The Fathers According to Rabbi Nathan* (New Haven, Yale University Press, 1955). See also K. Kohler in G. A. Kohut (ed.), *Semitic Studies in Memory of A. Kohut* (Berlin, Calvary, 1897), 277–8.

[5] Denis, *Introduction*, 101.

[6] M. Philonenko, 'Le Testament de Job. Introduction, traduction et notes', *Semitica* 18 (1968), 9, 61–3.

[7] *Ibid.*, 61, n. 2.

[8] B. Schaller, *Das Testament Hiobs*, JSHRZ, III, 3 (Gütersloh, Gerd Mohn, 1979), 317, n. 135.

[9] Philonenko, 'Le Testament de Job', 63.

Old Church Slavonic (AD X ?)

Three MSS, only one complete, of an Old Church Slavonic version of T. Job were critically edited by G. Polívka[10] in 1891, just a few years prior to the initial studies of James and Kohler. With a textual procedure similar to that of Brock,[11] Polívka printed as his text a MS known to have been owned by P. J. Šafarik (1795–1861),[12] placing in a critical apparatus the variant readings of two other MSS (Belgrade, National Library no. 149 (= N); Moscow, Rumjancov Museum, no. 1472 (= S)). N had been edited earlier by S. Novaković,[13] who had high praise for the work as an artistic tale. Since nearly half of N was missing, Novaković put the remainder into Serbocroatian from Migne's French translation.[14] Brock's edition of T. Job cites the Slavonic version in selected instances, but 'only where it clearly supports a Greek variant'.[15]

Greek manuscripts

T. Job survives mainly through four very late Greek MSS preserved in European libraries:

1. Paris, Bibliothèque Nationale, Fonds grec 2658, folia 72^r–97^r, AD XI (= P). According to the descriptive catalogue,[16] this MS contains (in order) four works: *Anonymi interpretatio nominum hebraicorum sacrae scripturae*; *Testamentum XII filiorum Jacob*; *Testamentum Jobi*; *Anastasii Sinaitae Interrogationes et responsiones*. It was this MS which James

---

[10] 'Apokrifna priča o Jovu', *Starine* (Antiquities: for the Yugoslav Academy of Sciences and Humanities, Zagreb) 24 (1891), 135–55. For details of additional Old Church Slavonic MSS not used by Polívka or Brock, see Schaller, *Das Testament*, 317, n. 134. No critical text for this version has been published.

[11] S. Brock, *Testamentum Iobi*, and J.-C. Picard, *Apocalypsis Baruchi*, PsVTG 2 (Leiden, E. J. Brill, 1967).

[12] The dates come from M. van Esbroeck, *Analecta Bollandiana* 86 (1968), 177, who observed in his review of Brock's edition that 'l'auteur parle comme si P. J. Šafarik (1795–1861) avait donné son nom à une ville pareille à Moscou ou Belgrade'.

[13] 'Apokrifna priča o Jovu', *Starine* 10 (1878), 157–70.

[14] By default then, a portion of T. Job exists in Serbocroatian.

[15] Brock, *Testamentum Iobi*, 7.

[16] H. Omont, *Inventaire sommaire des manuscrits grecs de la Bibliothèque Nationale et des autres bibliothèques de Paris et des départements* (4 vols., Paris, Ernest Leroux, 1886–98), 3.20.

published for the first time and Brock used as the basis of his edition.

2. Paris, Bibliothèque Nationale, Fonds grec 938, folia 172^v–192^v, AD XVI (= P^2). According to the MS catalogue,[17] T. Job appears as the last of a dozen (apparently Christian) works – again following Test12Patr. This MS is a copy of P.

3. Messina (Sicily) San Salvatore 29, folia 35^v–41^v, AD 1307[18] (= S). According to Brock,[19] the text of S is 'equal in value and indeed in places superior, to that of P'. The orthography of S 'is throughout very wild', and on fourteen occasions it doubles an intervocalic v.

4. Rome, Vatican gr. 1238, folia 340^v–349^v, AD 1195 (= V).[20] Both James[21] and Brock[22] adjudged V secondary on the basis of its expansive tendencies. It resembles the so-called Western text inasmuch as it stylizes, paraphrases, and harmonizes the text. Brock found that some of V's changes were 'carelessly made', while others showed a 'slightly Semitic flavor', which 'should be attributed to reminiscences of Septuagint Greek, rather than pointing to traces of a Semitic original'.

Modern research

Collations

1. Conybeare. In an article that gives the appearance of being incomplete and unclear in purpose, F. Conybeare reproduced T. Job

---

[17] *Ibid.*, 1.180.

[18] A description is given by A. Mancini, *Codices graeci monasterii messanensis S. Salvatoris* (Messina, D'Amico, 1907), 44–67. While Brock (p. 3) gives the date of this MS as AD 1307, a date of AD 1308 appears in the MS catalogue, H. Delehaye, 'Catalogus codicum hagiographicorum ...', *Analecta Bollandiana* 23 (1904), 33; cf. 41.

[19] *Testamentum Iobi*, 8–9.

[20] This MS is a palimpsest, whose lower script dates to the twelfth century: 'Die obere Schrift des Palimpsestes stammt aus dem Jahre 1195' (A. Ehrhard, *Überlieferung und Bestand der hagiographischen Literatur der griechischen Kirche*, vol. I = TU 50, (Leipzig, J. C. Hinrichs, 1937), 334, n. 2).

[21] *Apocrypha Anecdota*, II, TSt V, 1 (Cambridge University Press, 1897), xciii–xciv.

[22] *Testamentum Iobi*, 9.

1.1–4 and 47.9–53.8 from V.[23] Brock remarked that Conybeare 'evidently had a low opinion of the work' and that 'the transcription is not very accurate as far as it goes'.[24] This collation is now merely of historical interest.

2. Spitta. For inclusion in Spitta's major study of T. Job published in 1907, James furnished to him about three dozen corrections to James' own edition derived from his own collation of V, which by then he had identified.[25] On the basis of these corrections – which he felt were not so far-reaching as Battifol's review had made them out to be[26] – Spitta proceeded with his study of T. Job approving James' preference for P.

3. Mancini. It was A. Mancini's collation of S which was to introduce a third witness.[27] What was needed, Mancini said, was a third witness to provide an independent assessment of P and V: S could do just that. Mancini concluded that S is closer to V than to P and that two parallel traditions arise from the original: P on the one hand, and S and V on the other. Brock's stemma[28] reflects a similar conclusion.

Editions

1. Mai. The *editio princeps* of T. Job was published in 1833 by A. Mai in his ten-volume *Scriptorum veterum nova collectio a Vaticanis codicibus edita.*[29] Mai drew his text from a single MS of the twelfth century, Vaticanus gr 1238 (= V). Apart from a brief introductory description in his preface, Mai added only one footnote – enough to show he took T. Job to be a Christian

---

[23] F. Conybeare, 'The Testament of Job and the Testaments of the XII Patriarchs', *JQR* 13 (1901), 111–29. Test12Patr precedes T. Job in V as it does also in P and P².

[24] *Testamentum Iobi*, 5.

[25] From Battifol's review (*RB* 7 (1898), 302–4)? See n. 37.

[26] Spitta, F., 'Das Testament Hiobs und das Neue Testament', *Zur Geschichte und Literatur des Urchristentums*, 3/2 (Göttingen, Vandenhoeck und Ruprecht, 1907), 145.

[27] A. Mancini, 'Per la critica del "Testamentum Job"', *Rendiconti della Reale Accademia dei Lincei. Classe di scienze morali, storiche e filologiche*, serie quinta, 20 (1911), 479–502.

[28] *Testamentum Iobi*, 14.

[29] (Rome, Typis Vaticanis, 1833), 7.180–91.

work.[30] T. Job did not appear in J. Fabricius' collection of OT pseudepigrapha published more than a century earlier, not only because the text was virtually unknown but also because he favoured the reading 'Testamentum Jacobi' for 'Testamentum Job' in the Gelasian Decree (5.6.4).[31]

2. *James.* The standard text in the first two-thirds of the twentieth century[32] was published in 1897 by M.R. James.[33] He based his work on a personal reading of P. As the Vatican MS was unknown to James at the time, he used Mai's edition for variant readings of V noted in his critical apparatus. This procedure made errors inevitable. Some corrections were furnished by James to F. Spitta, who included them in his major study of T. Job published a decade later. James noted biblical parallels in the margin, provided a useful introduction and divided the text into the currently used fifty-three chapters. Struck both by its Jewish character and the abundance of NT words and phrases, James proposed that T. Job was produced by a second-century Christian, Jewish by birth, who — with no visible interest in patently Christianizing the text — freely put into Greek a Hebrew original and added his own Greek material, including T. Job 46−52 and the hymns (T. Job 25, 32, 33, 43).[34]

3. *Kohler.* In the same year that James' text was published, K. Kohler reprinted Mai's text, adding an English translation and an introduction that is valuable for its information concerning Jewish and Arabian folklore on Job.[35] Kohler concluded that T. Job had arisen in Essene circles, and specifically amongst the Therapeutae, and that the book was therefore pre-Christian. It is Kohler's introduction, rich in rabbinic lore, that is of abiding value and not his (= Mai's) text or the resultant translation.[36]

---

[30] *Scriptorum veterum nova collectio*, 7.191.

[31] Fabricius, *Codex pseudepigraphus veteris testamenti* (2 vols., 1, Hamburg, Sumptu Christiani Liebezeit, 1713; 2, Hamburg, Apud Felgineriam et Bohnium, 1741), 1.799.

[32] It was used for example in G. Lampe's *Patristic Greek Lexicon* (London, Clarendon Press, 1961−8), which treats T. Job vocabulary not found in H. Liddell and R. Scott, *A Greek−English Lexicon*, 9th edn (Oxford, Clarendon Press, 1940).

[33] M.R. James, *Apocrypha anecdota*, II, lxxii−cii, 104−37.

[34] *Ibid.*, xciii−xciv.

[35] K. Kohler, pp. 264−338 (addenda and corrigenda, 611−12), in Kohut (ed.), *Semitic Studies*.

[36] 'réédité, de façon parfois défectueuse' (Denis, *Introduction*, 100, n.1).

4. Brock. Since James had used, in addition to P, only Mai's edition of V – rather than Vaticanus gr 1238 itself – a new edition was necessary.[37] But it was seventy years in coming. In 1967 the current major edition of the text was published by S. P. Brock as volume 2 in the series Pseudepigrapha veteris testamenti graece.[38] After the publication of James' edition, A. Mancini had brought S to light and had published a collation of it with James' text. A.-M. Denis furnished Brock with photocopies of P, S and V;[39] Brock then produced a text consisting essentially of P with the variants of V and S in a critical apparatus, and with the variants of the Old Church Slavonic tradition – but for the most part only where these clearly support a Greek variant. In a few obvious cases, Brock relegated P to the apparatus and followed S or V (or, rarely, his own conjecture) for the text. He also provided a concise introduction wholly concerned with textual matters. Brock's text remains the standard until publication of the Coptic version will permit preparation of a full critical edition in the light of all known evidence. This is true even though Brock's edition, in his own words, 'does not aim at providing an eclectic text'.[40]

5. Kraft. As an outcome of rising interests in Jewish Greek literature, the Society for Biblical Literature (SBL) Pseudepigrapha Group specified T. Job as the topic for its 1974 annual meeting. R. Kraft, of the University of Pennsylvania, utilized his graduate seminar in the Spring of 1974 to prepare a fresh edition of T. Job. Continuing the intent of the SBL 'Texts and Translations' project – provision of inexpensive but reliable editions of original texts with facing translations – Kraft's seminar group published *The Testament of Job According to the SV Text*[41] in time for the 1974 annual meeting. Brock had based his edition on P, but Kraft produced an edition of the text which argued for affinities between S (which

---

[37] In a review of James' text (*RB* 7 (1898), 304), P. Battifol chided James for over-looking his own earlier identification of Mai's source as Vat gr 1238 published in *Bulletin critique* 10 (1889), 113.

[38] Brock, *Testamentum Iobi.*

[39] *Ibid.*, 5.

[40] *Ibid.*, 6.

[41] R. Kraft *et al.*, *Testament of Job According to the SV Text*, Texts and Translations, 5, Pseudepigrapha Series, 4 (Missoula, Montana, SBL, 1974). See 1974 bibliographic entries for J. J. Collins and H. C. Kee for two major studies of T. Job prepared for the same seminar.

spittler

Mancini had collated) and V. Kraft's edition of the Greek text with its accompanying English translation makes it the leading working edition in English.

The existence of two recent editions of the Greek text of T. Job (Brock and Kraft) yielded something like an embarrassment of riches that led one reviewer to a forgivable lament.[42]

Translations

1. French. The earliest translation into a modern language appeared during 1858 in J. Migne's French rendition of Mai's text for inclusion in his *Dictionnaire des apocryphes.*[43] A century later, M. Philonenko produced[44] a new French translation with brief notes and an introduction reviving Kohler's theory of a provenance among the Therapeutae.[45]

2. German. P. Riessler published the first German translation[46] as a part of his 1928 collection, *Altjüdisches Schrifttum ausserhalb der Bibel übersetzt und erklärt.*[47] He added a page of useful notes, in which he followed James in viewing T. Job as a first-century BC Jewish work subsequently paraphrased into Greek. Riessler added verse divisions to the chapter divisions of James, and the resulting chapter–verse enumeration has now become standard.

A half-century later, the publication of B. Schaller's new German translation put at the disposal of modern readers a competent

[42] N. Walter, *TLZ* 102 (1977), 359: 'Ein wenig bedauert man freilich, dass nun das Testament Hiobs gleich in zwei modernen Ausgaben vorliegt (die Textabweichungen sind so gering, dass man nicht einmal von zwei 'Rezensionen' sprechen kann), während andere ähnliche Pseudepigrapha immer noch in Ausgaben von vor 1900 schwer erreichbar sind.'

[43] Troisième et dernière encyclopédie théologique, 23–4 (2 vols., Paris, J. P. Migne, 1858), 2.401–20. Migne thought it useful to index a few fifteenth- to seventeenth-century plays inspired by the canonical book of Job. He provides a few notes, often textual.

[44] 'Le Testament de Job', *Semitica* 18 (1968).

[45] An origin among the Therapeutae had been maintained a decade earlier by Philonenko: 'Le Testament de Job et les Therapeutes', *Semitica* 8 (1958), 41–53.

[46] T. Job was not included in E. Kautzsch (ed.), *Die Apokryphen und Pseudepigraphen des Alten Testaments* (2 vols., Tübingen, J. C. B. Mohr, 1900). Nor was it included in the major English collection of R. H. Charles, *The Apocrypha and Pseudepigrapha of the Old Testament in English* (2 vols., Oxford, Clarendon, 1913).

[47] (Augsburg, B. Filser, 1928), 1104–34, 1333–4.

translation with very full notes and an introduction unexcelled in richness and insight.[48] This translation is part of an extensive series, 'Jüdische Schriften aus hellenistisch–römischer Zeit', which is an outcome of the renaissance in pseudepigraphic studies. Schaller also investigated 'Das Testament Hiobs und die Septuaginta-Übersetzung des Buches Hiob',[49] firmly concluding the priority of the LXX over T. Job.

3. English. K. Kohler included an English translation of Mai's transcription of V in his study published the same year as that of James (1897).[50] In a few cases Kohler's notes to his translation attempted recovery of what he believed to be the Hebrew original. James himself, near the end of his long and distinguished career,[51] published what amounts to be a (pseudo-!) Bible story book[52] which he dedicated to his grandchildren. His story of Job therein, based on T. Job, was never intended to be more than a simplified and selective paraphrase.[53] But it does yield a glimpse of James' overall understanding of the text. A second English paraphrase – restyled from Kohler's translation – was given as a sample of 'Re-Reading a Biblical Work' by N. Glatzer in 1961.[54] The paraphrase appears without notes and is appreciably abridged.

For his 1971 Harvard dissertation, R. Spittler prepared 'The Testament of Job: Introduction, Translation, and Notes'. Though Brock's text was mainly followed, significant variants were included with the translation in an apparatus. The translation from this dissertation underlay that which appeared in Kraft's edition, but it was modified according to the textual principles applied by Kraft in that edition. On the basis of his earlier work, Spittler revised

---

[48] Schaller, *Das Testament Hiobs*, 303–74; cf. n. 8.

[49] In *Biblica* 61 (1980), 377–406.

[50] K. Kohler in Kohut (ed.), *Semitic Studies*, 264–338 (addenda and corrigenda, 611–12).

[51] Towards a biography of James, see S. Lubbock, *A Memoir of Montague Rhodes James* (Cambridge University Press, 1939), and M. R. James, *Letters to a Friend*, ed. Gwendolen McBryde (London, Edward Arnold, 1956).

[52] *Old Testament Legends. Being Stories Out of Some of the Less-Known Apocryphal Books of the OT* (London, Longmans, Green and Company, 1913).

[53] T. Job 13, for example – difficult in translation – was entirely omitted from the paraphrase.

[54] N. Glatzer, *The Rest is Commentary: A Source Book of Judaic Antiquity* (Boston, Beacon Press, 1961), 98–112.

his translation and provided an introduction for T. Job in the Double-day pseudepigrapha.[55]

In 1984, Clarendon Press published *The Apocryphal Old Testament*.[56] It was originally intended and eventually published as a companion volume to M.R. James, *The Apocryphal New Testament*.[57] Clarendon Press was also the publisher of R.H. Charles' long-standard two-volume edition of *The Apocrypha and Pseudepigrapha of the Old Testament*.[58] The two smaller volumes provided a compact twin edition of 'apocryphal' works related to both of the Christian testaments. R. Thornhill provided the translation of T. Job included in the Clarendon volume, along with notes limited to matters of text and translation. The editor of the volume, H.F.D. Sparks, prepared the brief introduction and bibliography.

4. Modern Hebrew. In 1936/37 A. Kahana included a trans-lation of ספר דברי איוב in his collection of 'outside books' (הספרים החיצונים),[59] with both general and particular introductions and notes. In somewhat more popular style, A. Hartom included דברי איוב in his similar collection published in 1965.[60] Hartom provides more extensive notes than Kahana (in pointed Hebrew, as against Kahana's unpointed notes: the translations of both are in pointed Hebrew). Curiously, Hartom superimposed Kohler's verse divisions over James' chapter enumeration (Kahana follows the more desirable Riessler/Brock scheme). Kahana indicates the readings of V in his notes: Hartom gives variant readings of P and V by a system of brackets in the text of his translation. Both take T. Job to be Jewish in character and origin, though Hartom's popular style precludes any serious assessment of the text.

5. Other languages. According to J.H. Charlesworth, translations of the pseudepigrapha are planned for the languages of Denmark,

[55] R. Spittler, 'Testament of Job', in J.H. Charlesworth (ed.), *The Old Testament Pseudepigrapha* (2 vols., Garden City, NY, Doubleday, 1983–5), 1.829–68.
[56] H.F.D. Sparks (ed.), *The Apocryphal Old Testament* (Oxford, Clarendon Press, 1984). T. Job occupies pp. 617–48.
[57] (Oxford, Clarendon Press, 1924).
[58] (Oxford, Clarendon Press, 1913).
[59] A. Kahana, הספרים החיצונים (2 vols., Tel Aviv, Masada, 1st edn. 1936/7, 2nd edn. 1956), 1.515–38.
[60] A. Hartom, הספרים החיצונים (6 vols., Tel Aviv, Yavneh, 1965), 6.5–43.

Japan, Spain and Greece.[61] T. Job is projected for inclusion in the Japanese and Spanish versions.

Thus, T. Job flourishes in recent and adequate translations into French, German, Hebrew and English – all prepared since 1960.

Studies

Directions for subsequent major studies of T. Job were cast in the two 1897 introductions of James (second-century Christian, expanding and paraphrasing in Greek a first-century BC Hebrew original) and Kohler (pre-Christian, Essenic midrash – possibly originating with the Therapeutae).

A decade later F. Spitta published an extensive essay examining 'Das Testament Hiobs und das Neue Testament'[62] – prodded, it seems, by James' mild reprimand[63] of Spitta for overlooking the relevance of T. Job to Spitta's arguments that the NT letter of James is not at all Christian but Jewish. A major thrust of Spitta's work traced parallels in T. Job to the NT.[64] More significant, however, are his conclusions (1) that T. Job is pre-Christian but *not* Essene[65] and (2) that T. Job and the *Hioblegende* as a

---

[61] J. H. Charlesworth, 'A History of Pseudepigrapha Research: The Re-emerging Importance of the Pseudepigrapha', in H. Temporini and W. Haase (eds.), *Aufstieg und Niedergang der römischen Welt: Geschichte und Kultur Roms im Spiegel der neueren Forschung.* Teil II: *Principat*, 19/1 (Berlin/New York, Walter de Gruyter, 1979), 56–88. See esp. 64–73, with nn. 90, 93, 94, 95.

[62] F. Spitta, *Zur Geschichte*, 139–206.

[63] 'It is to be wished that he had taken into account the Testament of Job in his investigations; but, so far as I can see, he has, in common with well nigh all modern writers been unaware of its existence' (James, *Apocrypha Anecdota*, II, p. lxxxvi). Spitta (p. 170) quoted James' remark and added 'in der Tat war mir die Herausgabe des Hiobtestaments durch Mai unbekannt geblieben, und die Ausgabe von James erschien erst ein Jahr nach meiner Untersuchung über den Jakobusbrief'. Cf. F. Spitta, *Der Brief des Jakobus untersucht* (Göttingen, Vandenhoeck und Ruprecht, 1896), 140–1.

[64] Spitta, *Zur Geschichte*, 169–97.

[65] 'Somit kann doch wohl von essenischem Ursprung des Hiobtestamentes nicht die Rede sein. Es lässt sich überhaupt keiner besonderen Richtung des späteren Judentums zuweisen, sondern ist ein Denkmal der Volksfrömmigkeit in der sich natürlich manches "Untalmudische" findet' (*ibid.*, 165).

whole furnished a specific model on which NT writers presented Jesus the sufferer.[66]

The distinction of reintroducing modern studies in T. Job – of initiating their post-Qumran stage in research – falls to M. Philonenko of Strasburg. In 1958 he revived and strengthened Kohler's thesis of an origin among the Therapeutae by drawing attention to Qumran parallels.[67] A decade later, he published a French translation with brief notes and introduction.[68]

Likewise a Continental scholar – and also in 1968 – M. Delcor made a very substantial study of T. Job and its antecedents.[69] He traced certain agreements of 4QPrNab with T. Job: a (1) north Arabian (2) king (3) becomes ill (4) for seven years (5) in connection with idolatry. More significantly, Delcor offers specific arguments concluding that (1) the LXX interpolation at Job 2.9 derived from T. Job and (2) the invasion of Palestine by the Parthian general Pacorus in 40 BC provides, with 17.2 in mind, a *terminus a quo* for the work.[70]

In 1967 D. Rahnenführer's thesis on 'Das Testament des Hiob in seinem Verhältnis zum Neuen Testament' was accepted at Halle-Wittenberg University.[71] His central interest lay in tracing similarities of expression in T. Job and the NT as James and Spitta before him had done less systematically. But he also drew

[66] One must agree with Spitta (*ibid.*, 198) that 'die Parallelen sind in der Tat schlagend': both Job and Jesus (1) are of royal lineage, (2) aid the poor, (3) are opposed by Satan, who vainly attempts to cause their apostasy, (4) suffer ignominiously, (5) mediate forgiveness, (6) 'werden aus der νεκρότης erlöst', (7) are buried, yet (8) are elevated to God's throne. In detail, see Spitta, *ibid.*, 198–206.

[67] M. Philonenko, 'Le Testament de Job et les Thérapeutes', *Semitica* 8 (1958), 41–53.

[68] M. Philonenko, 'Le Testament de Job. Introduction, traduction et notes', *Semitica* 18 (1968), 1–75. This work originated as his 'thèse complémentaire' and does not reach the degree of thoroughness found in the same author's *Joseph et Aséneth: Introduction, texte critique, traduction et notes* (Leiden, E. J. Brill, 1968).

[69] Delcor, 'Le Testament de Job, la prière de Nabonide et les traditions targoumiques', 57–74.

[70] Riessler had earlier suggested Pacorus and the Arsacids (*Altjüdisches Schrifttum ausserhalb der Bibel* (Augsburg, Filser, 1928), 1337).

[71] Results published as D. Rahnenführer, 'Das Testament des Hiob und das Neue Testament', *ZNW* 62 (1971), 68–93.

some conclusions regarding date (late first century BC) and provided useful tables of 'Wortstatistik'.[72]

In 1982 Peter H. Nicholls submitted to the Hebrew University a thesis investigating the intent and literary structure of T. Job.[73] He discerns four underlying documents from which T. Job was edited, and he views the finally edited work as an effort to relieve God of any blame for Job's suffering. Nicholls dates the work in the first century BC, originating possibly in Egypt.

But use of T. Job has been made also in related studies, where T. Job was not the primary focus of investigation. Apart from its use in the major commentaries on the canonical Job,[74] T. Job was a major source for L. Ginzberg's *Legends of the Jews*.[75] Although P. Volz apparently did not use T. Job when (1903) he traced *Jüdische Eschatologie von Daniel bis Akiba*,[76] he knew it well (post-Spitta!) by 1910 in *Der Geist Gottes*.[77]

G. Gerleman made mature use of T. Job in his study of the LXX Job.[78] In a 1960 dissertation R. Carstensen relied heavily on evidence from T. Job in arguing that post-biblical Elihu traditions reflect

---

[72] Words in T. Job which occur only in the second century or later (162–3); words in T. Job which appear neither in NT nor LXX (164–8); words in T. Job which do not appear in the NT (169–76). 'Ungefähr 213 Wörter des TH [= T. Job] begegnen nicht in NT, doch 132 davon finden sich in der LXX. Lediglich 16 Vokabeln sind erst im 2. Jh. n. Chr. (9) oder später (7) belegt. Der Wortschatz des TH umfasst nahezu 1150 Vokabeln' (Rahnenführer, 178f.). Although this thesis has been carefully done, it is more concerned with lexical than with textual matters. The absence of συγχώρησις (T. Job 43.4 V) from the first of these lists suggests that Rahnenführer used only P in James' edition. (Page references in this note refer to the original dissertation, not to the published article.)

[73] P. H. Nicholls, 'The Structure and Purpose of the Testament of Job', doctoral dissertation, Hebrew University, Jerusalem.

[74] Such as those by Dhorme, Hölscher, Pope, Tur-Sinai.

[75] Trans. H. Szold and P. Radin (7 vols., Philadelphia, 1909–38). Stories about Job are collected in 2.225–42, notes in 5.381–90.

[76] (Tübingen and Leipzig, J. C. B. Mohr, 1903).

[77] See *Der Geist Gottes und die verwandten Erscheinungen im Alten Testament und im anschliessenden Judentum* (Tübingen, J. C. B. Mohr, 1910). E.g. p. 137, n. 2: 'Jede Engelssphäre hat ihre besondere Stimme (die "Engelszunge"), vgl. Hen 40 und besonders Test. Hiob 48–50; dies ist die Wurzel des Terminus ἐν γλώσσαις λαλεῖν.' T. Job also appeared (pp. 51, 269) in the second edition of *Jüdische Eschatologie von Daniel bis Akiba* published as *Die Eschatologie der jüdischen Gemeinde im neutestamentlichen Zeitalter* (Tübingen, J. C. B. Mohr, 1934).

[78] In *Studies in the Septuagint. I, Book of Job* (Lund, C. W.K. Gleerup, 1946).

proto-gnostic interests.[79] S. Currie included T. Job in his survey of extra-NT evidence for γλώσσαις λαλεῖν.[80] T. Job's relation to the canonical work figured in M. Glatzer's pursuit of the folklorist successors to biblical Job,[81] and its affinities with Merkabah mysticism were cited by E. Urbach.[82]

In 1982, under the supervision of J. Charlesworth, James A. Dumke drew heavily on T. Job for his study of the suffering of the righteous in nineteen Jewish apocryphal texts.[83]

It is also true that T. Job does not appear where one might expect, or hope, it would. So far as I can tell, it was not used in Strack – Billerbeck's *Kommentar zum NT aus Talmud und Midrasch* (4 vols., Munich, C. H. Beck, 1922–8) – certainly not at James 5.17; or in H. Bietenhard's *Die himmlische Welt im Urchristentum und Spätjudentum* (Tübingen, J. C. B. Mohr, 1951), where a treatment of T. Job 33 (e.g. ἐμοῦ ὁ θρόνος ἐν τῷ ὑπερκοσμίῳ ἐστίν) may have been appropriate. Although G. Scholem earlier methodologically ruled out the pseudepigrapha (*Major Trends in Jewish Mysticism* (New York, Schocken Books, 1946), 40), if he can speak of ApocAbr as 'a text that more closely resembles a Merkabah text than any other in Jewish apocalyptic literature' (*Jewish Gnosticism*, 2nd edn (New York, Jewish Theological Seminary, 1976), 23) one may hope that the relevance of such passages as T. Job 33.9 for Merkabah affinities might be considered also.

As for inclusion in *Einleitungen* to the OT and to the apocrypha and pseudepigrapha and in histories of Jewish literature and religion,

[79] 'The Persistence of the "Elihu" Point of View in Later Jewish Literature', unpublished Ph.D. dissertation, Vanderbilt University, 1960. Summarized as R. Carstensen, 'The Persistence of the "Elihu" Tradition in Later Jewish Writings', *Lexington Theological Quarterly* 2 (1967), 37–46.

[80] ' "Speaking in Tongues", Early Evidence outside the NT bearing on "glossais lalein" ', *Interpretation* 19 (1965), 274–94.

[81] N. Glatzer, *The Dimensions of Job* (New York, Schocken Books, 1969), 12–16. The same writer earlier produced an abridged translation of T. Job in *The Rest is Commentary*.

[82] 'The Traditions about Merkabah Mysticism in the Tannaitic Period' is the English title given for the article (in modern Hebrew) on pp. כה – א (= 1–28) in E. Urbach *et al.* (eds.), *Studies in Mysticism and Religion*, G. Scholem Festschrift (Jerusalem, Magnes Press, 1967).

[83] James A. Dumke, 'The Suffering of the Righteous in Jewish Apocryphal Literature', unpublished dissertation, Duke University, 1982. Summary in *Dissertation Abstracts International* 42 (July 1981), 261–A.

T. Job earlier in the century did not fare well. It was barely mentioned by Steuernagel, Strack or Székely,[84] and was not mentioned at all by Winter–Wünsche, Beek, Lods or Eissfeldt.[85] Two pages were devoted to it in the early Schürer[86] (who upheld James' view of T. Job as Christian, a view also supported by Boussett–Gressmann[87]). C. Torrey's important introduction to *The Apocryphal Literature*[88] anticipated contemporary studies in T. Job: his proposal for an Aramaic original was followed by R. Pfeiffer's *History of NT Times*.[89] With the publication of A.-M. Denis' *Introduction*[90] T. Job has achieved its deserved recognition.[91]

[84] C. Steuernagel, *Lehrbuch der Einleitung in das Alte Testament* (Tübingen, J. C. B. Mohr, 1912), 834; H. Strack, *Einleitung in das Alte Testament, einschliesslich Apokryphen und Pseudepigraphen* (Munich, C. H. Beck, 1898), 168, 233; S. Székely, *Bibliotheca apocrypha* (Freiburg im B., B. Herder, 1913), 1.383, 486.

[85] J. Winter and A. Wünsche, *Die jüdische Literatur seit Abschluss des Kanons* (3 vols., Berlin, M. Poppelaver, 1894–7); M. Beek, *Inleiding in de Joodse Apocalyptiek* (Haarlem, De Erven F. Bohn, 1950); A. Lods, *Histoire de la littérature hébraïque et juive* (Paris, Payot, 1950); O. Eissfeldt, *The Old Testament: An Introduction, Including the Apocrypha and Pseudepigrapha* (New York, Harper, 1965).

[86] E. Schürer, *Geschichte des jüdischen Volkes im Zeitalter Jesu Christi* (4 vols., Leipzig, J. C. Hinrichs, 3rd/4th edn, 1901–9), 3 (1909), 406–7.

[87] W. Bousset and H. Gressmann, *Die Religion des Judentums*, 3rd edn (Tübingen, J. C. B. Mohr, 1926), 45: 'in leichter christlicher Bearbeitung'; cf. 296–7, 396.

[88] (New Haven, Yale University Press, 1945), 140–5.

[89] (New York, Harper, 1949), 70–2. The same author listed T. Job among 'Palestinian Pseudepigrapha' in *The Interpreter's Bible*, 1 (1952), 421, 425.

[90] Denis, *Introduction*, 100–4. Some other introductions to apocryphal and pseudepigraphic literature are listed by Denis, p. XVIII, n. 18. An indication of the changing fortunes of T. Job emerges in its omission from L. Rost's *Einleitung in die alttestamentlichen Apokryphen und Pseudepigraphen einschliesslich der grossen Qumran-Handschriften* (Heidelberg, Quelle & Meyer, 1971; ET by D. Green as *Judaism Outside the Hebrew Canon: An Introduction to the Documents* (Nashville, Abingdon, 1976)) at midpoint in this thirty-year period – coupled with the inclusion of T. Job in a similar work at the end of the time by D. S. Russell, *The Old Testament Pseudepigrapha: Patriarchs and Prophets in Early Judaism* (Philadelphia, Fortress, 1987).

[91] Articles in encyclopaedias, past and present, give a mixed picture in regard to T. Job. The most important of these include K. Kohler, *Jewish Encyclopedia*, 7.200–2; J. Frey, *Supplément au Dictionnaire de la Bible*, 1.455; R. Meyer, *RGG*, 3rd edn, 3.361. *IDB* mentions T. Job under 'Pseudepigrapha' (3.961) but has no separate article on T. Job – even though the 'Book of the Resurrection of Christ by Bartholomew the Apostle', one of the fifth-/sixth-century AD 'Coptic fantasies', rates nearly a column (1.360–1). Others: G. Beer, *Realencyklopädie für protestantische Theologie und Kirche*, 16, 3rd edn (1905), 256; I. Bernfield, *Encyclopaedia Judaica*, 8 (1931), 74–5; H. Fuchs, *JüdLex*, 2 (1928), 1613; J. E. H. Thomson,

Thus, there have been two fertile periods in modern investigation of T. Job. The first was a fifteen-year period (1897–1911) spanning the turn of the century (James, Kohler, Spitta, Mancini). This period resulted in the first modern texts (James, Kohler), the first English translation (Kohler) and the first modern investigation (Spitta).

But then the fortunes of T. Job precisely illustrate what Charlesworth has identified as the 'Dark Clouds over Intertestamental Judaism (1914–1949)' – a period spanning the two World Wars and the Nazi era.[92] Other than the translations of Riessler and Kahana and notice by Torrey, scant attention was paid to T. Job during that period.

With the investigation of T. Job by Philonenko in 1958, the second fertile era of studies of T. Job – a thirty-year period (1958–1988) – began very slowly. Interest rose sharply following the publication of Brock's text in 1967. Since then two critical, though penultimate, editions of the Greek text have appeared. Fresh translations were prepared in French, German and English. At least three dissertations focused on T. Job. At midpoint in this period, the Society of Biblical Literature (1974) devoted one of its seminars to T. Job (Kraft, Collins, Kee). By the end of this period, the Studiorum Novi Testamenti Societas had devoted its pseudepigrapha seminar during two succeeding annual meetings (1986, 1987) to T. Job.

The early and middle 1980s, in fact, have gathered abundant harvest from the reassessment of Judaism at the turn of the era arising from the renaissance in the study of the apocrypha and pseudepigrapha.[93]

International Standard Bible Encyclopedia, 1 (1943 (1915)), 177–8: T. Job, 52, 53, 'decidedly … additions'; F. Spadafora, *Enciclopedia Cattolica* 6 (1951), 413–4; R. H. Pfeiffer, *Twentieth-Century Encyclopedia of Religious Knowledge*, 2 (1955), 925; M. Philonenko, *Biblisch-historisches Handwörterbuch*, 2 (1964), 726–7; R. J. Zwi Werblowsky and G. Wigoder (eds.), *Encyclopedia of the Jewish Religion* (New York, Holt, Rinehart, and Winston, 1966), 213: 'probably written in answer to the problem of pagan domination'.
[92] J. H. Charlesworth, *The Old Testament Pseudepigrapha and the New Testament* (Cambridge University Press, 1985), 10. See also D. Harrington, 'Research on the Jewish Pseudepigrapha During the 1970s', *CBQ* 42 (1980), 147–59.
[93] T. Job received full attention, for example, in G. Nickelsburg, *Jewish Literature Between the Bible and the Mishnah: A Historical and Literary Introduction* (Philadelphia, Fortress, 1981), 241–8; J. Collins, *Between Athens and Jerusalem: Jewish Identity in the Hellenistic Diaspora* (New York, Crossroad, 1983), 220–4; and the same author's chapters on (1) 'Testaments' in M. E. Stone (ed.), *Jewish Writings of the Second Temple Period; Apocrypha, Pseudepigapha, Qumran*

Despite remaining unclarities about its origin, T. Job is a clear contributor to the kaleidoscopic varieties of Hellenistic Judaism.

Still awaited for T. Job are (1) a critical edition of the Old Church Slavonic version using the MSS noticed by Schaller, (2) publication of the fifth-century Coptic MS and (3) eventual preparation of a critical edition of the text of T. Job.

Nearly a century ago, M.R. James complained that T. Job 'has attracted extremely little attention'.[94] The neglect has been rectified.

The Testament of Job: An Annotated Bibliography in Chronological Order

This bibliography surveys the history of research on T. Job. Some entries (especially certain encyclopaedia articles) are included for completeness, even though they may offer little that is original or new. The compiler would be deeply grateful to readers who would send notice of other items for inclusion. Address: Prof. R. Spittler, Fuller Theological Seminary, Pasadena, CA 91182, USA.

1833   Mai, A. *Scriptorum veterum nova collectio e Vaticanis codicibus edita* (Rome, Typis Vaticanis), 7.180–91. *Editio princeps*, using the V text. The sole note to the text concludes from the past tense of the term ἀνέστησε in the subscript (counting Job among those whom the Lord 'raised up') that the work is Christian.

1858   Migne, J.P. *Dictionnaire des apocryphes*, Troisième et dernière encyclopédie théologique, 23–4 (Paris, Migne), 2.401–20. First translation into a modern language. Based on Mai's text (= V).

1878   Novaković, S. 'Apokrifna priča o Jovu', *Starine: na sviet izdaje Jugoslavenska Akademija Zananosti i Unjetnosti* (Antiquities:

Sectarian Writings, Philo, Josephus (Assen, Van Gorcum; Philadelphia, Fortress, 1984), 325–55, and (2) 'The Testamentary Literature in Recent Scholarship', in R. Kraft and G. Nickelsburg (eds.), *Early Judaism and its Modern Interpreters* (Philadelphia, Fortress; Atlanta, Scholars Press, 1986), 268–85. Finally, the 'new Schürer' summarizes recent studies on T. Job: E. Schürer, *The History of the Jewish People in the Age of Jesus Christ, A New English Version*, revised and edited by G. Vermes, F. Millar and M. Goodman (4 vols., Edinburgh, T. & T. Clark, 1973–87), 3.1 (1986), 552–5.
[94] *Apocrypha Anecdota*, II, lxxii.

for the Yugoslav Academy of Sciences and Humanities, Zagreb), 10.157–70. An edition of one (= N) of the Old Church Slavonic MSS. Since half of the MS was missing, the editor put that portion of T. Job into Serbocroatian from Migne's French translation.

1891   Polívka, G. 'Apokrifna priča o Jovu', *Starine* 24.135–55. Critical edition of three Old Church Slavonic MSS. For details on other Old Church Slavonic MSS, see Schaller, *Das Testament Hiobs*, 317, n. 134.

1897   James, M. R. *Apocrypha anecdota*, II, TSt V,1 (Cambridge University Press). Introduction to T. Job lxxii–cii; Greek text of P (with some V variants noted from Mai) 104–37. Earlier standard text, with chapter divisions, used until Brock. Helpful introductory material; biblical parallels cited. 'If we think of [the author] as a Jew by birth, a Christian by faith, and as living in Egypt in the second or third century, we shall not, I believe, be far wrong ... He was putting into Greek a Hebrew Midrash on Job ... His work is not a literal translation of a Hebrew original: it is rather a paraphrase thereof in Greek ... Our author felt at liberty to make some additions to his original ... the longer speeches, the hymns [in chs. 25, 32, 33, 43], the similes [in chs. 4, 18, 27], and the whole of chs. 46–52, will have been inserted by the man who put the story into Greek' (xciv–xcvi). A similar technique of Christian Greek paraphrasing to that used in History of Asenath. Reviews: N. Bonwetsch, *TLZ* 19 (1897), 510: mentions Slavonic sources; P. Battifol, *RB* 7 (1898), 302–4.

Kohler, K. 'The Testament of Job: An Essene Midrash on the Book of Job Reedited and Translated with Introductory and Exegetical Notes', in *Semitic Studies in Memory of A. Kohut*, ed. G. A. Kohut (Berlin, Calvary), 264–338 (with addenda and corrigenda on 611–12). Mai's Greek text (= V) with English translation (sometimes flawed) and chapter/verse divisions differing from those of James. (A 'Concordance to the Chapter Numeration in James and Kohler' in Brock, *Testamentum Iobi*, 17.) Introduction focuses on Semitic, especially rabbinic and Muslim, folklore about Job. Sees T. Job as originating from Therapeutae 'in the outskirts of Palestine in the land of Haran, where the Nabateans lived, and the Essene brotherhoods spread it all over the Arabian lands' (295).

1900   Ehrhard, A. *Die altchristliche Literatur und ihre Erforschung von 1884–1900*. Erste Abteilung: *Die vornicänische Literatur*,

Strasburger theologische Studien, Supplementband 1 (Freiburg i. B., Herdersche Verlagshandlung, 1900; repr., Hildesheim/New York, George Olms Verlag, 1982), 179–80. Brief summary of Mai and James.

1901   Conybeare, F. 'The Testament of Job and the Testaments of the XII Patriarchs', *JQR* 13.111–27 transcribes the V text of 1.1–2 and 47.10–end, without significant comment.

Kohler, K. (and Toy, C.H.). 'Job, Testament of', in *Jewish Encyclopedia*, 7.200–2. Brief survey of scholarship followed by lengthy summary of contents. 'The work is one of the most remarkable productions of the pre-Christian era, explicable only when viewed in the light of ancient Hasidean practice.'

1904   Reitzenstein, R. *Poimandres: Studien zur griechisch-ägyptischen und frühchristlichen Literatur* (Leipzig, B.G. Teubner), 56–9. T. Job 'zwischen Christentum und Judentum steht ...' The episode of Job's daughters using the language of the angels illumines the pagan gnostic text Poimandres.

1905   Beer, G. 'Pseudepigraphen des AT' (no. 32 = T. Job), in *Real-encyklopädie für protestantische Theologie und Kirche* 16.256 (= *New Schaff Herzog Encyclopaedia of Religious Knowledge*, 9 (1911), 340). Bare mention of T. Job.

Nestle, E. 'Miscellen: 8. Zum Testament Hiobs', *ZAW* 25 (1905), 208–9. Conybeare's work (1901) could have been eased considerably had he known and used James (1897). 'Warum keine der neuen Sammlungen (Kautzsch, Hennecke) eine Übersetzung desselben [T. Job] brachte, weiss ich nicht.' A few corrections to James are made.

1907   Spitta, F. 'Das Testament Hiobs und das Neue Testament', *Zur Geschichte und Literatur des Urchristentums*, 3/2 (Göttingen, Vandenhoeck und Ruprecht), 132–206. T. Job is a pre-Christian but not Essene product of Jewish popular piety. It furnished NT writers with a model for Jesus as sufferer. Includes some corrections of Mai's text of V provided by James.

1909   Schürer, E. *Geschichte des jüdischen Volkes im Zeitalter Jesu Christi*, 3rd/4th edn (Leipzig, Hinrichs), 3.406–7. Earlier editions contained no mention of T. Job. Follows James, despite Spitta's arguments, in seeing T. Job as a Christian work. See below (1986) for the 'new Schürer'.

1910/25 Ginzberg, L. *Legends of the Jews* (Philadelphia, Jewish Publication Society), 2.225–42, and notes in 5.381–90. Synthetic overview of Jewish materials on Job, including T. Job.

1911   Charles, R.H. 'Apocalyptic Literature', *Encyclopedia Brittanica*, 11th edn, 2.169–75. Refers favourably to Kohler's theory of Essenic origin for T. Job. Charles did not include T. Job in his 1913 collection of *Apocrypha and Pseudepigrapha of the OT*.

        Mancini, A. 'Per la critica del Testamentum Job', *Rendiconti della Reale Accademia dei Lincei. Classe di scienze morali, storiche e filologiche*, serie quinta, 20.479–502. Collation of S with P (James) and V (Mai), with some philological and text-critical observations.

1913   James, M.R. *Old Testament Legends, Being Stories out of Some of the Less-Known Apocryphal Books of the OT* (London, Longmans, Green and Company). A simplified and selective paraphrase of T. Job appears in this storybook dedicated to James' grandchildren. Not a technical work.

1915   Thomson, J.E.H. 'Apocalyptic Literature IV: Testaments, (4) Testament of Job', *International Standard Bible Encyclopedia*, 1.177–8. Palestinian (?) Jewish work translated into Greek by a Christian, with some additions.

1920   James, M.R. *The Lost Apocrypha of the OT – Their Titles and Fragments*, Translations of Early Documents, 1/14 (London, SPCK), 93. Reports the suggestion of H. Bate that T. Job 20.9 is alluded to by Tertullian in *De patientia* 13.

1926   Bousset, W. and Gressman, H. *Die Religion des Judentums im späthellenistischen Zeitalter*, Handbuch zum NT 21, 3rd edn, (Tübingen, J.C.B. Mohr), 45. T. Job contains Jewish legends with traces of Christian editing (see p. 396).

1928   Frey, J.B. 'Apocryphes de l'Ancien Testament' (no. 16 = Quelques apocryphes plus tardifs ou fragmentaires: 2° le Testament de Job), in *Supplément au Dictionnaire de la Bible*, 1.455. General summary of past research.

        Riessler, P. *Altjüdisches Schrifttum ausserhalb der Bibel* (Augsburg, Filser), 1104–34 (German translation with new versification later followed by Brock), and 1333–4 (introduction and notes). Sees T. Job as an Essenic Hebrew midrash on Job composed in the first century BC and later rendered paraphrastically into Greek.

1931   Bernfeld, I. 'Hiobs Testament', in *Encyclopedia Judaica*, 8.74–5. A propaganda document emphasizing conversion of pagans to Judaism; potentially useful for Christians as well as Jews.

1936/7 Kahana, A. הספרים החיצונים (Tel Aviv, Masada), 1.515–38.

Modern Hebrew translation using Riessler's chapter/verse divisions (2nd edn, 1956).

1945   Torrey, C.C. *The Apocryphal Literature: A Brief Introduction* (New Haven, Yale University Press), 140–5. Posits first-century BC Aramaic original.

1946   Gerleman, G. *Studies in the Septuagint* I, *Book of Job*, Lund Universitets Årsskrift, 43/2, (Lund, C.W.K. Gleerup), 60–3. The appendix to LXX Job may derive from a possible Hebrew original of T. Job.

1947   Stevenson, W.B. *The Poem of Job: A Literary Study with a New Translation* (London, Oxford University Press), 78–80. As received, not a unity. Contains 'what may be called Gnostic elements'. T. Job provides evidence of an independent folk tradition about Job, along with references ranging from Babylonian theodicy, through James 5.11, the Visio Pauli, Theodore of Mopsuestia and the Koran to Yemenite and Moroccan Spanish folklore.

1949   Pfeiffer, R.H. *History of NT Times* (New York, Harper), 70–2. See also his article in *The Twentieth Century Encyclopedia of Religious Knowledge*, 2 (1955), 925. 'A pre-Christian legendary biography [midrash] written in Aramaic [in Palestine], ... probably ... in the last century before our era, and translated soon after'. LXX Job used T. Job as a source. 'The religious teaching of the book is characteristic of the Hasidim.'

1951   Spadafora, F. 'Giobbe V: Testamento de G.', in *Enciclopedia Cattolica*, 6.413–4. Jewish, from AD second century.

1958   Philonenko, M. 'Le Testament de Job et les Thérapeutes', *Semitica* 8.41–53. Additional arguments drawing also on Qumran parallels, in support of Kohler's thesis of an origin among the Egyptian Jewish sectarian group described by Philo.

1959   Meyer, R. 'Hiobstestament', in *RGG*, 3rd edn, 3.361. T. Job is probably a freely reworked Christian edition of a Hebrew, possibly Essenic, *Vorlage*.

1960   Carstensen, R. 'The Persistence of the "Elihu" Point of View in Later Jewish Literature', unpublished Vanderbilt University Ph.D. dissertation, summarized in *Lexington Theological Quarterly* 2 (1967), 37–46. Relies heavily on T. Job material to argue that post-biblical Elihu traditions reflect proto-gnostic interests.

1961   Glatzer, N. *The Rest is Commentary. A Source Book of Judaic*

Antiquity, Beacon Texts in the Judaic Tradition, 1 (Boston, Beacon). Chapter 5 contains an abridged English translation of T. Job.

1962 Fritsch, C. 'Pseudepigrapha', in *IDB*, 3.961. Aramaic midrash on Job from first century BC.

1964 Philonenko, M. 'Hiobs Testament', in *Biblisch-historisches Handwörterbuch*, 2.726–7.

1965 Currie, S. ' "Speaking in Tongues", Early Evidence outside the NT bearing on "glossais lalein" ', *Interpretation* 19.274–94. Discusses T. Job 48–50.

Hartom, A. S. הספרים החיצונים (Tel Aviv, Yavneh), 6.1–42. Modern Hebrew translation mixing Kohler's verse divisions with James' chapter divisions. More popular in style than Kahana's 1936/7 rendering.

1966 Glatzer, N. 'The Book of Job and its Interpreters', in *Biblical Motifs*, ed. A. Altman, Brandeis Studies and Texts, 3 (Cambridge, Massachusetts, Harvard University Press), 197–200. T. Job is the best documentation of Job pictured as a saint. Hebrew original probably composed in first century BC.

Werblowsky, R. J. Zwi and Wigoder, G., 'Job, Testament of', in the *Encyclopedia of the Jewish Religion*, 213. 'Probably written in answer to the problem of pagan domination.'

1967 Brock, S. P. *Testamentum Iobi*, and Picard, J.-C. *Apocalypsis Baruchi graece*, PsVTG, 2 (Leiden, E. J. Brill). Re-edits P, noting all significant variations in S and V, and selected variants in Slav. Useful introduction covering the characteristics and interrelations of the text witnesses. Reviews: G. Fohrer, *ZAW* 80 (1968), 428–9; M. van Esbroeck, *Analecta Bollandiana* 86 (1968), 177–9.

Rahnenführer, D. 'Das Testament des Hiob in seinem Verhältnis zum NT', Halle-Wittenberg University doctoral dissertation. Focuses on lexical correspondences with NT vocabulary. Dates T. Job in late first century BC. See Rahnenführer, 1971.

Urbach, E. 'The Traditions about Merkabah Mysticism in the Tannaitic Period' (in modern Hebrew), in E. Urbach *et al.* (eds.), *Studies in Mysticism and Religion*, Festschrift for G. Scholem (Jerusalem, Magnes Press), 1–28. Includes discussion of affinities of T. Job materials with Merkabah mysticism.

1968 Delcor, M. 'Le Testament de Job, la prière de Nabonide et les traditions targoumiques', in S. Wagner (ed.), *Bibel und Qumran*,

H. Bardtke Festschrift (Berlin, Evangelische Hauptbibel-
gesellschaft), 54–74. Concludes that the Greek interpolation at
Job 2.9LXX derives from T. Job and that T. Job 17.1 alludes
to the invasion of Palestine by Pacorus in 40 BC, after which
T. Job was composed.

Philonenko, M. 'Le Testament de Job. Introduction, traduction
et notes', *Semitica* 18.1–75. French translation with brief
notes and introduction. Original language of T. Job not
determined – at least parts come from Hebrew (e.g. ch. 43).
An authentically Jewish writing from an Egyptian Therapeutic
origin, from first Christian century (pre-AD 70). Also announced
existence of the Coptic version.

1969 Glatzer, N. *The Dimensions of Job* (New York, Schocken). 'The
Folk Tale Tradition' is traced on pp. 12–16, including T. Job
material.

1970 Denis, A.-M. *Introduction aux pseudépigraphes grecs d'Ancien
Testament*, SVTP, 1 (Leiden, E. J. Brill), 100–5. Summarizes
and catalogues previous work.

Jacobs, I. 'Literary Motifs in the Testament of Job', *JJS* 21.1–10.
T. Job is an early sample of Jewish martyr literature, distinctively
featuring a convert who suffers for his faith.

1971 Spittler, R. 'The Testament of Job: Introduction, Translation, and
Notes', unpublished Harvard Ph.D. dissertation. Favours
Kohler–Philonenko theory of origin among the Therapeutae
but also suggests possibility of Montanist redaction around the
year AD 194. Closely literal English translation and extensive
notes. Revised and published in J. H. Charlesworth, *The Old
Testament Pseudepigrapha* (Doubleday, 1983), 1.829–68.

Rahnenführer, D. 'Das Testament des Hiob und das Neue Testament', *ZNW* 62.68–93. Summarizes his 1967 doctoral dissertation at Halle-Wittenberg. Pre-Christian, originally Greek,
example of Hellenistic Jewish missionary literature. Useful
data on the vocabulary of T. Job and its affinities with the NT.

Wacholder, B.-Z. 'Job, Testament of', in *EncJud*, 2nd edn,
10.129–30. The present Greek text is 'closely linked with the
Greco-Jewish historian Aristeas ... and with the Greek version of
Job', and is based on a Hebrew or Aramaic model (from
Palestinian–Qumranic background), with later additions and
probably also abridgements. No Christian editing is present.
Therapeutae produced the Greek form. Referred to in James
5.11.

1974 Collins, J. J. 'Structure and Meaning in the Testament of Job', in G. MacRae (ed.), *Society of Biblical Literature: 1974 Seminar Papers*, 1.35–52 (Cambridge, Massachusetts, SBL). Views T. Job as a coherent first-century AD product of Egyptian Judaism. Valuable suggestions regarding opposition between Job and others (notably Satan, his friends, and his wife) as a possible clue to the underlying structural unity of the work. The same author describes structure, summarizes content and sketches the low view of womankind in M. E. Stone (ed.), *Jewish Writings of the Second Temple Period* (Philadelphia, Fortress Press, 1984), 349–54.

Kee, H. C. 'Satan, Magic, and Salvation in the Testament of Job', in G. Macrae (ed.), *Society of Biblical Literature: 1974 Seminar Papers*, 1.53–76 (Cambridge, Massachusetts, SBL). T. Job is a first-century AD text, originally Greek, most closely aligned with magical and mystical features of early Merkabah mysticism. Its eschatology is a temporal process – modelled by Job's endurance – and hence not gnostic.

Kraft, R. A. (ed.), with H. Attridge, R. Spittler and J. Timbie. *The Testament of Job According to the SV Text*, Texts and Translations, 5, Pseudepigrapha series, 4 (Missoula, Montana, SBL). Valuable notes on the textual history of T. Job and an extensive bibliography. Reviews: B. Malina, *CBQ* 38 (1976), 112; N. Walter, *TLZ* 102 (1977), 358f.; G. Mayer, *ThR* 44 (1979), 223.

1977 Licht, J. 'The Significance of the Book "Testament of Job"', in A. Shinan (ed.), *Proceedings of the Sixth World Congress of Jewish Studies: Hebrew University, August 13–19, 1973* (Jerusalem: World Union of Jewish Studies), 1.147–51 (in modern Hebrew). Origins unclear, but T. Job is unique and worthy. Closest to T. Abr and T. Isaac. Stresses leading Jewish themes: struggle with evil, everlasting life, proper burial. Unlike canonical Job, T. Job only hints at a God behind the scenes.

1979 Dautzenberg, G. 'Glossolalie', *RAC*, 11.225–46. T. Job as a Hellenistic Jewish text which equates glossolalia with the language of the angels points towards a Jewish Christian origin for speaking in tongues.

Schaller, B. *Das Testament Hiob*, JSHRZ, III, 3 (Gütersloh, Gütersloher Verlagshaus Gerd Mohn, 1979). Now the major German translation, with introduction and notes. Sees T. Job as of strictly Jewish origin, composed in Greek between 100 BC and AD 150, but its exact origin must be left open.

1980   Dumke, James A. 'The Suffering of the Righteous in Jewish
        Apocryphal Literature', Ph.D. dissertation, Duke University.
        T. Job figures prominently among the nineteen pseudepigrapha
        treated.

        von Nordheim, E. *Die Lehre der Alten*, I, *Das Testament als
        Literaturgattung im Judentum der hellenistisch-römischen Zeit*,
        ALGHJ, 13.1 (Leiden, E. J. Brill), 119–35. Except for the
        absence of future predictions characteristic of the genre, 'uns
        im TestHiob durchaus die Form des Testamentes wieder-
        begegnet'.

        Schaller, B. 'Das Testament Hiobs und die Septuaginta-Übersetzung
        des Buches Hiob', *Biblica* 61.377–406. Concludes that T. Job
        always derives from the LXX and that it does not provide the
        source, as M. R. James had suggested, for LXX additions to the
        Hebrew text of the biblical Job.

1981   VanderKam, J. C. 'Intertestamental Pronouncement Stories',
        Semeia 20 (1981), 65–72. A survey of most of the pseud-
        epigraphic literature shows T. Job to be second only to Ahiqar
        in the use of the apophthegmatic form. All ten examples found
        in Ahiqar are of the 'Inquiry' type. Six 'corrections' and two
        'commentaries' appear in T. Job.

1982   Nicholls, P. H. 'The Structure and Purpose of the Testament of
        Job', Ph.D. dissertation, Hebrew University. Four written
        sources lie behind T. Job: one in T. Job 1–27, two in T. Job
        28–46, and a fourth accounts for the shift in person at T. Job
        46–52. T. Job relieves God of any blame for Job's illness.
        Composed in Greek in the first century AD.

1983   Spittler, R. P. 'The Testament of Job', in J. H. Charlesworth (ed.),
        The Old Testament Pseudepigrapha (New York, Doubleday),
        1.829–68. English translation, notes, and introduction revised
        from his 1971 Harvard dissertation.

1984   Thornhill, R. 'The Testament of Job', in H. F. D. Sparks (ed.),
        The Apocryphal Old Testament (New York, Oxford University
        Press), 617–48. English translation with notes limited to text
        and translation. Brief introduction by Sparks.

1986   Van der Horst, P. W. 'The Role of Women in the Testament
        of Job', *NedThT* 40 (1986), 273–89. Despite her noble sacrificial
        labour to feed her impoverished and ill husband, Job's first
        wife is easily duped by Satan and figures as a model of the
        unilluminated. The daughters mentioned in T. Job 46–53,
        on the other hand, are virtually transformed into heavenly

beings by the glossolalia-inducing capacities of the golden girdles given them by Job. T. Job 46–53 thus comes from a different hand – probably from an unidentified Jewish mystical and ecstatic circle, and possibly from one such woman herself. See below, pp. 93–116 (a revised version).

Schürer, E. *The History of the Jewish People in the Age of Jesus Christ*, A New English Version revised and edited by G. Vermes, F. Millar and M. Goodman (4 vols., Edinburgh, T. & T. Clark, 1973–87), 3.1 (1986), 552–5. Composed in Greek, probably before AD 200. 'There is nothing indisputably Christian in any of the work, and its Jewish origin should be accepted.' The proposal for a later Montanist redaction is 'very hypothetical'.

Supplement

1987   Philonenko, M. 'Le Testament de Job', in A. Dupont-Sommer et M. Philonenko (eds.), *La Bible: écrits intertestamentaires* (Paris: Gallimard), 1605–45. Translation with very brief annotations.

Piñero, A. 'Testamento de Job', in A. Diez-Macho (ed.) *Apocrifos del Antiguo Testamento*. Tomo V: *Testamentos o discursos de adios* (Madrid: Ediciones Cristiandad), 161–216. Introduction, Spanish translation, extensive annotation.

Russell, D.S. *The Old Testament Pseudepigrapha: Patriarchs and Prophets in Early Judaism* (Philadelphia, Fortress), 60–8. May have originated amongst the Therapeutae, 'but in any case is a Jewish work with, perhaps, some degree of Christian influence'.

3

P. KÖLN INV. NR. 3221: DAS TESTAMENT DES HIOB IN KOPTISCHER SPRACHE. EIN VORBERICHT

Cornelia Römer und Heinz J. Thissen
Institut für Altertumskunde der Universität zu Köln

Die Papyrussammlung am Institut für Altertumskunde der Universität Köln besitzt seit 1964 umfangreiche Teile eines Papyruskodex in koptischer Sprache. Bald nach dem Erwerb wurde der Inhalt des Kodex von L. Koenen und M. Weber identifiziert. Es handelt sich um eine Sammlung apokrypher Texte, unter denen das Testament Hiobs und das Testament Abrahams den größten Anteil haben. Größere Textpartien sind außerdem aus den Acta Petri et Andreae erhalten. Ein kleines Fragment, ebenfalls zum Kodex gehörig, trägt wenige Zeilen aus dem Testament des Adam.

Der interessanteste Text dieser Sammlung dürfte das Testament Hiobs sein. Der Kölner Kodex ist der einzige Textzeuge in koptischer Sprache und der früheste Textzeuge überhaupt. Die älteste Handschrift des griechischen Textes stammt aus dem 11. Jahrhundert. Unser Kodex dürfte dagegen schon dem 5. Jahrhundert angehören. In einem Addendum zur Übersetzung des Testamentum Hiobs von Mark Philonenko[1] hatte Manfred Weber 1968 bereits auf die Bedeutung des Kölner Kodex hingewiesen. So konnte Berndt Schaller in seiner Übersetzung des griechischen Textes von 1979[2] schon eine von ihm selbst erstellte erste Abschrift des koptischen Textes in seinem kritischen Apparat verwerten.

Zu Beginn dieses Jahres wurde die Bearbeitung des Kodex den obengenannten übertragen.

Wir haben uns bisher nur mit dem Testament Hiobs beschäftigt, den Text weitgehend kontrolliert und an einigen Stellen gegenüber der Erstabschrift verbessern können. Trotz dieser Beschränkung auf den

---

[1] 'Le Testament de Job', *Semitica* 18 (1968), 61–3.
[2] JSHRZ, III, 3; s. besonders S. 318 mit Anm. 144.

Text des Testamentum Hiobs war es nötig, sich eine Vorstellung vom
Aussehen des gesamten erhaltenen Kodexteiles zu machen, um
eventuell noch Fragmente zusammenfügen zu können und eine bessere
Einsicht über noch fehlende Textpartien zu bekommen.

Die Fragmente waren bisher unsystematisch nur ihrer laufenden
Nummer folgend verglast. Es gibt 110 Fragmente. Die Mühe, die
Fragmente zu Seiten zusammenzufügen, wobei die vorhandene
laufende Numerierung half, hat sich gelohnt. Über den Kodex läßt
sich jetzt folgendes sagen:
In der Kölner Sammlung befinden sich 40 fragmentarische Blätter.
Davon entfallen 24 1/2 Blätter = 49 Seiten auf das Testament Hiobs.
Die Reihenfolge der Schriften im Kodex war:
Testament Adams; Testament Hiobs; Testament Abrahams; Acta
Petri et Andreae. Der Kodex besteht nur aus einer Lage. Die Mitte
der Lage befindet sich im ersten Drittel des erhaltenen Teiles; es fehlen
also nach vorne hin mehr Blätter als nach hinten; wieviele insgesamt,
läßt sich bisher nicht sagen.
Jede Seite trägt eine Kolumne mit 26 Zeilen. Der Schriftspiegel liegt
bei etwa 14 cm x 22 cm. Ränder sind bisweilen erhalten, jedoch ist
kein einziges Blatt vollständig.

An dem Kodex haben zwei verschiedene Schreiber gearbeitet. Die
Testamente Adams, Hiobs und Abrahams stammen von anderer
Hand als die Acta Petri et Andreae. Die Zugehörigkeit zu demselben
Kodex ist jedoch dadurch gesichert, daß die Acta Petri et Andreae auf
der Rückseite der Schlußpassage des Testamentum Abrahae beginnen.
Die Schriften lassen sich dann auch beide dem 5. Jahrhundert, und
hier eher der ersten Hälfte, zuordnen. Die Buchstaben haben die
Tendenz, sich einem Quadrat anzupassen, doch sind Haar- und
Schattenstriche noch unregelmäßig unterschieden.

Für den Text des Testaments Hiobs ergibt sich nach der Neuanord-
nung der Fragmente folgendes:
Anfang und Ende der Schrift sind erhalten. Im ersten Teil bis Kapitel
25 existieren jedoch nur die unteren Seitenhälften mit jeweils etwa
8 Zeilen auf Vorder- und Rückseite. Da die Tinte hier an einigen
Stellen abgerieben ist, wird die Lesung Schwierigkeiten bereiten. Wir
sind jedoch zuversichtlich, auch dort mit viel Geduld und UV-Licht

den Text entziffern zu können. Es darf wohl damit gerechnet werden,
daß auch von dem ersten Teil des Textes bis Kapitel 25 noch weit mehr
als 'wenige, kleine Bruchstücke', wie Berndt Schaller in seiner
Edition noch schreiben mußte,[3] identifiziert und publiziert werden
können.

Ab Kapitel 25 ist der Text abgesehen von kleineren Lücken durchgehend vorhanden. Gegenüber der Liste von Berndt Schaller, Anm.
144, konnten jedoch einige Textstellen mehr identifiziert werden.
Dazu ein Beispiel:

Da der Kodex einmal der Breite nach geknickt worden war, sind
alle Seiten in eine obere und eine untere Hälfte zerfallen. Bis Kapitel
38 haben wir daher auf jeder Seite abgesehen von fehlenden Zeilen
vor allem am oberen Rand einen Textverlust von etwa 3 Zeilen
zwischen der oberen und unteren Seitenhälfte. Unsere Hoffnungen,
hier Anschlußstücke finden zu können, haben sich bisher nicht
erfüllt. Es war aber möglich, bisher nicht identifizierbare Stücke als
Ober- bzw. Unterteil von schon identifizierten Stücken zu lokalisieren.
Dieses ist der Fall bei den Fragmenten 7 und 8. Die Fragmente tragen
auf der Rückseite 8 Zeilen mit Kapitel 30, 4—5. Die Feststellung,
30, 5 sei im koptischen Text ganz weggefallen, wie Manfred Weber
bemerkte, ist damit widerlegt. Zu diesem Irrtum konnte es kommen,
da der koptische Text an dieser Stelle wortreicher ist. Er nimmt
nämlich in 30, 1 das ⲚⲀⲨⲠⲀⲢⲬⲞⲚⲦⲀ (sie sprachen über 'meine Habe')
aus dem vorigen Kapitel 30, 4 wieder auf. Der griechische Text
begnügt sich an der zweiten Stelle mit einem οὕτως (sie sprachen
'so').

Andererseits läßt sich nun für Kapitel 31, 2—5 mit Sicherheit fest-
stellen, daß der Text des koptischen Kodex hier erheblich verkürzt
gewesen sein muß. Was im griechischen gedruckten Text bei Brock[4]
7 Zeilen einnimmt, dafür sind im koptischen Kodex nur 5 Zeilen frei.

Zur Sprache

Der Grunddialekt des Kodex ist Sahidisch, jedoch mit den Inkonse-
quenzen, die nach P. E. Kahle, *Bala'izah*[5] für die frühen sahidischen
Texte typisch sind:

---

[3] *Ibid.*, Anm. 144.
[4] S. P. Brock, *Testamentum Iobi* (PsVTG, 2, Leiden, 1967).
[5] *Bala'izah. Coptic Texts from Deir el-Bala'izah in Upper Egypt* (London, 1954).

1. fr. 7/8 Rs.,1: [ⲁⲩ₂ⲙⲟⲥ] ergänzt nach fr. 94 Rs.,9: ⲁ ϥ ₂ⲙⲟⲥ ; daneben kommt auch die Form ⲁⲩ₂ⲙⲟⲟⲥ (fr. 13 Vs.,6) vor. Zu ⲟ = ⲟⲟ vgl. Kahle I 83, Nr. 48.

2. fr. 95 Vs.,3: ⲛⲉⲙⲁ ⲓ (vgl. auch fr. 97 Vs.,3: ⲛⲉⲙⲁⲕ) ist ein Bohairicismus, nach Kahle I 101, Nr. 78A jedoch in einer Anzahl früher Texte belegt.

3. Die Verwendung von ⲛ ⲓ - (in fr. 94 Rs.,7: ⲡ ⲓ ⲛⲟⲟ₂ⲉ), ⳼- (in fr. 9 Rs.,6: ⳼ⲥⲉ ⲛ̄ⲧⲣⲁⲡⲉⲍⲁ), ⲛ ⲓ - (in fr. 94 Vs.,6: ⲛ ⲓ ₂ⲏ [ⲃ ⲥ], 7: ⲛ ⲓ ⲗⲩⲭⲛ ⲓ ⲁ) könnte als Bohairicismus gedeutet werden; da jedoch im griech. Text der best. Artikel verwendet wird, d.h. die aufgezählten Tatsachen als bekannt vorausgesetzt werden, möchten wir annehmen, daß es sich um den Demonstr.-Artikel handelt, vgl. auch Kahle I 122/3, Nr. 94A.

4. fr. 94 Rs.,2.6.11 uö.: ⲁ ϥ ⲛⲉ ϣ ⲛ̄ⲙⲁ und fr. 94 Rs.,9: ⲁ ϥ ₂ⲙⲟⲥ können B oder A sein, obwohl in diesem Falle das für A typische ⲉ fehlt; es bliebe also B (oder M) übrig, doch weist der Text sonst keine für diese Dialekte kennzeichnenden Formen auf.

5. fr. 7/8 Rs.,5: ⲙⲛ] ⲧⲣⲙⲙⲉⲟ, vgl. fr. 36/37 Vs.,8:] ⲣⲙⲙⲉⲟ: diese weder bei Crum noch bei Westendorf genannte Form könnte auf Einfluß durch A, A₂ zurückzuführen sein, vgl. Kahle I 68, Nr. 21.

Bei Würdigung dieser und anderer, später zu beschreibender Eigentümlichkeiten möchten wir nicht von 'Sahidisch, beeinflußt durch diesen oder jenen Dialekt' sprechen, sondern lieber von einem noch nicht standardisierten sahidischen Text, also einem relativ frühen Text. Dazu gehört, daß ⲛ vor ⲡ (bzw. ⲙ) durchweg nicht zu ⲙ assimiliert ist, vgl. fr. 7/8 Rs.,3: ⲙ̄ⲙⲟⲥ , aber 95 Vs.,9: ⲙ̄ⲙⲟ ⲓ, in der Rede des Eliphas: ⲁ ϥ ⲛ̄ⲉ ϣ ⲛ̄ⲙⲁ , ⲛ̄ⲡⲉⲕⲑ ⲣⲟⲛⲟⲥ .
Die Schreibung des 'i' ist schwankend: fr. 35 Vs.,8: ⲛⲛⲁⲉ ⲓ, vlg. fr. 86 Rs.,4: ⲛⲁ ⲓ̈, 9: ⲛⲁⲉ ⲓ 'mir', ibid. 6: ⲓ̈ⲛⲉ .
Die Edition wird alle diese Eigenheiten verzeichnen.
Die dem ausgewählten Textstück beigegebene Übersetzung ist bewußt wörtlich gehalten, um die Eigenständigkeit der koptischen Fassung zum Ausdruck zu bringen. Die Einzelheiten brauchen nicht besprochen zu werden, der Unterschied zeigt sich im Vergleich mit den griechischen Versionen; auf einiges hat M. Weber (bei Philonenko) schon hingewiesen:

Wiederholung des Refrains: 'der Ruhm Deines Thrones ...',
dabei werden auch Teile des Refrains wiederholt (wenn
unsere Ergänzungen richtig sind).
Die Strophen sind stark verkürzt: 'der vom Herdenbringen',
'der von den 60 Tischen ...' etc.
In fr. 35 Vs., 4–5 wird eine Strophe über die Frau Jobs hin-
zugefügt, deren Wortlaut leider verstümmelt ist.

Im Vergleich mit den griechischen Fassungen macht die koptische
Version einen durchaus selbständigen Eindruck; es ist uns noch nicht
klar, was dies für die griechische Vorlage bedeuten soll.

Frag.7 und 8 Rs.: **30,4-5**

- - - - - - - - - - - - - - - -

1 [ⲀⲨϨⲘⲞⲤ ⲆⲈ ⲈⲨⲀ]ⲒⲀⲔⲢⲒⲚ[Ⲉ ⲈⲚ]
  [ⲈⲦⲚ̄ⲤⲰⲒ ⲀⲨⲰ Ⲧ]ⲂⲚⲞⲞⲨⲈ ⲈⲨⲰⲀ
  [ⲊⲈ ⲈⲚⲀϨⲨⲠⲀⲢⲬ]ⲞⲚⲦⲀ ⲈⲨⲊⲰ Ⲙ̄ⲘⲞⲤ
4 [ⲊⲈ Ⲛ̄ⲦⲰⲦⲚ̄ ⲘⲎ]Ⲛ̣ⲦⲈⲦⲚ ⲤⲞⲞⲨⲚ ⲀⲚ
  [Ⲛ̄ⲦⲀⳙⲎ Ⲛ̄ⲦⲘⲚ]ⲦⲢ̄Ⲙ̄ⲘⲈⲞ ⲈⳙⲀⲨ
  [ⲦⲚⲚⲞⲨⲤ ⲈϨⲢ]Ⲁ̣Ⲓ̈ ⲈⲚⲠⲞⲖⲈⲒⲤ ⲈⲦ
  [Ⲙ̄ⲠⲔⲰⲦⲈ Ⲛ̄ⲤⲰ]ⲞⲨ Ⲛ̄ⲚⲈⲦⲢⲀⲢⲰ
8 [ϨⲚ̄ⲠⲈ]ⳙⲎⲒ̈
Es fehlen wohl 3 Zeilen.

Frag.95 Vs.: **31,1-2**

1 [ⲤⲀⳙ̣ϥ Ⲛ̄Ϩ]ⲞⲞⲨ ⲈⲨⳙⲞⲞⲠ̣ [Ⲙ̄ⲘⲀⲨ Ⲛ̄ⲘⲞ]
  ⲞⲨ ⲈⲦ̣ⲂⲈ ⲚⲀϨⲨⲠⲀⲢⲬⲞⲚⲦ̣[Ⲁ ⲀⲨ]
  ⳙⲀⲊⲈ ⲚⲈⲘⲀⲒ ⲈⲠⲦⲎⲢϥ Ⲉ̣[ϥⲊⲰ Ⲛ̄]
4 ⲆⲈ ⲠⲈⲊⲈ ⲈⲖⲒ⳯ⲀⲤ ⲚⲚⲈϥⲔⲈ̣[ⳙⲂ]
  Ⲣ̄ⲢⲞ ⲆⲈ ⲦⲰⲞⲨⲚ Ⲛ̄ⲦⲚϨⲰⲚ ⲈϨ[ⲞⲨⲚ]
  ⲈⲢⲞϥ Ⲛ̄ⲦⲚⲀⲚⲞⲨϥ ⲀⲔⲢⲒⲂ̣[ⲰⲤ]
  ⲊⲈ Ⲛ̄ⲦⲞϥ ⲢⲰ ⲠⲈ Ⲁ̣[ⲈⲚ Ⲙ̄ⲘⲞⲚ Ⲛ̄]
8 ⲦⲞⲞⲨ Ⲛ̄ⲆⲈ ⲀⲨⲞ̣ϨⲈ̣ [ⲈⲂⲞⲖ ⲈⲨ]
  ⲞⲨⲎⲞⲨ Ⲛ̄ⲘⲞⲒ Ⲛ̣[ⲞⲨ6ⲞⲤ Ⲛ̄ⲤⲦⲀ]
  ⲀⲒⲞⲚ ⲈⲦⲂⲈ Ⲥ̣[ϯⲂⲰⲰⲚ Ⲙ̄ⲠⲀⲤⲰⲘⲀ]

Rand

Sie saßen, indem sie meine Lage und das
Vieh erörterten, indem sie über meine Habe
sprachen, indem sie sagten:
'Ihr, wißt ihr nicht von der Menge des Reichtums, den man in die Städte der Umgebung
schickte, außer dem, was ... in seinem
Hause ...

... (nach) sieben Tagen, die sie verbrachten
wegen meiner Lage, da sprachen sie mit mir
im Allgemeinen. Da ergriff Eliphas das Wort und
sagte zu seinen Mitkönigen: 'Erhebt euch, auf
daß wir uns ihm nähern und ihn genau fragen,
ob er es nun ist oder nicht.'

Sie aber standen da, indem sie eine halbe Stadie
von mir entfernt waren wegen des üblen Geruches
meines Leibes ...

Frag.9 Vs. : **31,6-32,1**

- - - - - - - - - - - -

```
   [          ϩⲚⲦⲠⲀϢⲉ ⲚⲦⲉⲨ]
1  ϣ[ⲏ ⲀⲨⲱ] ⲀⲓϢⲀⲀ[ⲉ ⲉⲣⲟϥ]
   Ⲭⲉ ⲀⲚⲟⲕ ⲡⲉ Ⲁϥⲣⲓ̈[ⲙⲉ Ⲛⲟⲩ]
   ⲚⲟϬ Ⲛⲣⲓⲙⲉ ⲘⲚⲟ[ⲨϨⲂⲉ Ⲛ]
4  ⲦⲘⲚⲦⲉⲣ̅ⲟ̅ ⲉⲨⲟⲩϣ[ϣ]ⲃ Ⲛ̅Ϭⲓ Ⲛⲉ]
   ⲕⲉϣ⟨ⲃ⟩ⲣ̅ⲣ̅ⲟ̅. ⲤⲱⲦⲘ [ⲚⲉⲗⲓⲫⲀⲤ]
   ⲉϥⲦⲀⲙⲟ Ⲛⲟⲩⲟⲛ Ⲛ[ⲓⲙ ⲉⲚⲉⲬⲣⲏⲙⲀ]
   Ⲛ̅ⲓⲱⲃ ˙ ⲚⲦⲟⲕ [ⲡⲉ ⲓⲱⲃ ⲉⲓⲤ ⲡⲉ]
8  ⲟⲟⲩ ⲡⲉⲟⲟⲩ Ⲛ̅[ⲡⲉⲕⲑⲣⲟⲚⲟⲤ]
   . ....[
```

Es fehlt wohl 1 Zeile.

Frag.94 Rs.: **32,2-4**

```
            ]...[          ⲡⲉⲟ]
   [ⲟⲨ] Ⲛ̅ⲡⲉⲕⲑⲣⲟⲚⲟⲤ ⲀϥⲚ̅ⲉϣⲛ̅[ⲙⲀ]
   [ⲚⲦ]ⲟⲕ ⲡⲉ ⲓ̈ⲱⲃ ⲠⲀⲠⲓϢⲟⲙⲚⲦ[Ⲛϣ]
4  ⲟ Ⲛ̅ϬⲀⲙⲟⲩⲗ ⲉⲦϥⲓ ϨⲀⲠⲀⲅⲀ[ⲑⲟⲚ]
   ⲚⲚ̅ϨⲎⲕⲉ ⲡⲉⲟⲩ Ⲛ̅ⲡⲉⲕⲉⲣⲟ[ⲚⲟⲤ]
   ⲀϥⲚ̅ⲉϣⲛ̅ⲙⲀ ⲚⲦⲟⲕ ⲡⲉ ⲓ̈ⲱⲃ ⲡ[Ⲁ]
   ⲠⲓⲚⲟⲟ[ϩⲉ ⲡ]ⲉⲟⲟⲩ ⲡⲉⲟⲟⲩ Ⲛ̅ⲡⲉⲕ
8  [ⲑⲣⲟⲚⲟⲤ ⲀϥⲚ̅]ⲉϣⲛ̅ⲙⲀ ⲠⲀⲠⲓⲙⲀ
   [Ⲛ̅ ⲕⲣⲀⲃⲀⲦⲦ]ⲟⲩⲤ ⲀϥϨⲙⲟⲤ ⲦⲉⲚⲟⲩ
   [ⲉⲦⲕⲟⲠⲣⲓⲀ ⲡⲉⲟ]ⲟⲩ Ⲛ̅ⲡⲉⲕⲑⲣⲟⲚⲟ[Ⲥ]
   [Ⲛ̅ⲡⲉⲕⲑⲣⲟⲚⲟⲤ] ⲀϥⲚ̅ⲉϣⲛ̅ⲙⲀ
```

Rand

'... in der Mitte der Nacht?'
Und ich sagte zu ihm: 'Ich bin es.' Er brach in
heftiges Weinen aus und in eine königliche
Klage, indem die Mitkönige antworteten.

Höret Eliphas, indem er alle die Reichtümer
des Job wissen läßt. 'Bist du Job? Siehe,
der Ruhm, der Ruhm deines Thrones ...

... der Ruhm deines Thrones, wo ist er?

Bist du es, Job, der mit den 3000 Kamelen, welche
die Güter zu den Armen brachten? Der Ruhm
deines Thrones, wo ist er?
Bist du es, Job, der vom Herdenbringen? Der Ruhm,
der Ruhm deines Thrones, wo ist er?
Der vom Ort der Betten, jetzt sitzt er auf dem
Müll. Der Ruhm deines Thrones,
deines Thrones, wo ist er?

Frag.9 Rs.: **32,6-7**

‒ ‒ ‒ ‒ ‒ ‒ ‒ ‒ ‒ ‒ ‒ ‒ ‒ ‒ ‒

1 [ΠΕΟΟΥ N̄ΠΕΚΘ]ΡΟΝΟΣ [ΑϤ]N̄
  [ΕϢN̄ΜΑ ΝΙΜ ΠΕ]ΝΤΑϤΤΟΛΜΑ Ε
  [ΡΤΕΚϨΕ ϨN̄ ΤΜ]ΗΤΕ ΝΝΕΚϢΗΡΕ
4 [ϨϢΣ ΒϢ N̄ΧΕΜ]ΠΕϨ ϨN̄ ΠΕΣΤΟΗ
  [N̄Σ†ΝΟΥϤΕ ΠΕ]ΟΟΥ N̄ΠΕΚΘΡΟ
  [ΝΟΣ ΑϤN̄ΕϢN̄Μ]Α ΠΑ†ΣΕ ΝΤΡΑ
  [ΠΕΖΑ ΕΥΤΗϢ N̄]ΝϨΗΚΕ ΕϤ
8 [ΤΑΧΡΟ N̄ΜΟΟΥ] N̄ΘΕ N̄ΟΥ
Es fehlen wohl 3 Zeilen.

Frag.94 Vs.: **32,8-10**

1 [Σ†ΝΟ]ΥϤΕ ΑϤϢϢΠ[Ε ϨN̄ ΟΥΣ†]
  ΒϢΝ ΠΕΟΟΥ N̄ΠΕΚΘΡΟ[ΟΝΟΣ ΑϤ]
  N̄ΕϢN̄ΜΑ ΠΕΤΕΠΕϤΝΕϨ[ΒΕ]
4 ϢΑϤΤϢϨΣ N̄ΜΟϤ ⟨N̄⟩ΟΥΣΟϬΕΝ [N̄]
  ΤΕΠΛΙΒΑΝΟΣ ΠΕΟΟΥ N̄ΠΕΚ[ΘΡΟ]
  ΝΟΣ ΑϤN̄ΕϢN̄ΜΑ Π[Α]ΝΙϨΗ[ΒΣ̄ N̄]
  N̄ΟΥΒ ϨΙΑΝ ΝΙΛΥΧ[ΝΙ]Α N̄[ϨΑΤ]
8 ΕΙΣ ϨΗΤΕ ϨϢϤ ϤΜ[ΟΥΝ ΕΒΟΛ ΤΕ]
  ΝΟΥ ⟨Ε⟩ΠΟΟϨ N̄[ΤΕϤΟΥΛΕΙΝΕ]
  ΠΕΟΟΥ N̄ΠΕ[ΚΘΡΟΝΟΣ ΑϤN̄ΕϢ]

Rand

Der Ruhm deines Thrones, wo ist er?
Wer ist der, der gewagt hat, wie du zu sein in
der Mitte deiner Kinder, wie ein Apfelbaum in
Wohlgeruch?
Der Ruhm deines Thrones, wo ist er?
Der von den 60 Tischen, die bestimmt waren
für die Armen, indem er sie befestigte wie ...

... Wohlgeruch, in üblen Geruch ist er geraten.
Der Ruhm deines Thrones, wo ist er?
Der, welcher seinen Nacken mit Salbe von Weihrauch
(Libanon) zu salben pflegte, der Ruhm deines Thrones,
wo ist er?
Der mit den goldenen Leuchtern auf den silbernen
Ständern, siehe, er wartet jetzt auf den Mond in seinem
Licht.

Der Ruhm deines Thrones, wo ist er?

Frag.35 Vs.: **32,11-33,2**

1 ̄ΝΜΑ ΠΕΤΕϢΑϤ[ϹΩΒΕ ΝϹΑ ̄ΝΡΕϤ̄Ρ]
   ΝΟΒΕ ΤΕΝΟΥ ϹΕϹϢ[ΒΕ ̄ΝϹΩΚ ΠΕΟΟΥ]
   ̄ΝΠΕΚΘΡΟΝΟϹ ΑϤ̄Ν[ΕϢ]̄ΝΜΑ ̄ΝΤΟϹ ΤΕ]
4 ΤΕΚϹϨΙΜΕ ΤΑϮΤΑΠ[ΑΝΗ
   ϹΟ ̄ΝϨΜϨΑΛ ΝΤΟΚ Π[Ε ΙΩΒ ΠΕΟΟΥ ̄ΝΠΕΚ]
   ΘΡΟΝΟϹ ΠΕΟΟΥ ̄ΝΠ̣[ΕΚΘΡΟΝΟϹ ΑϤ̄ΝΕϢ]
   ̄ΝΜΑ ̄ΝΤΕΡΕϤϢϹΚ ̄Ν[ϬΙ ΕΛΙΦΑϹ ΕϤ]
8 ΧΩ ΝΝΑΕΙ ΕΥΟΥΩϢ[Β ̄ΝϬΙ ΠϢΟΜΝΤ̄Ν]
   ΕΡΩΟΥ Μ̄Ν ΠΕϹΤΡΑΤ̣[ΕΥΜΑ ̄ΝΜΑΤΟΙ]
   ϨΩϹΤΕ ̄ΝΤΕ ΟΥΝΟϬ Ν[ϢΤΟΡΤΡ ϢΩΠΕ]
   ΑΝΟΚ ϨΩ ΛΕΙΩΧ̣[Ν ̄ΝΜΟΟΥ ΕΒΟΛ]
12 ϨΜ̄ ΠΕΥΛϢΚ[ΑΚ ΑΥΩ ΛΕΙϢΑΧΕ ΕΙ]
   ΧΩ ̄ΝΜΟϹ Χ̣[Ε ΚΑΡΩΤ̄Ν ΤΑΤΑΜΩΤ̄Ν]
   [Μ]ΠΟΟΥ

Der, welcher über die Sünder zu lachen pflegte –
jetzt lacht man über dich. Der Ruhm deines
Thrones, wo ist er? Ist es
deine Frau, die vom Aufwand (?) ... Sie
ist Diener (?). Bist du es, Job? Der Ruhm deines
Thrones, der Ruhm deines Thrones, wo ist er?
Als Eliphas verweilte, indem er dies sagte, indem
die drei Könige und das Heer der Soldaten antworteten,
so daß große Unruhe entstand,

da ließ ich sie aufhören mit ihrem Geschrei, und ich
sprach: 'Seid ruhig, auf daß ich euch jetzt belehre
...

4

ZUR KOMPOSITION UND KONZEPTION DES TESTAMENTS HIOBS*

Berndt Schaller

Georg-August-Universität Göttingen

Die Erforschung des Testaments Hiobs hat in den letzten zwanzig Jahren – entscheidend angestoßen durch die von S. Brock besorgte neue, kritische Ausgabe des griechischen Textes[1] – einen merklichen Aufschwung genommen. Das Werk ist mehrfach in ihm eigens gewidmeten Untersuchungen insgesamt oder zu einzelnen Fragen bearbeitet worden.[2] Es ist inzwischen in verschiedenen modernen Übersetzungen zugänglich gemacht[3] und wird in der judaistischen wie in der neutestamentlichen Forschung[4] zunehmend beachtet.

---

* Überarbeitete und durch Anmerkungen erweiterte Fassung eines vor der Pseudepigrapha-Gruppe der SNTS am 25.8.1987 in Göttingen gehaltenen Vortrags.

[1] S. P. Brock, Testamentum Iobi, PsVTG, 2 (Leiden, Brill 1967).

[2] S. die Literaturübersicht von R. P. Spittler in diesem Band.

[3] Deutsch: B. Schaller, Das Testament Hiobs, JSHRZ, III, 3 (Gütersloh, Gütersloher Verlagshaus G. Mohn, 1980), 325–74.

Englisch: R. P. Spittler, Testament of Job, in: The Old Testament Pseudepigrapha, ed. J. H. Charlesworth, I (London, Darton, Longman & Todd; New York, Doubleday 1983), 839–68; R. Thornhill, The Testament of Job, in: The Apocryphal Old Testament, ed. H. F. D. Sparks (Oxford, Clarendon Press, 1984), 622–48.

Französisch: M. Philonenko, Le Testament de Job, Semitica 18 (1968), 25–59; ders. Testament de Job, in: La Bible. Ecrits intertestamentaires, ed. A. Dupont-Sommer–M. Philonenko (Paris, Editions Gallimard, 1987), 1605–45.

Spanisch: A. Piñero, Testamento de Job, in: Apocrifos del Antiguo Testamento V, ed. A. Diez-Macho (Madrid, Ediciones Cristiandad, 1987), 157–213.

[4] S. dazu Schaller, JSHRZ, III, 3, 321; ferner: K. Berger, Die Amen-Worte Jesu, BZNW, 39 (Berlin, de Gruyter 1970), 52ff., 126f.; ders., Die Gesetzesauslegung Jesu, I, WMANT, 40 (Neukirchen-Vlyn, Neukirchener Verlag, 1972), *passim*; ders., Materialien zur Form- und Überlieferungsgeschichte neutestamentlicher Gleichnisse, NovTest 15 (1973), 2–9; ders., Die Auferstehung des Propheten und die Erhöhung des Gerechten, StUNT, 13 (Göttingen, Vandenhoeck & Ruprecht, 1976), *passim*; H. C. C. Cavallin, Life After Death, CB, NTSer, 7, 1 (Lund, Gleerup, 1974), 160ff.; G. Dautzenberg, Glossolalie, RAC, 11 (1981), 233f.; A. von Dobbeler, Glaube als Teilhabe, WUNT, II, 22 (Tübingen, Mohr-Siebeck, 1987), 28.131; A. L. Lincoln, Paradise Now and Not Yet, SNTSt, Mon Ser, 43 (Cambridge University Press, 1981), 112. 149; H.-P. Müller, Hiob und seine Freunde, ThSt B, 103 (Zürich, EVZ-Verlag,

Unsere Kenntnis dieses umfänglichsten und wohl bedeutendsten Zeugnisses der Hiobhaggada des antiken Judentums ist dadurch deutlich verbreitet und vertieft worden. Man kann — gemessen an der älteren Forschung — ohne Übertreibung von nicht unerheblichen Fortschritten sprechen. Dennoch läßt sich nicht übersehen: an manchen, auch an entscheidenden Stellen gibt es nach wie vor mehr Fragen als Antworten.

Das trifft u. a. auch im Hinblick auf die literarische Komposition und die darin zum Ausdruck kommende sachliche Konzeption des ganzen Werkes zu.

Wie ist das Testament Hiobs literarisch gestaltet? Warum und wozu ist es geschrieben worden?

Diese für das Verständnis der Schrift grundlegenden Fragen sind bis heute nicht wirklich geklärt. In der Forschung hat man sich zwar mehrfach dazu geäußert. Zu einem befriedigenden, fundierten und darum weithin anerkannten Ergebnis ist man indes nicht gelangt. Im Gegenteil, die Ansichten gehen nach wie vor weit auseinander. Bald wird von einer Werbe- und Missionsschrift,[5] bald von einem paränetischen Traktat,[6] bald von einer mystischen Abhandlung,[7] bald von einem apologetischen Propagandatext[8] gesprochen. Ebenso unterschiedlich eingeschätzt wird die literarische Eigenart. Das Werk gilt teils als zusammenhängende, von einer Hand gestaltete

---

1970), 9–16.19; G. Nebe, 'Hoffnung' bei Paulus, StUNT, 16 (Göttingen, Vandenhoeck & Ruprecht, 1983), 349–54; E. Noort, Een duister duel. Over de theologie van het boek Job, Kampen cahiers 59 (Kampen, 1986), 19–23; E. von Nordheim, Die Lehre der Alten I, ALGHJ, 13 (Leiden, Brill, 1980), 119–35; E. Schürer, G. Vermes, F. Millar und M. Goodman, The History of the Jewish People in the Age of Jesus Christ, III, 1 (Edinburgh, Clark, 1986), 552ff.; G. Theissen, Psychologische Aspekte paulinischer Theologie, FRLANT, 131 (Göttingen, Vandenhoeck & Ruprecht, 1983), 289ff.; E. E. Urbach, The Sages (Jerusalem, Magnes Press, 1979²), 411f., 867f.

[5] D. Rahnenführer, Das Testament des Hiob in seinem Verhältnis zum Neuen Testament, Diss. theol. Halle, 1967, 180–5; ders., Das Testament des Hiob und das Neue Testament, ZNW 62 (1971), 88ff.; I. Jacobs, Literary Motifs in the Testament of Job, JJS 21 (1970), 1–10.

[6] Schaller, JSHRZ, III, 3, 314.

[7] K. Kohler, The Testament of Job, in: Semitic Studies in memory of Rev. Dr. Alexander Kohut, ed. G. A. Kohut (Berlin, Calvary, 1897), 272; M. Philonenko, Le 'Testament de Job' et les Thérapeutes, Semitica 8 (1958), 49.

[8] Spittler, Testament of Job (s. Anm. 3), 834.

Komposition,[9] teils als Ergebnis einer mehrstufigen Entwicklung und darum als literarisches Konglomerat.[10]

Wie weit es gelingt, in diesen Fragen noch zu einer Klärung zu gelangen, kann angesichts dieser Meinungsvielfalt zweifelhaft erscheinen. Dennoch soll im folgenden ein neuer Versuch unternommen werden.

I

Methodisch ist es angebracht, zunächst die Frage nach der Komposition zu erörtern.

Von der äußeren Disposition her kann man das Testament Hiobs durchaus als 'durchsichtig'[11] bezeichnen. Es gibt einen Erzählkern und einen Erzählrahmen. Der Kern besteht aus einem Bericht Hiobs über sein Leben und Leiden (Kap. 2–45). Er ist in zwei Teile geteilt. Der erste (2–27) erzählt vom Kampf Hiobs mit dem Satan, der zweite (28–44) von den Auseinandersetzungen Hiobs mit den Freunden. Beide Teile schließen jeweils mit einer Paränese (27, 7/45, 1–3). Der Rahmen ist am Anfang (Kap. 1) gestaltet als knapp gehaltene Einleitung, die den Ort und Anlaß beschreibt; das Ende (Kap. 46–53) bildet ein längerer Schluß, der von der Verteilung des Erbes Hiobs und dem Tod Hiobs handelt.

Daß diese Disposition auf eine bewußte Gestaltung hinweist, steht zu vermuten; dennoch gibt es Anlaß zu fragen, ob sie sich einer durchgehend und einheitlich gestalteten Komposition verdankt. Hier sind durchaus Zweifel angebracht. Genau besehen enthält das Testament Hiobs in Stil und Darstellungsweise, vor allem aber auch im Erzählstoff mancherlei Spannungen, ja Brüche. Was erzählt und

---

[9] J. J. Collins, Structure and Meaning in the Testament of Job, SBL 1974 Seminar Papers, 1 (1974), 46ff.; Schaller, JSHRZ, III, 3, 304ff.

[10] M. R. James, The Testament of Job, Apocrypha Anecdota, II, TSt V, 1 (1897), lxxxix, xcvi; Philonenko, Semitica 8 (1958), 47ff.; ders., Semitica 18 (1968), 10; Rahnenführer, Diss., 76, 129; Spittler, Testament of Job (s. Anm. 3), 834.

[11] F. Spitta, Das Testament Hiobs und das Neue Testament, in: ders., Zur Geschichte und Literatur des Urchristentums, III, 2 (Göttingen, Vandenhoeck & Ruprecht, 1907), 153.

dargestellt wird, setzt sich aus recht verschiedenen Szenen- und Motivkreisen zusammen, die in der Sache oft wenig zusammenpassen und in der Form nicht immer recht zusammengepaßt sind. Besonders auffällig ist dies im Verhältnis der Schlußkapitel zu den beiden Hauptteilen der Fall. Die Erzählung vom wunderwirkenden Erbe, das Hiob seinen Töchtern vermacht, und vom ebenso wundersamen Ende Hiobs hebt sich von den vorausgehenden Berichten über Hiobs Auseinandersetzungen mit dem Satan und seinen Freunden stark ab. Nicht nur hat die Person des Erzählers von Hiob zu einem vorher nicht genannten, plötzlich auftauchenden Hiob-Bruder namens Nereus gewechselt, vor allem stellt sich auch das Sprach- und Sachmilieu völlig anders dar: Im Mittelpunkt stehen die Töchter Hiobs, nicht Hiob selbst; es ist von wunderwirkenden Gürteln die Rede; geradezu mystische, ja magische Verwandlungen finden statt, die himmlische Welt, Engelmächte treten in Erscheinung. Von dem allen war vorher so nicht die Rede.

Diese Diskrepanz ist bereits von M. R. James[12] in seiner vor neunzig Jahren veröffentlichten und die gesamte Forschung lange bestimmenden Untersuchung über das Testament Hiobs beobachtet worden und hat ihn zu einer umfassenden, literarkritischen Bearbeitungs- und Ergänzungshypothese veranlaßt.

Nach James ist das Testament Hiobs ein in zwei Stufen entstandenes Werk. Die Grundlage bildet ein ursprünglich vermutlich hebräisch geschriebener Hiob-Midrasch. Dieser ist später frei ins Griechische übertragen und zugleich durch eingeschobene bzw. angehängte Zusätze erweitert worden. Neben den Schlußkapiteln (46−52) gelten als solche Zusätze − ohne daß dies weiter begründet wird − die in die eigentliche Hiob-Erzählung eingestreuten Hymnen (25, 1−8; 32, 2−12; 33, 3−9; 43, 4−17) sowie auch die Gleichnisabschnitte (18, 6−8; 27, 3−6), ferner − ohne genauer bezeichnet zu werden − einige längere Redestücke.

Mit dieser Sicht hat sich James zwar nicht restlos durchgesetzt, aber doch die weitere Forschung entscheidend bestimmt.[13] In der neueren

---

[12] James (s. Anm. 10), xciii−xcvi.

[13] S. die in Anm. 10 aufgeführten Autoren, ferner: H. Fuchs, Hiobs Testament, JüdLex, II (1928), 1613; R. Meyer, Hiobstestament, RGG³, III (1959), 361; B. Z. Wacholder, Testament of Job, EncJud², 10 (1971), 129f.; Müller (s. Anm. 4), 9;

Zeit ist sie vor allem von R. Spittler[14] neu belebt worden. Der Unterschied zwischen James und Spittler besteht wesentlich in der historischen Einordnung und der sachlichen Bestimmung der hinter dem Testament Hiobs stehenden Textbearbeitung. Während James von einer hebräisch verfaßten Grundschrift ausgeht und diese in Palästina ansiedelt und die Endfassung einem griechischsprechenden Judenchristen zuschreibt, der im zweiten oder dritten Jahrhundert in Ägypten lebte, denkt Spittler an eine griechisch verfaßte Grundschrift, die der in Ägypten lebenden jüdischen Gruppe der Therapeuten entstammen soll; die spätere Überarbeitung weist er einem gegen Ende des zweiten Jahrhunderts in Phrygien beheimateten, christlichen Montanistenkreis zu und stuft sie als Ausdruck montanistischer Apologetik und Propaganda ein. Es ist hier nicht der Ort, die Berechtigung der einen oder anderen Position zu beurteilen.[15] In der literarkritischen Analyse fußt Spittler ganz auf den Überlegungen von James. Er hat sie zwar durch ein paar sprachliche Beobachtungen ergänzt,[16] im übrigen aber nicht weiter ausgebaut oder am Gesamttext des Testaments Hiobs überprüft. Eine solche Überprüfung ist in jedem Fall aber nötig. Denn jedes Einzelstück eines Textes kann literarkritisch sinnvoll nur beurteilt werden, wenn die literarische Eigenart des Gesamttextes erfaßt ist.

Diesen Grundsatz nicht beachtet zu haben, ist ein entscheidender Mangel bei allen bisherigen Bemühungen, die Frage nach der Entstehungsgeschichte des Testaments Hiobs literarkritisch zu lösen.

Freilich wird man nicht verschweigen dürfen, daß auch bei den gegenläufigen Versuchen, das Testament Hiobs als literarisch geschlossen darzustellen, eine umfassende Textanalyse noch nicht geliefert worden ist.

J.J. Collins,[17] der erstmals eine eigene Untersuchung über die Struktur und die Bedeutung des Testaments Hiobs vorgelegt und

---

P. Schäfer, Testament des Hiob, Kleines Lexikon des Judentums (Stuttgart, Katholisches Bibelwerk, 1981), 143.

[14] R.P. Spittler, The Testament of Job, Diss. phil., Harvard, 1971, 58–69; ders., Testament of Job (s. Anm. 3), 833f.

[15] Vgl. dazu meine Bemerkungen in JSHRZ, III, 3, 306, 369.

[16] Spittler, Diss., 62ff.

[17] Collins (s. Anm. 9), 35–52.

sich mit Nachdruck gegen die Ergänzungs- und Überarbeitungs-Hypothese von James und Spittler gewandt hat, hat sich im wesentlichen darauf beschränkt, in den verschiedenen Teilen des Testaments Hiobs die tragenden Leitmotive samt den jeweiligen Kompositions-strukturen herauszuarbeiten und die neben den vorhandenen Differenzen bestehenden Gemeinsamkeiten aufzuzeigen. Dabei kommen in der Tat mancherlei Beziehungen zutage, aber diese betreffen wesentlich nur die beiden Hauptteile der Hioberzählung und nicht auch die für die ganze Frage nach der literarischen Eigenart des Testaments Hiobs doch zumindest mitentscheidenden Schluß-kapitel.[18] Aber auch abgesehen davon ist Collins Vorgehen unzu-reichend, denn er hat den zweiten Schritt vor dem ersten getan. Eine solche Motivanalyse ist erst dann wirklich sinnvoll, wenn die vorausgesetzten Beziehungen auch literarisch umfassend abgesichert sind.

In der Einleitung der von mir vorgelegten Übersetzung und Kommen-tierung des Testaments Hiobs in JSHRZ[19] habe ich selbst auf solche literarischen Verklammerungen und Verzahnungen und auf sonstige Anzeichen planvoller Zusammenstellung hingewiesen, daraus gefolgert, das Testament Hiobs sei 'als ganzes konzipiert und aller Wahrscheinlichkeit nach von einer Hand geschrieben',[20] und die Unausgeglichenheiten auf die schlichte Tatsache zurückgeführt, 'daß der Verfasser aus unterschiedlichen Quellen geschöpft hat und nicht sonderlich bemüht war, die vorgegebenen Stoffe und Überlieferungen zu einem in sich abgerundeten Werk zu verarbeiten'.[21] Die Belege für diese These konnten aber nur anmerkungsweise und auszugsweise geliefert werden. Eine spätere Untersuchung sollte die fehlenden Einzelnachweise liefern. Dies ist aber bisher unterblieben.

Am ausführlichsten und eingehendsten hat sich zuletzt P.H. Nicholls[22] in einer leider nicht veröffentlichten und daher bislang wenig bekannten und beachteten Jerusalemer Dissertation geäußert.

[18] Ebd., 47f.
[19] JSHRZ, III, 3, 304ff.
[20] Ebd., 306.
[21] Ebd., 306.
[22] P.H. Nicholls, The Structure and Purpose of the Testament of Job, Diss. phil., Jerusalem, 1982.

Nicholls hat ebenfalls – ohne meinen Beitrag zu kennen – die literarische Geschlossenheit des Testaments Hiobs mit der Annahme von verarbeiteten Quellen verfochten. Sein Hauptaugenmerk ist dabei darauf gerichtet, den Nachweis für die Benutzung von Quellen im Gesamttext des Testaments Hiobs zu führen. Methodisch setzt er ähnlich wie Collins bei der Verteilung der Leitmotive ein, darüber hinaus spielen im Text vorhandene formale und sachliche Brüche und Spannungen eine Rolle. Insgesamt meint Nicholls, im Testament Hiobs vier verschiedene literarische Quellen erheben zu können.[23] Ob seine Quellenanalyse im Ergebnis wirklich stichhaltig ist, wird noch zu prüfen sein. Im methodischen Ansatz verdient sie in jedem Fall beachtet zu werden. Denn wenn es zutrifft, daß die Kernerzählung des Testaments Hiobs Anzeichen für die Benutzung von Quellen enthält, dann ist die auf die Besonderheit der Schlußkapitel begründete Annahme einer sekundären Überarbeitung und Ergänzung alles andere als zwingend.

Um die These belegen zu können, das Testament Hiobs sei in seiner heute vorliegenden Gestalt als ein Gesamtwerk konzipiert, genügt es freilich nicht, auf die Benutzung von Quellen abzuheben; ebenso wichtig, ja wichtiger ist es, der literarischen Gestaltung auf die Spur zu kommen. Was läßt sich darüber im Text des Testaments Hiobs ausmachen?

II

Bereits eine oberflächliche Lektüre des Testaments Hiobs zeigt, daß die in ihm dargebotene Erzählung nicht einspurig, sondern auf verschiedenen Ebenen verläuft und die beteiligten Personen und die verhandelten Themen vielfach wechseln. Vom Handlungsablauf her ergibt sich ein Aufriß in folgende Erzählblöcke:[24]

---

[23] Ebd., 57; s.u. S. 79f.
[24] Der Aufriß (vgl. bereits JSHRZ, III, 3, 304) richtet sich nach dem Handlungsablauf, nicht nach dem Umfang des Erzählstoffes. – Eine etwas andere Einteilung nimmt Spittler, Testament of Job (s. Anm. 3), 839–68 vor:
Prologue (1)
I. Job and the Revealing Angel (2–5)
II. Job and Satan (6–27)
   A. Satan's attack and Job's tragedy (6–8)
   B. Job's generosity and piety (9–15)

Einleitung:

A (1, 1–6): Ort und Anlaß der Erzählung, beteiligte Personen und ihre Vorgeschichte.

B *Erster Hauptteil*:
Die Auseinandersetzung Hiobs mit dem Satan.

B I (2, 1–5, 3) Hiobs Zweifel an der Verehrung eines Götzen und sein Vorgehen gegen das Götzenheiligtum, veranlaßt und bestärkt durch eine himmlische Offenbarung und Verheißung.

B II (6, 1–8, 3) Die erste Auseinandersetzung zwischen Hiob und dem Satan.

B III (9, 1–15, 9) Hiobs Wohltätigkeit gegenüber Armen, Witwen, Waisen und Fremden aufgrund seines Reichtums.

B IV (16, 1–20, 9) Erneutes Vorgehen des Satans gegen Hiob, seinen Besitz und seine Kinder sowie seine eigene Person.

B V (21, 1–26, 6) Auftreten der Frau Hiobs: Ihre Fürsorge für Hiob und ihre Vorwürfe gegen Hiob.

B VI (27, 1–7) Erneute Auseinandersetzung Hiobs mit dem Satan: Sieg der Standhaftigkeit Hiobs.

C *Zweiter Hauptteil*:
Die Begegnung und Auseinandersetzungen Hiobs mit seinen Freunden.

C I (28, 1–38, 8) Besuch der befreundeten Könige bei und ihre ersten Auseinandersetzungen mit Hiob.

C II (39, 1–40, 14) Erneutes Auftreten der Frau Hiobs, ihre Klage über Hiobs Geschick, ihre Bitte für die verstorbenen Kinder, ihr Ende.

C III (41, 1–6) Weiteres Vorgehen der Könige, insbesondere des Elihu gegen Hiob.

C IV (42, 1–43, 17) Das Kommen Gottes, sein Urteil über die Könige.

    C. Job's losses (16–26)
    D. Job's triumph and Satan's defeat (27)
  III. Job and the three kings (28–45)
    A. Job recognized and the kings astonished (28–30)
    B. Eliphas laments Job's losses (31–4)
    C. Baldad tests Job's sanity (35, 1–38, 5)
    D. Sophar offers the royal physicians (38, 6–8)
    E. Sitis laments her children, dies, and is buried (39–40)
    F. Job's recovery and vindication (41–5)
  IV. Job and his three daughters (46–50)
  Epilogue (51–3).

C V (44, 1–5) Die Wiederherstellung Hiobs, seiner Gesundheit und seiner Besitztümer.

C VI (45, 1–4) Abschiedsrede Hiobs an seine Kinder.

D *Schlußteil*:
Das Erbe der Hiob-Töchter und Hiobs Ende.

D I (46, 1–51, 4) Die Erbschaft der Hiob-Töchter.

D II (52, 1–53, 8) Hiobs Ende: Die Himmelfahrt seiner Seele, Begräbnis des Leibes und Totenklage.

Wie weit steht hinter der Zusammenstellung und Gestaltung dieser Erzählblöcke ein erkennbares Verfahren kompositorischer Arbeit? Um diese Frage zu beantworten, darf man nicht allein auf inhaltliche, sachliche Stimmigkeiten achten. Gerade wenn es zutreffen sollte, daß im Testament Hiobs vorgegebenes Material, ja Quellen verarbeitet sind, führen Vergleiche der Inhalte nicht weiter. In erster Linie wird man nach formalen Anzeichen kompositorischer Arbeit zu fragen haben. Gibt es Verklammerungen zwischen aufeinanderfolgenden Erzählblöcken? Bestehen Verzahnungen im Motiv- und Sprachmaterial? Wie weit sind bestimmte Sprach- und Stileigentümlichkeiten verbreitet?

Geht man den Text des Testaments Hiobs durch, so ergibt sich folgendes Bild:

1. Verklammerungen

Verklammerungen zwischen den einzelnen Erzählblöcken sind nahezu überall klar zu erkennen. Sie zeigen sich in der Form von Stichwortverknüpfungen.
In den meisten Fällen verlaufen diese unmittelbar zwischen den jeweiligen End- und Anfangssätzen:

1. B I/II 5,3 καὶ οὕτως ἀνεχώρησα εἰς τὸν οἶκόν μου κελεύσας ἀσφαλισθῆναι τὰς θύρας

6,2 ἅμα γὰρ εἰσῆλθον εἰς τὸν οἶκόν μου καὶ τὰς θύρας μου ἀσφαλισάμενος ἐνετειλάμην

2. B II/III 8,3 καὶ ἦρέν μοι σύμπαντα τὸν πλοῦτον
9,1 ὑποδείξω γὰρ ὑμῖν πάντα ... τὰ ἀρθέντα μοι

3.   B IV/V   20,6f.   καὶ ἐπάταξέν με <u>πληγὴν</u> σκληρὰν ...
καὶ ... <u>ἐξῆλθον τὴν πόλιν</u> καὶ καθεσθεὶς
<u>ἐπὶ τῆς κοπρίας</u>

            21,1   καὶ ἐποίησα ἔτη ... <u>ἐν τῇ κοπρίᾳ ἐκτὸς</u>
<u>τῆς πόλεως</u> ἐν ταῖς <u>πληγαῖς</u>

4.   B V/VI   26,6   ἆρα σὺ οὐχ ὁρᾷς τὸν διάβολον <u>ὄπισθέν</u>
<u>σου</u> <u>στήκοντα</u> ...; βούλεται γάρ σε
δεῖξαι ὥσπερ μίαν τῶν ἀφρόνων
<u>γυναικῶν.</u>

            27,1   ἐγὼ δὲ πάλιν στραφεὶς πρὸς <u>τὸν</u>
<u>Σατανᾶν</u> εἶπον, <u>ὄπισθεν</u> <u>ὄντα</u> τῆς
<u>γυναικός</u> <u>μου</u>

5.   B VI/C I   27,5   οὕτω καὶ σύ, Ιωβ, ὑποκάτω <u>ἧς</u> καὶ
<u>ἐν πληγῇ</u>

            28,1   καὶ ὅτε ἐπλήρωσα ... <u>ἔτη</u> <u>τυγχάνων</u>
<u>ἐν τῇ πληγῇ</u>

6.   C I/II   38,1   <u>καὶ ἐγὼ πρὸς ταῦτα εἶπον</u>

            38,8   <u>ἀποκριθεὶς δὲ εἶπον</u>

            39,1   <u>καὶ ἐμοῦ ταῦτα πρὸς αὐτοὺς λέγοντος</u>

7.   C II/III   40,14   τὸν μὲν οὖν θρῆνον ... εὑρήσετε ἐν τοῖς
παραλειπομένοις ‹Ελιφα›[25]

            41,1   <u>Ελιφας</u> δὲ καὶ οἱ λοιποὶ μετὰ ταῦτα
παρεκάθισάν μοι

8.   C VI/D I   45,4   ἰδοὺ οὖν, τεκνία μου, <u>διαμερίζω ὑμῖν</u>
<u>πάντα</u> <u>ὅσα</u> <u>μοι</u> <u>ὑπάρχει</u> πρὸς τὸ
δεσπόζειν ἕκαστον τοῦ <u>μέρους</u> ἑαυτοῦ
ἀκωλύτως

            46,1   οἱ δὲ παρήνεγκαν <u>τὰ ὄντα εἰς μερισμόν</u>

Zum Teil reichen sie aber auch in den weiteren Kontext zurück:

---

[25] In den Handschriften fehlt der Name, was jedoch kaum ursprünglich sein kann
(vgl. 41,6; 49,3; 50,3). Wie bereits Spitta (s. Anm. 11), 152 erkannt hat, liegt
eine Haplographie zugrunde.

9.	A/B I	1,1	βίβλος λόγων Ιωβ τοῦ καλουμένου Ιωβαβ
		2,1f.	ἐγω γάρ εἰμι <u>Ιωβαβ πρὶν ἢ ὀνομάσαι</u> <u>με ὁ κύριος Ιωβ. ὅτε Ιωβαβ ἐκαλούμην</u>
10.	C III/IV	41,1	παρεκάθισάν μοι ἀνταποκρινόμενοι καὶ <u>μεγαλορημονοῦντες</u> κατ ἐμοῦ
		42,1	μετὰ τὸ παύσασθαι αὐτὸν τῆς <u>μεγαλο-</u> <u>ρημοσύνης</u> αὐτοῦ
11.	C IV/V	43,2	ἀναλαβὼν Ελιφας πνεῦμα εἶπεν <u>ὕμνον</u> ἐπιφωνούντων αὐτῷ τῶν ἄλλων φίλων καὶ τῶν στρατευμάτων <u>πλησίον τοῦ</u> <u>θυσιαστηρίου</u>
		44,1	μετὰ δὲ τὸ παύσασθαι Ελιφαν τοῦ <u>ὕμνου</u> ὑποφωνούντων αὐτῷ πάντων <u>καὶ κυκλούντων τὸ θυσιαστήριον</u>
12.	C V/VI	44,3	καὶ παρεγένοντο πρός με πάντες οἱ φίλοι μου καὶ ὅσοι ᾔδεισαν <u>εὐποιεῖν</u> καὶ ἠρώτησάν με λέγοντες Τί παρ' ἡμῶν νῦν αἰτεῖς; ἐγὼ δὲ ἀναμνησθεὶς <u>τῶν πτωχῶν</u> τοῦ πάλιν <u>εὐποιεῖν</u> ἠτησάμην ...
		45,2	<u>εὐποιήσατε τοῖς πτωχοῖς</u>
13.	D I/II	51,3	ἐκαθεζόμην <u>πλησίον τοῦ</u> Ιωβ ἐπὶ <u>τῆς</u> <u>κλίνης</u> μου
		52,1	μετὰ τρεῖς ἡμέρας ποιουμένου Ιωβ νοσεῖν ἐπὶ <u>τῆς κλίνης</u>

Keine Anbindung durch Stichwortverknüpfung gibt es nur in einem Fall: zwischen den Blöcken B III/IV (9–15/16–20). Der Block B IV setzt übergangslos nach Block B III ein; immerhin bezieht er sich deutlich auf den Abschluß des Blockes B II, so daß man auch hier von einer kompositorischen Verklammerung sprechen kann.

14. B II/IV 8,1ff. ἀπελθὼν ὑπὸ τὸ στερέωμα ὥρκωσεν
τὸν κύριον ἵνα λάβῃ ἐξουσίαν ... καὶ
τότε λαβὼν τὴν ἐξουσίαν ἦλθεν καὶ
ἦρέν μου σύμπαντα τὸν πλοῦτον

16,1ff. ἐμοῦ δὲ τοῦτο ποιοῦντος ἐν τοῖς ἑπτὰ
ἔτεσιν ... εἶτα μετὰ τὸ εἰληφέναι τὴν
ἐξουσίαν τὸν Σατανᾶν, τότε λοιπὸν
ἀνηλεῶς κατῆλθεν καὶ ἐφλόγισεν ...

2. Verzahnungen

Beispiele sachlicher Verzahnungen finden sich – was zu erwarten ist
– innerhalb einzelner Erzählblöcke, darüber hinaus aber auch nicht
selten zwischen den Erzählblöcken, und zwar zwischen benachbarten
wie auch zwischen auseinanderliegenden:

1. *1,2* (A) Ιωβ ... ἐν ᾗ γὰρ ἡμέρᾳ νοσήσας[26]

52,1 (D II) καὶ μετὰ τρεῖς ἡμέρας ποιουμένου τοῦ
Ιωβ νοσεῖν

2. *1,2* (A) ἐκάλεσεν τοὺς ἑπτὰ υἱοὺς καὶ τὰς τρεῖς
θυγατέρας αὐτοῦ

17,5 (B IV) ἔχει ἑπτὰ υἱοὺς καὶ θυγατέρας τρεῖς

46,4 (D I) ὑμῖν ἔπεμψα κληρονομίαν κρείττονα τῶν
ἑπτὰ ἀδελφῶν

52,12 (D II) προηγουμένων τῶν τρίων θυγατέρων αὐτοῦ

3. *1,3* (A) Ημερα, Κασια, Αμαλθειας κερας
46,5; 47,1; 48,1; 49,1; 50,1 (D I)
52,3f. (D II)

4. *1,4* (A) περικυκλώσαντες,[27] τέκνα μου, περι-
κυκλώσατέ με

53,5 (D II) περιεκύκλωσαν πᾶσαι αἱ χῆραι καὶ οἱ
ὀρφανοί

---

[26] νοσεῖν außerdem nur 35,3.
[27] περικυκλοῦν sonst im TestHi an keiner Stelle.

5.   *1,6* (A)   <u>δηλώσω ὑμῖν τὰ συμβεβηκότα μοι</u>

       9,1 (B III)   <u>ὑποδείξω</u> γὰρ <u>ὑμῖν τὰ συμβεβηκότα μοι</u>

       23,4 (B V)   ἀγνοεῖς <u>τὰ συμβεβηκότα ἡμῖν</u> πονηρά

       28,9 (C I)   <u>ἐδηλώθη</u> αὐτοῖς <u>τὰ συμβεβηκότα μοι</u>

6.   *1,6* (A)   <u>ἡ</u> γὰρ <u>προτέρα μου, γυνὴ ἐτελεύτησεν</u>

       21,2 (B V)   ὥστε ἰδεῖν ... <u>τὴν πρώτην μου γυναῖκα</u>

       40,6 (C II)   (<u>ἡ γυνή μου</u>) <u>ἐκοιμήθη καὶ τετελεύτηκεν</u>

7.   *2,4* (B I)   ἄρα πῶς <u>γνώσομαι</u>;

       3,2 (B I)   <u>ὑποδείξω</u> σοι τίς ἐστιν οὗτος ὃν <u>γνῶναι</u> θέλεις

8.   *3,4* (B I)   <u>κατέπεσα ἐπὶ τὴν κλινήν</u>[28] μου

       51,3 (D I)   <u>ἐκαθεζόμην</u> πλησίον τοῦ Ιωβ <u>ἐπὶ τῆς κλίνης</u> μου

       52,1 (D II)   ποιουμένου τοῦ Ιωβ <u>νοσεῖν ἐπὶ τῆς κλίνης</u>

9.   *3,6* (B I)   δός μοι ἐξουσίαν ἵνα ... <u>καθαρίσω αὐτοῦ τὸν τόπον</u>

       4,1 (B I)   <u>καθαρίσαι</u> τοῦτον <u>τὸν τόπον</u> δυνήσῃ

       4,4 (B I)   ἐὰν ἐπιχειρήσεις <u>καθαρίσαι τὸν τόπον</u> τοῦ Σατανᾶ

       5,2 (B I)   εἰς <u>τὸν ναὸν τοῦ εἰδωλίου</u> ἀπελθὼν κατήνεγκα αὐτὸ εἰς τὸ ἔδαφος

       17,4 (B IV)   καὶ <u>τὸν</u> μὲν <u>ναὸν τοῦ μεγάλου Θεοῦ</u> καθελὼν καὶ ἀφανίσας <u>τὸν τόπον τῆς</u> σπονδῆς

10. *3,7* (B I)   τίς ἐστιν ὁ κωλύων <u>με βασιλεύοντα</u>[29] ταύτης τῆς χώρας;

       28,7 (C I)   ποῦ <u>Ιωβαβ</u> ὁ τῆς Αἰγύπτου ὅλης <u>βασιλεύων</u>;

---

[28] κλίνη sonst im TestHi an keiner Stelle.
[29] βασιλεύειν sonst im TestHi an keiner Stelle.

11. *4,1* (B I) ἐμοὶ εἶπεν τὸ φῶς ... ὑποδείκνυμί σοι πάντα ἅπερ ἐνετείλατό μοι κύριος μεταδιδόναι σοι

    16,1 (B IV) μετὰ τὸ τόν ἄγγελον ὑποδεῖξαί μοι

    47,9 (D I) ὁ δὲ κύριος ἐλάλησέν μοι ... ὑποδείξας μοι τὰ γενόμενα καὶ τὰ μέλλοντα

12. *4,4* (B I) ἐπαναστήσεταί σοι μετὰ ὀργῆς εἰς πόλεμον[30]

    18,5 (B IV) μνησθεὶς ... τοῦ προσημανθέντος μοι πολέμου ὑπὸ τοῦ κυρίου διὰ τοῦ ἀγγέλου αὐτοῦ

13. *4,4* (B I) ἐπιφέρει[31] δέ σοι πληγὰς πολλάς

    7,13 (B II) ἕτοιμός εἰμι ὑποστῆναι ἅπερ ἐπιφέρεις μοι

    20,2 (B IV) ᾐτήσατο τὸ σῶμά μου παρὰ τοῦ κυρίου ἵνα ἐπενέγκῃ μοι πληγήν

    37,3 (C I) ἐπήνεγκέν σοι τὰς πληγὰς ταύτας;

       5 ἐπενέγκων σοι τὰς πληγὰς ταύτας

14. *4,5* (B I) ἀφαιρεῖταί σου τὰ ὑπάρχοντα

    8,2 (B II) ὥρκωσεν τὸν κύριον ἵνα λάβῃ ἐξουσίαν κατὰ τῶν ὑπαρχόντων μου. καὶ τότε ... ἦρέν μου σύμπαντα τὸν πλοῦτον

    16,7 (B IV) καὶ τῶν ὑπαρχόντων μοι ἀνήγγειλάν μοι τὴν ἀπώλειαν

    20,1 (B IV) καὶ τῶν ὑπαρχόντων μοι πάντων ἀπολομένων

    26,3 (B V) ὑποφέρεις καὶ τὴν τῶν τέκνων ἡμῶν ἀπώλειαν καὶ τῶν ὑπαρχόντων

    37,3 (C I) τίς ἀφείλατο τὰ ὑπάρχοντά σου;

       4 ἀφελόμενός σου τὰ ὑπάρχοντα

---

[30] πόλεμος nur noch 16,1 (V).
[31] ἐπιφέρειν außerdem noch 11,11, aber in medialer Form.

15.   4,5 (B I)   τὰ παιδία σου ἀναιρήσει

      18,1 (B IV)   κατέβαλεν τὴν οἰκίαν ἐπὶ τὰ τέκνα μου
                       καὶ ἀνεῖλεν αὐτά

      19,1 (B IV)   ἐλθόντος δὲ τοῦ ἐσχάτου ἀγγέλου καὶ
                       δηλώσαντός μοι τὴν τῶν ἐμῶν τέκνων
                       ἀπώλειαν

      20,4 (B IV)   καὶ προσῆλθέν μοι ... πενθοῦντι τὴν τῶν
                       τέκνων μου ἀπώλειαν

      26,3 B V)   ὑποφέρεις καὶ τὴν τῶν τέκνων ἀπώλειαν

16.   4,8 (B I)   ἵνα γνῷς ὅτι ἀπροσωπολημπτός³² ἐστιν

      43,13 (C IV)   παρ' ᾧ οὐκ ἔστιν προσωπολημψία

17.   4,11 (B I)   τότε γνώσει ὅτι δίκαιος καὶ ἀληθινὸς καὶ
                       ἰσχυρὸς ὁ κύριος

      43,13 (C IV)   δίκαιός ἐστιν κύριος, ἀληθινὰ αὐτοῦ τὰ
                       κρίματα

18.   4,10 (B I)   ἔσῃ γὰρ ὡς ἀθλητὴς³³ πυκτεύων καὶ
                       καρτερῶν³⁴ πόνους

      27,3 (B VI)   ἐγένου γὰρ ὃν τρόπον ἀθλητής μετὰ
                       ἀθλητοῦ

      4   καὶ ἐνέγκαντος αὐτοῦ τὴν καρτερίαν

19.   4,11 (B I)   τότε γνώσει ὅτι δίκαιος καὶ ἀληθινὸς καὶ
                       ἰσχυρὸς ὁ κύριος, ἐνισχύων³⁵ τοὺς
                       ἐκλεκτοὺς αὐτοῦ

      47,7 (D I)   καὶ λοιπὸν τὸ σῶμά μου ἐνίσχυσεν διὰ
                       κυρίου

---

³² Die aus der hebr. Wendung *nasaʿ panim*, griech. πρόσωπον λαμβάνειν hervor-
gegangene adjektivische bzw. substantivische Wortverbindung ist nur hier im
TestHi, sonst ausschließlich in christlichen Quellen belegt: vgl. W. Bauer,
Griechisch-deutsches Wörterbuch zum Neuen Testament und übrigen urchristlichen
Schrifttum (Berlin, de Gruyter, 1963⁵), 1429.
³³ ἀθλήτης sonst im TestHi nicht vorhanden.
³⁴ καρτερεῖν/καρτερία ausschließlich im vorliegenden Zusammenhang.
³⁵ ἐνισχύειν sonst im TestHi nicht verwendet.

20. 6, 4 (B II)   ὁ Σατανᾶς μετασχηματισθεὶς[36] εἰς ἐπαίτην

     17, 2 (B IV)   (ὁ διάβολος) μετασχηματισθεὶς εἰς βασιλέα
                     τῶν Περσῶν

     23, 1 (B V)   καὶ ὁ Σατανᾶς ... μετεσχηματίσθη εἰς
                     πράτην

21. 7, 8 (B II)   καὶ ἔκλαυσεν μετὰ λύπης μεγάλης ἡ παῖς
                     λέγουσα

     34, 5 (C I)   Ελιφας ἔκλινεν ἀπ᾽ αὐτῶν ἐν μεγάλῃ λύπῃ
                     λέγων

22. 8, 3 (B II)   ἦρέν μου σύμπαντα τὸν πλοῦτον[37]

     26, 3 (B V)   ἵνα ἀπαλλοτριωθῶμεν τοῦ μεγάλου
                     πλούτου

     28, 5 (C I)   ἐπειδὴ ᾔδεισάν με πρὸ τούτων τῶν κακῶν
                     ἐν πολλῷ πλούτῳ ὄντα

     32, 1   ἀκούσατε οὖν τοῦ κλαυθμοῦ τοῦ Ε.
                     ὑποδεικνύοντος τοῖς παισὶν τὸν πλοῦτον
                     τοῦ Ιωβ

23. 9, 2f. (B III) εἶχον γὰρ ἑκατὸν τριάκοντα χιλιάδας
                     προβάτων καὶ ἀφώρισα ἀπ᾽ αὐτῶν χιλιάδας
                     ἑπτὰ καρῆναι εἰς ἔνδυσιν[38] ὀρφανῶν καὶ
                     χηρῶν καὶ πενήτων καὶ ἀδυνάτων

     16, 3 (B IV)   καὶ ἐφλόγισεν τὰς ἑπτὰ χιλιάδας προβάτων
                     τὰ ταγέντα εἰς ἔνδυσιν τῶν χηρῶν

     32, 2 (C I)   σὺ εἶ ὁ τὰ ἑπτακισχίλια πρόβατα ἐκτάξας
                     εἰς ἔνδυσιν τῶν πτωχῶν;

     44, 2 (C V)   πάλιν ἐπεζήτησα εὐεργεσίας ποιεῖν τοῖς
                     πτωχοῖς

---

[36] μετασχηματίζειν ausschließlich an den aufgeführten Stellen im Zusammenhang mit der Gestalt des Satan/Teufels.

[37] πλοῦτος außerdem nur 18, 6.

[38] ἔνδυσις außerdem nur 25, 7 das Verb ἐνδύεσθαι 39, 5; in beiden Fällen bezogen auf die Frau Hiobs.

4		δότε μοι ἕκαστος ἀμνάδα μίαν εἰς ἔνδυσιν τῶν πτωχῶν τῶν ἐν γυμνώσει
45,2 (C VI)		εὐποιήσατε τοῖς πτωχοῖς, μὴ παρίδητε τοὺς ἀδυνάτους
53.1 (D II)		σὺν τοῖς πένησιν καὶ ὀρφανοῖς καὶ πᾶσιν τοῖς ἀδυνάτοις κλαίουσιν
2		ἦρται ἡ δύναμις τῶν ἀδυνάτων
3		ἦρται ὁ πατὴρ τῶν ὀρφανῶν ἦρται ἡ ἔνδυσις τῶν χηρῶν
24.	9,4f. (B II)	εἶχον δὲ καμήλους ἐννακισχιλίους καὶ ἐξ αὐτῶν ἐξελεξάμην τρισχιλίας ἐργάζεσθαι πᾶσαν πόλιν καὶ γομώσας³⁹ ἀγαθῶν ἀπέστειλα εἰς τὰς πόλεις καὶ εἰς τὰς κώμας … ἐπιδιδόναι τοῖς ἀδυνάτοις καὶ τοῖς ὑστερουμένοις καὶ ταῖς χηραῖς πάσαις
	16,3 (B IV)	ἐφλόγισεν … καὶ τὰς τρισχιλίας καμήλους
	25,4 (B V)	ἧς αἱ κάμηλοι γεγομωμέναι ἀγαθῶν ἀπέφερον εἰς τὰς χώρας τοῖς πτωχοῖς
	30,5 (C I)	μὴ οὐκ οἴδαμεν τὰ πολλὰ ἀγαθὰ τὰ ἀποστελλόμενα ὑπ' αὐτοῦ εἰς τὰς κώμας καὶ εἰς τὰς κύκλῳ πόλεις διαδίδοσθαι τοῖς πτωχοῖς
	32,2 (C I)	σὺ εἶ ὁ τὰς τρισχιλίας καμήλους ἐκτάξας εἰς μεταφορὰν τῶν ἀγαθῶν τοῖς πένησιν
25.	9,6 (B III)	εἶχον δὲ ἑκατὸν τεσσαράκοντα χιλιάδας ὄνων νομάδων καὶ ἀφώρισα ἐξ αὐτῶν πεντακοσίας
	16,3 (B IV)	ἐφλόγισεν … καὶ τὰς πεντακοσίας ὄνους
26.	9,6 (B III)	διδόναι τοῖς πένησιν καὶ ἐπιδεομένοις⁴⁰

---

³⁹ γομεῖν ausschließlich 9,5 und 25,4 verwendet.
⁴⁰ V. 1.: V δεομένοις.

17,3 (B IV)   ὁ διαδεδωκὼς τοῖς ἐπιδεομένοις[41] καὶ
                τυφλοῖς καὶ χωλοῖς

27.   10,1 (B III)   ἦσαν δέ μοι τράπεζαι ἱδρυμέναι[42] τριάκοντα
                ἐν τῷ οἴκῳ μου ἀκίνητοι ... τοῖς ξένοις

        25,5 (B V)   ἴδε ἡ ἔχουσα ἑπτὰ τραπέζας ἀκινήτους
                ἐπὶ τῆς οἰκίας εἰς ἃς ἦσθιον οἱ πτωχοὶ καὶ
                πᾶς ξένος

        32,7 (C I)   σὺ εἶ ὁ τὰς ἱδρυμένας ἑξήκοντα τραπέζας
                τοῖς πτωχοῖς στηρίξας

28.   10,2 (B III)   εἶχον δὲ καὶ τῶν χηρῶν ἄλλας δώδεκα
                τραπέζας κειμένας

        13,4 (B III)   ἀπέκαμνον δὲ καὶ οἱ δοῦλοί μου οἱ τὰ τῶν
                χηρῶν ἐδέσματα ἑψοῦντες

29.   10,3 (B III)   ἀνάγκην εἶχεν[43] τρέφεσθαι
        12,3 (B III)   ἀνάγκην ἔχεις λαβεῖν

30.   10,5f. (B III) εἶχον δὲ τρισχίλια καὶ πεντακόσια ζεύγη
                βοῶν καὶ ἐξελεξάμην ἐξ αὐτῶν ζεύγη
                πεντακόσια καὶ ἔστησα εἰς ἀροτριασμὸν[44]
                ... καὶ τὸν καρπὸν αὐτῶν ἀφορίζειν τοῖς
                πένησιν

        16,3 (B IV)   ἐφλόγισεν ... τὰ πεντακόσια ζεύγη βοῶν

        32,3 (C I)   σὺ εἶ ὁ τὰς χιλίας βοῦς ἐκτάξας τοῖς
                πένησιν εἰς ἀροτρίαν

31.   11,1 (B III)   ἐπεθύμησαν καὶ αὐτοὶ ὑπηρετεῖν τῇ
                διακονίᾳ

        12,1 (B III)   βούλομαι μέντοι κἂν διακονῆσαι τοῖς
                πτωχοῖς

---

[41] V. 1.: S δεομένοις.
[42] ἱδρυμέναι ausschließlich in 10,1 und 32,7 verwendet.
[43] ἀνάγκην ἔχειν sonst im TestHi nicht vorhanden.
[44] ἀροτριασμός (10,5; 32,3 SV)/ἀροτρία (32,3P) sonst im TestHi nicht verwendet.

	15,1 (B III)	καὶ τὰ ἐμὰ τέκνα μετὰ τὴν ὑπερησίαν τῆς <u>διακονίας</u>
	4	καὶ οἱ υἱοί μου ἀνέκειντο τοῖς ἀρρενικοῖς δούλοις τοῖς <u>διακονοῦσιν</u>
32.	*14,1* (B III)	εἶχον δὲ ἓξ ψαλμοὺς καὶ δεκάχορδον κιθάραν
	2	καὶ ἐλάμβανον τὴν κιθάραν[45] καὶ ἔψαλλον αὐτοῖς
	52,3 (D II)	καὶ εὐθέως ἀναστὰς ἔλαβεν <u>κιθάραν</u> καὶ ἔδωκεν τῇ θυγατρὶ αὐτοῦ
33.	*17,3* (B IV)	ὁ διαδεδωκὼς[46] τοῖς ἐπιδεομένοις καὶ τυφλοῖς καὶ χωλοῖς
	30,5 (C I)	<u>διαδίδοσθαι</u> τοῖς <u>πτωχοῖς</u>
	53,3 (D II)	ἦρται τὸ φῶς <u>τῶν τυφλῶν</u>
34.	*18,1* (B IV)	ἀπῆλθεν καὶ κατέβαλεν τὴν οἰκίαν ἐπὶ τὰ <u>τέκνα μου</u> καὶ ἀνεῖλεν αὐτά
	39,8 (C II)	κελεύσατε τοῖς στρατιώταις ὑμῶν ἵνα σκάψωσιν τὴν πτῶσιν τῆς οἰκίας τῆς ἐπιπεσούσης τοῖς <u>τέκνοις μου</u>
35.	*20,8* (B IV)	καὶ ἰχῶρες τοῦ σώματος <u>σκώληκες</u> πολλοὶ ἦσαν ἐν τῷ σώματί μου
	24,3 (B V)	σὺ δὲ αὐτὸς κάθῃ ἐν σαπρίᾳ <u>τῶν σκωλήκων</u>
	26,1 (B V)	ὑφιστάμενος τοὺς <u>σκώληκας</u> τοὺς ἐν τῷ σώματί μου
	34,4 (C I)	αὐτὸς ἐν ταλαιπωρίᾳ <u>σκωλήκων</u> κάθηται
	47,4 (D I)	τούτων με κατηξίωσεν ὁ κύριος ἐν ἡμέρᾳ ᾗ ἠβουλήθη με ἐλεῆσαι καὶ περιγραφῆναι ἐκ τοῦ σώματος τὰς πληγὰς καὶ τοὺς <u>σκώληκας</u>

---

[45] λαμβάνειν κίθαραν sonst im TestHi nicht verwendet.
[46] διαδιδόναι kommt sonst im TestHi nicht vor, ebenso τυφλός.

	6	καὶ εὐθέως ἀφανεῖς ἐγένοντο ἀπὸ τότε οἱ σκώληκες <u>ἀπὸ τοῦ σώματος</u> καὶ αἱ πληγαί
36.	*21,3* (B V)	ὦ τῆς ἀλαζονείας τῶν ἀρχόντων τῆς πόλεως ταύτης· πῶς χρῶνται τῇ γαμετῇ μου ὡς <u>δουλίδι</u>
	39,2 (C II)	ἀποδράσασα ἐκ τῆς τοῦ οἰκοδεσπότου <u>δουλείας ᾧ ἐδούλευεν</u>
	40,4 (C II)	ἡ γυνή μου … εἶπεν … ἀνακτήσομαι πρὸ τῆς ὑπουργείας τῆς <u>δουλείας</u> μου.
	5	καὶ ἀπελθοῦσα εἰς τὴν πόλιν εἰσῆλθεν εἰς τὴν ἔπαυλην τῶν βοῶν αὐτῆς τῶν ἁρπασθέντων ὑπὸ <u>τῶν ἀρχόντων οἷς ἐδούλευεν</u>
37.	*22,2* (B V)	καὶ αὐτὴ <u>λαμβάνουσα διεμέριζεν αὐτῇ τε καὶ ἐμοί</u>
	24,5 (B V)	μόλις τὴν ἐμὴν τροφὴν <u>λαμβάνω</u> καὶ <u>διαμερίζω σοί τε καὶ ἐμοί</u>
38.	*22,2* (B V)	λέγουσα μετ' <u>ὀδύνης</u>
	24,4 (B V)	ἐργαζομένη ἡμέρας <u>ὀδυνομένη</u>
	47,8 (D I)	τῶν ἐν καρδίᾳ <u>ὀδυνῶν</u> λήθην ἔσχον
	52,1 (D II)	ἄνευ … <u>ὀδύνης</u>
39.	*24,1* (B V)	<u>ἀνακράξασα μετὰ</u> κλαυθμοῦ λέγει
	40,9 (C II)	<u>ἀνέκραξαν μετὰ</u> μυκήματος <u>κλαυθμοῦ</u>
40.	*24,6* (B V)	οὐκ ἀρκετὸν εἶναί σε ἐν <u>πόνοις</u>
	25,10 (B V)	ἀπαλλαγήσομαι ἀκηδίας διὰ <u>πόνου</u> σου τοῦ σώματος
	26,2	οὐκ ἐβαρήθη ἡ ψυχή μου διὰ τοὺς <u>πόνους</u> ὅσον διὰ τὸ ῥῆμα
	52,1 (D II)	ἄνευ <u>πόνου</u> μέντοι
41.	*24,9* (B V)	καὶ ἐμὲ δὲ δεῖξαι τὴν <u>ἀπορίαν ἡμῶν</u>

	32,10 (C I)	νυνὶ δὲ ἐν <u>ἀπορίᾳ ὤν</u>
42.	25,1 (B V)	<u>τίς οὐκ ἐξεπλάγη</u>[47]
	35,5 (C I)	<u>τίς γὰρ οὐκ ἂν ἐκπλαγείη</u>
43.	25,7 (B V)	νῦν δὲ φορεῖ <u>ῥακκώδη</u>[48]
	39,1 (C II)	ἡ γυνή μου Σιτιδος ἐν ἱματίοις <u>ῥακκώδοις</u>
44.	25,8 (B V)	βλέπε τὴν <u>τοὺς κραββάτους χρυσοῦς καὶ ἀργυρέους ἔχουσαν</u>
	32,4 (C I)	<u>σὺ εἶ ὁ τοὺς χρυσέους κραββάτους ἔχων</u>
45.	28,2 (C I)	ὅπως ἐπισκεψάμενοι <u>παραμυθήσονταί με</u>
	34,2 (C I)	ἵνα <u>παραμυθησώμεθα αὐτόν</u>
	5	ἵνα <u>παραμυθησώμεθα αὐτόν</u>
46.	29,3 (C I)	εἶπεν, <u>σὺ εἶ Ιωβαβ</u>
	31,5 (C I)	εἶπέν μοι, <u>σὺ εἶ Ιωβαβ</u>
	36,1 (C I)	λέγων, <u>σὺ εἶ Ιωβ</u>
47.	31,2 (C I)	διὰ τὴν <u>δυσωδίαν</u> τοῦ σώματός μου
	32,8 (C I)	νυνὶ ἐν <u>δυσωδίᾳ</u> ὑπάρχεις
	34,4 (C I)	αὐτὸς ἐν ταλαιπωρίᾳ σκωλήκων κάθηται καὶ <u>δυσωδίαις</u>
	35,2 (C I)	οὐκ ἰσχύσαμεν προσεγγίσαι αὐτῷ διὰ τὴν <u>δυσωδίαν</u>
48.	31,7 (C I)	καὶ οὕτως <u>κλαύσας κλαυθμὸν μέγαν</u>
	39,6 (C II)	τότε <u>κλαύσαντες κλαυθμὸν μέγαν</u>
49.	31,8 (C I)	<u>ὑποφωνούντων</u>[49] καὶ τῶν ἄλλων βασιλέων καὶ τῶν στρατευμάτων αὐτῶν
	33,1 (C I)	<u>ὑποφωνούντων</u> αὐτῷ τῶν συμβασιλέων
	43,3 (C IV)	<u>ἐπιφωνούντων</u> αὐτῷ τῶν ἄλλων φίλων καὶ τῶν στρατευμάτων

[47] ἐκπλήσσειν sonst im TestHi nicht verwendet.
[48] ῥακκωδός nur als Bezeichnung des Gewandes der Frau Hiobs verwendet.
[49] ὑπο/ἐπιφωνεῖν sonst im TestHi nicht verwendet.

	44,1 (C V)	ὑποφωνούντων αὐτῷ
50.	*32,9* (C I)	σὺ εἶ ὁ τοὺς χρυσέους λύχνους ἐπὶ τὰς ἀργυρᾶς λυχνίας ἔχων
	43,5 (C IV)	ὁ λύχνος αὐτοῦ σβεσθείς
51.	*33,2* (C I)	νῦν ὑποδείξω ὑμῖν τὸν θρόνον μου
	3	ἐμοῦ ὁ θρόνος ἐν τῷ ὑπερκοσμίῳ ἐστίν
	5	ἐμοὶ δὲ ὁ θρόνος ὑπάρχει ἐν τῇ ἁγίᾳ γῇ
	41,4 (C III)	λελάληκεν λέγων ἔχειν τὸν ἑαυτοῦ θρόνον ἐν οὐρανοῖς
52.	*33,2* (C I)	εἶπεν αὐτοῖς Ιωβ, σιωπήσατε
	34,1 (C I)	ἐμοῦ ταῦτα λέγοντος πρὸς αὐτοὺς ἵνα σιωπήσωσιν
	39,6 (C II)	γενόμενοι ἐν διπλῇ ἀκηδίᾳ ἐσιώπησαν
53.	*33,4* (C I)	ὁ κόσμος ὅλος παρελεύσεται
	8	οὗτοι οἱ βασιλεῖς παρελεύσονται
	34,4 (C I)	βασιλεῖαι παρέρχονται
	43,7 (C IV)	ἡ βασιλεία αὐτοῦ παρῆλθεν
54.	*34,2* (C I)	Ελιφας εἶπεν τοῖς ἄλλοις φίλοις
	43,3 (C IV)	Ελιφας … εἶπεν ὕμνον ἐπιφωνούντων αὐτῷ τῶν ἄλλων φίλων
55.	*35,4f.* (C I)	μήτι ἄρα ἐξέστη αὐτοῦ ἡ καρδία …τίς γὰρ οὐκ ἂν … μανῇ ὑπάρχων ἐν πληγαῖς;
	39,13 (C II)	τίς πάλιν οὐκ ἐρεῖ ὅτι ἐξεστήκεις καὶ μαίνει
56.	*35,4* (C I)	μήτι ἄρα μνήσκεται αὐτοῦ τῆς εὐδαι-μονίας[50] τῆς προτέρας
	41,4 (C III)	ἀναμνησκόμενος τῆς εὐδαιμονίας τῆς προτέρας
57.	*36,2* (C I)	ἄρα ἐν τῷ καθεστηκότι ἡ καρδία σου;

---

[50] εὐδαιμονία im TestHi ausschließlich hier verwendet.

	37,8 (C I)	εἰ ἐν τῷ καθεστηκότι ὑπάρχεις
	38,6 (C I)	εἰ ἐν τῷ καθεστηκότι ὑπάρχεις
58.	*36,3* (C I)	ἐν δὲ τοῖς ἐπουρανίοις συνέστηκεν ἡ καρδία μου
	38,3 (C I)	ἵνα οὖν γνῶτε ὅτι συνέστηκεν ἡ καρδία μου
59.	*38,1* (C I)	διὰ τί οὖν μὴ λαλήσω τὰ μεγαλεῖα τοῦ κυρίου
	51,3 (D I)	ἤκουσα ἐγὼ τὰ μεγαλεῖα μιᾶς ὑποσημειουμένης τῇ μιᾷ
	4	καὶ ἀναγραψάμην τὸ βιβλίον ὅλον ... σωτήριον ταῦτα εἶναι ὅτι ταῦτά ἐστιν τὰ μεγαλεῖα τοῦ θεοῦ
60.	*41,6* (C III)	οἵτινες ἀναγεγραμμένοι[51] εἰσὶν ἐν τοῖς παραλειπομένοις τοῦ Ελιφα
	50,3 (D I)	εὑρήσει ἀναγεγραμμένα ἐν ταῖς εὐχαῖς τῆς Αμαλθειας κερας
	51,4 (D I)	καὶ ἀνεγραψάμην τὸ βιβλίον ὅλον
61.	*47,6* (D I)	ἐγὼ δὲ λαβὼν περιεζωσάμην
	47,11 (D I)	περιζώσασθε αὐτάς
	49,1 (D I)	καὶ τότε ἡ Κασια περιεζώσατο
	50,1 (D I)	καὶ τότε περιεζώσατο καὶ ἡ ἄλλη
	52,1 (D II)	διὰ τὸ σημεῖον τῆς περιζώσεως ἧς περιεζώσατο
	12	τῶν τριῶν θυγατέρων ... περιεζωσμένων
62.	*51,1* (D I)	ἐμοῦ Νηρείου ἀδελφοῦ ὄντος τοῦ Ιωβ
	53,1 (D II)	καὶ ἐγὼ Νηρευς ὁ ἀδελφὸς αὐτοῦ

Zum großen Teil erfolgen die Verzahnungen in Form der Wiederaufnahme längerer oder kürzerer Wendungen bzw. Ausdrücke. Man kann mitunter geradezu von textinternen Zitaten oder Anspielungen

---

[51] ἀναγράφειν kommt sonst im TestHi nicht vor.

sprechen.[52] Daneben ergeben sich die Bezüge durch die Verwendung markanter, im Testament Hiobs sonst nie oder selten gebrauchter Stichworte.[53] Was die Verbreitung anlangt, so ist keiner der Blöcke von einer solchen Verzahnung ausgenommen. Jeder ist mit wenigstens einem, meist sogar mit mehreren anderen verbunden.

Die Zahl der Bezüge und die Verteilung schwanken allerdings nicht unerheblich. Im einzelnen stellen sie sich folgendermaßen dar:

A   : B III(1) − B IV(1) − B V(2) − C I(1) − C II(1) − D I(2) − D II(4)

B I   : B II(2) − B IV(10) − B V(2) − B VI(2) − C I(5) − C IV(2) − D I(3) − D II(1)

B II : B IV(1) − B V(2) − C I(3)

B III : B IV(5) − B V(2) − C I(5) − C V(2) − C VI(1) − D II(3)

B IV : B V(2) − C I(2) − C II(1) − D I(2) − D II(1)

B V : C I(3) − C II(5) − C I(1) − D II(2)

C I   : C II(3) − C III(2) − C IV(4) − C V(1) − D I(2)

C III : D I(2)

D I   : D II(3)

Am häufigsten und zugleich verbreitetsten kommen die Bezüge zu B I vor (28 Fälle, 8 Blöcke). Es folgen: B III (18 Fälle, 6 Blöcke), A (12 Fälle, 7 Blöcke), C I (12 Fälle, 6 Blöcke), B V (11 Fälle, 4 Blöcke), B IV (8 Fälle, 5 Blöcke), B II (6 Fälle, 3 Blöcke), D I (3 Fälle, 1 Block), C III (2 Fälle, 1 Block).

Diese zahlenmäßige Verteilung besagt für sich genommen noch nicht viel. Man muß den Umfang der Blöcke berücksichtigen und auch die Art der Verteilung. Immerhin lassen sich einige Sachverhalte bereits erheben. Zunächst ist unverkennbar: Textpassagen von Block B I spielen im gesamten Testament Hiobs eine starke Rolle.[54] Das ist gewiß kein Zufall, sondern spiegelt die sachliche Bedeutung dieses Blockes für den Gesamttext wider: es handelt sich in ihm um die Exposition der gesamten Erzählung des Testaments Hiobs (2, 1−5, 3).

---

[52] Vgl. Nr. 2. 5. 9. 13. 14. 15. 20. 23. 24. 25. 26. 28. 30. 35. 44. 46. 51. 53. 55. 56. 58. 61.
[53] Vgl. Nr. 1. 4. 8. 10. 11.12. 16. 17. 18. 19. 21. 22.27. 29. 31. 32. 33.36. 38. 39. 40. 41. 42. 43. 45. 47. 48. 49. 50. 52. 54. 57. 59. 60.
[54] S. Nr. 7−19.

Ebenso deutlich ist das Gewicht des Blockes B III (9–15),[55] der den Bericht über Hiobs Reichtum und Wohltätigkeit enthält, und des Einleitungsblockes A[56] für den Gesamttext, ferner das Gewicht des Blockes C I (28–38) zumindest für den zweiten Hauptteil der Hioberzählung, der die Auseinandersetzung zwischen Hiob und seinen Freunden betrifft.

Geht man mehr ins Detail, so stößt man auf drei weitere Befunde:

(a) Die beiden Hauptteile der Hioberzählung (B/2–27 und C/28–45) sind über mehrere unterschiedliche Blöcke verknüpft: B I mit C I(3), C IV(2); B II mit C I(3); B III mit C I(5), C V(2), C VI(1); B IV mit C I(2), C II(1); B V mit C I(3), C II(5).

(b) Die hymnisch gestalteten Texte in B V (25,1–8), C I (32,2–12; 33,3–9) und C IV (43,4–17) sowie D II (53,2–4) sind z. T. untereinander verzahnt (vgl. Nr. 44.50.53), daneben aber vor allem auch mit sonstigen Textabschnitten (vgl. Nr. 16.23.24. 27.30.33).

(c) Schließlich, auch in den beiden Blöcken der Schlußkapitel mangelt es nicht an Querverbindungen zu den vorausgehenden Textblöcken; im Gegenteil, sie begegnen im Verhältnis gesehen recht häufig: D I : A(2), B I(3), B IV(2), C I(2), C II(2) D II: A(4), B I(1), B III(3), B IV(1), B V(2), C VI(3).

3. Verbreitete Stil- und Sprachmittel

In Stil und Sprache bietet das Testament Hiobs kein einheitliches Bild. Z. T. finden sich gewählte Redefiguren,[57] daneben aber auch recht einfach gehaltene, bisweilen sogar ungefüge Ausdrucksformen.[58] An verbreiteten Stil- und Sprachmitteln ist nur wenig zu greifen. Immerhin in einigen Fällen sind sie durchaus vorhanden.

---

[55] S. Nr. 23–30.

[56] S. Nr. 1–6.

[57] Vgl. JSHRZ, III, 3, 305 Anm. 3.

[58] Vgl. ebd., 304 Anm. 2.

Auffällig ist einmal der Gebrauch des Genitivus absolutus. Er begegnet an 17 Stellen:

3,1 (B I)*   καὶ ἐν τῇ νυκτὶ κοιμωμένου μου
6,4 (B II)   καὶ ἐμοῦ ἔνδον ὄντος
16,1 (B IV)*   ἐμοῦ δὲ τοῦτο ποιοῦντος ἐν τοῖς ἑπτὰ ἔτεσιν μετὰ τό ...
19,1 (B IV)*   ἐλθόντος δὲ τοῦ ἐσχάτου ἀγγέλου καὶ δηλώσαντός μοι τὴν τῶν ἐμῶν τέκνων ἀπώλειαν
20,1 (B IV)*   τῶν οὖν ὑπαρχόντων μοι πάντων ἀπολομένων
25,9 (B V)*   ἀπαξαπλῶς ... Ιωβ, πολλῶν ὄντων τῶν εἰρημένων
30,2 (C I)*   καὶ ταραχθέντων τῶν στρατευμάτων αὐτῶν βλεπόντων
31,8 (C I)   ὑποφωνούντων καὶ τῶν στρατευμάτων αὐτῶν
33,1 (C I)*   τοῦ δὲ Ε. μακρύναντος τὸν κλαυθμὸν ὑποφωνούντων αὐτῷ τῶν συμβασιλέων
34,1 (C I)*   καὶ ἐμοῦ ταῦτα λέγοντος πρὸς αὐτούς
39,1 (C II)*   καὶ ἐμοῦ ταῦτα πρὸς αὐτοὺς λέγοντος
43,3 (C IV)   ἐπιφωνούντων αὐτῷ τῶν ἄλλων φίλων
44,1 (C V)*   μετὰ τὸ ... ὑποφωνούντων αὐτῷ πάντων καὶ κυκλούντων τὸ θυσιαστήριον
51,1 (D I)*   μετὰ δὲ τὸ ... ἐπικειμένου τοῦ κυρίου καὶ ἐμοῦ Νηρειου ἀδελφοῦ ὄντος τοῦ Ιωβ, ἐπικειμένου δὲ καὶ τοῦ ἁγίου πνεύματος
52,1 (D II)*   καὶ μετὰ τρεῖς ἡμέρας ποιουμένου τοῦ Ιωβ νοσεῖν
9 (D II)   βλεπουσῶν τῶν τριῶν θυγατέρων καὶ αὐτοῦ τοῦ πατρὸς βλέποντος, ἄλλων δέ τινων μη βλεπόντων
12 (D II)   προηγουμένων τῶν τριῶν θυγατέρων αὐτοῦ καὶ περιεζωσμένων, ὑμνολογουσῶν ἐν ὕμνοις τοῦ πατρός.

Das sind gemessen am Gesamttext des Testaments Hiobs nicht übermäßig viel. Immerhin ist es bemerkenswert, daß der Gebrauch sich über den ganzen Text hin erstreckt – er begegnet in 11 der 15 Erzählblöcken. Da es sich dazu überwiegend um Texte handelt, mit denen neue Abschnitte eingeleitet bzw. Übergänge markiert werden,[59] liegt es nahe, hier ein bewußt eingesetztes Stilmittel anzunehmen.

---

[59] In der Auflistung mit * gekennzeichnet.

Das gleiche gilt im Hinblick auf die Verwendung der Präposition μετά mit anschließendem substantivierten Infinitiv. Auch sie begegnet über das Testament Hiobs verstreut (in 6 Blöcken) und zwar wiederum meist bei 'Neueinsätzen'.

5,2 (B I)   καὶ μετὰ τὸ σφραγισθῆναί με ὑπὸ τοῦ ἀγγέλου
             ἀνέλθοντος ἀπ' ἐμοῦ, τότε ἐγώ
14,2 (B III) καὶ διεγειρόμην ... μετὰ τὸ τρέφεσθαι τὰς χήρας
16,1f.(B IV) ... μετὰ τὸ τὸν ἄγγελον ὑποδεῖξαί μοι, εἶτα μετὰ τὸ
             εἰληφέναι τὴν ἐξουσίαν τὸν Σατανᾶν, τότε λοιπόν
42,1 (C IV)   μετὰ δὲ τὸ παύσασθαι αὐτὸν τῆς μεγαλορημοσύνης
4   καὶ μετὰ τὸ παύσασθαι τὸν κύριον λαλοῦντα
44,1 (C V)   μετὰ δὲ τὸ παύσασθαι Ελιφαν τοῦ ὕμνου ...
51,1 (D I)   μετὰ δὲ τὸ παύσασθαι τὰς τρεῖς ὑμνολογούσας ...

In vier Fällen, aus drei verschiedenen Blöcken, stimmt der Wortlaut überein;[60] in zwei Fällen, aus zwei Blöcken, ist die Konstruktion verbunden zusätzlich mit einem Genitivus absolutus.[61]

An sprachlichen Eigentümlichkeiten, die mehrfach vorkommen, sind zu vermerken:
die Einleitung von Erzählblöcken mit ἀκούσατέ (μου)

1,6 (B I)   ἀκούσατε οὖν μου, τέκνα, καὶ δηλώσω
6,1 (B II)   ἀκούσατέ μου, τέκνια, καὶ θαυμάσατε
9,1 (B III)   ἀκούσατε οὖν, ὑποδείξω
32,1 (C I)   ἀκούσατε οὖν τοῦ κλαυθμοῦ
38,3 (C I)   ἀκούσατε, ὃ ἐπερωτῶ ὑμᾶς
41,5 (C III) τοίνυν ἐμοῦ ἀκούσατε καὶ γνωρίσω ὑμῖν

die Einleitung der paränetischen Abschlüsse der beiden Hauptteile mit νῦν τέκνα μου

27,7 (B VI)   νῦν οὖν, τέκνα μου, μακροθυμήσατε
45,1 (C VI)   καὶ νῦν τέκνα μου, ... μὴ ἐπιλάθεσθε

der Gebrauch der adverbialen Akkusative ἀκμήν – λοιπόν

7,11 (B II)   ἀκμὴν καὶ τοῦτό σοι ἔδωκα
27,4 (B VI)   ἐφώνησεν ἀκμὴν ὁ ἐπάνω

---

[60] 42,1.4; 44,1; 51,1.
[61] 16,1; 51,1.

34,4 (C I)	καὶ ἀκμὴν ἐπαίρεται
5 (C I)	καὶ ἀκμὴν κατέλυσεν ἡμᾶς
16,2 (B IV)	τότε λοιπὸν ἀνηλεῶς κατῆλθεν
17,5 (B IV)	καὶ λοιπὸν ἐπαναστάντες ἀποκτείνωσιν ἡμᾶς
30,4 (C I)	καὶ λοιπὸν ἐκάθισαν ἐν ταῖς ἑπτὰ ἡμέραις
47,7 (D I)	καὶ λοιπὸν τὸ σῶμά μου ἐνίσχυσεν
50,3 (D I)	καὶ ὁ βουλόμενος λοιπὸν ἴχνος ἡμέρας καταλαβεῖν
53,4 (D II)	τίς λοιπὸν οὐ κλαύσει ἐπὶ τὸν ἄνθρωπον τοῦ θεοῦ

Faßt man die genannten Befunde zusammen, so ist das Ergebnis aufs Ganze gesehen eindeutig, selbst wenn in dem einen oder anderen Fall die Auswertung strittig sein sollte. Namentlich die formalen Verklammerungen und sprachlich-sachlichen Verzahnungen, aber auch ergänzend dazu die genannten stilistischen und sprachlichen Eigenheiten weisen insgesamt darauf hin, daß die verschiedenen Erzählblöcke des Testaments Hiobs literarisch zusammengebunden sind und zusammengehören.

Angesichts dessen wird man mit literarkritischen Operationen, die zwischen einer Grundschrift und in diese nachträglich eingefügte bzw. angehängte Zusätze unterscheiden, der Eigenart des Testaments Hiobs kaum gerecht. Das Testament Hiobs will gemessen an Aufriß und Ausführung in seinem textlichen Gesamtbestand einschließlich der Schlußkapitel als ein zusammenhängendes von einer Hand gestaltetes und zusammengefügtes Werk betrachtet werden.

Daß es literarisch aus einem Guß besteht, ist damit freilich nicht gesagt. Bei der Abfassung dürften Erzählmaterialien unterschiedlicher Herkunft und Art verwendet worden sein. Schon die inhaltliche Vielfalt des Erzählten legt dies nahe. Wie weit sich diese Materialien im einzelnen noch quellenmäßig genauer ermitteln lassen, bleibt indes zu fragen. Die Antwort betrifft nicht unwesentlich auch die Einschätzung des kompositorischen Verfahrens, dem das Testament Hiobs seine Gestaltung verdankt.

III

Versucht man, das im Testament Hiobs angewandte kompositorische Verfahren sich klar zu machen, so stößt man auf einen merkwürdigen Widerspruch.

Auf der einen Seite gibt es Anzeichen planvoller Zusammenstellung, nicht nur in den Verklammerungen, sondern auch im Aufbau. Vor allem die beiden Hauptteile der Erzählung verlaufen in vielem parallel zueinander. Am Ende finden sich jeweils paränetische Abschlüsse, eingeleitet mit derselben Formel.[62] In beiden Teilen gibt es je eine Episode mit der Frau Hiobs im Mittelpunkt,[63] ebenso werden jeweils Stücke hymnischer Prägung eingefügt[64] als Mittel dramatischer Steigerung. Schließlich und vor allem: die beiden Teile sind in ihren Grundzügen aufeinander abgestellt. Es gibt einen Text, der das deutlich zu erkennen gibt: die Offenbarungsrede des Engels an Hiob. Sie steht sachlich im Mittelpunkt der Exposition der Gesamterzählung (4, 3−11) und bildet geradezu den Schlüsseltext für alles Folgende bis zum Abschluß des Ganzen.

Der Text, der mit der Botenformel τάδε λέγει ὁ κύριος eingeleitet wird und so höchste Legitimation zur Sprache bringt, benennt nahezu alle grundlegenden Motive der weiteren Erzählung: Zerstörung des Götzentempels (5, 1−3), Gegnerschaft des Satans, bezeichnet als 'Krieg' (vgl. 18, 5; 27, 1), in Form körperlicher Leiden (πληγή, vgl. 20, 2.6; 21, 1; 26, 1; 27, 2.5//28, 1; 35, 1.5; 37, 3.5//47, 4.6), Raub der Habe (τὰ ὑπάρχοντα, vgl. 8, 2; 16, 7; 20, 1; 26, 3; 28, 9; 30, 4; 37, 3.5), Tod der Kinder (vgl. 17, 6; 18, 1; 19, 1; 26, 1; 39, 8ff.), Mahnung zur Geduld (Motiv nur in 1−27), Verheißungen (berühmter Name, vgl. 53, 8; doppelte Erstattung der verlorenen Habe, vgl. 44, 5; Auferweckung, vgl. 53, 7), Erkenntnis des wahren Wesens Gottes (vgl. 33; 40, 4; 49, 3). Darüber hinaus enthält er im Kern bereits auch den Abriß der Gesamterzählung: Vorgehen Hiobs gegen den Götzentempel als Herausforderung des Satans − die Leiden Hiobs als Antwort des Satans, die Geduld Hiobs und sein Beharren auf der Einsicht in die himmlische Wirklichkeit, Wiederherstellung der irdischen Existenz Hiobs und die Öffnung der himmlischen Welt.

Daß in dem allen ein kompositorisches Bemühen steckt, läßt sich kaum bestreiten. Umso auffälliger ist es, daß sich im Testament Hiobs

[62] 27, 7; 45, 1ff.
[63] 21, 1−26, 6 (B V); 39, 1−40, 14 (C II).
[64] 25, 1−8; 32, 1−12; 33, 3−9; 43, 4−17.

daneben auch eine ganze Reihe von kompositorischen Mängeln und Fehlern bemerkbar machen.[65]

Es sind mehrfach Spannungen, Brüche und sonstige Ungereimtheiten vorhanden, vor allem auch innerhalb der beiden Hauptteile.

1. Es finden sich Texte, in denen auf Begebenheiten Bezug genommen wird, von denen vorher nicht die Rede war.

18,8 wird im Abschluß des Gleichnisses von der Seefahrt des Kaufmanns (18,6ff.) von der Stadt gesprochen, 'περὶ ἧς λελάληκέν μοι ὁ ἄγγελος'. In der Sache wird damit wohl auf die Verheißung der eschatologischen Zukunft durch den Offenbarungsengel in Kapitel 4 Bezug genommen.[66] Aber unter den dort verwendeten Bildern kommt das Motiv der eschatologischen Stadt gerade nicht vor.

Ähnlich verhält es sich in 19,1. Hiob berichtet vom Kommen des 'letzten Boten' (ἔσχατος ἄγγελος), der das Ende der Kinder meldet. Die Wendung setzt im Grunde voraus, daß bereits andere Boten erwähnt waren. Das ist nicht der Fall. Das Wort ἄγγελος kommt zwar in den vorhergehenden Abschnitten mehrfach vor,[67] bezieht sich aber stets auf die Gestalt des Offenbarungsengels, nie auf einen irdischen Boten. Von solchen Boten ist vorher nur indirekt in einer Nebenbemerkung die Rede. 16,7 heißt es: καὶ τῶν ὑπαρχόντων μοι ἀνήγγειλάν μοι τὴν ἀπώλειαν.

Reichlich unvermittelt ist auch die Art, wie in Kapitel 28 die mit Hiob befreundeten Könige ins Spiel gebracht werden. Sie werden eingeführt, als ob sie längst bekannt wären. Für den Leser, der nur das Testament Hiobs kennt, trifft das indes nicht zu.

Im Hymnus auf Hiobs Reichtum in Kapitel 32 fällt auf, daß unter den dort beschriebenen Reichtümern z. T. auf vorher geschilderte Sachverhalte Bezug genommen wird,[68] daneben aber auch ganz neue

[65] Auf den Sachverhalt haben bereits James und Spitta hingewiesen.
[66] Vgl. 4,9f.
[67] 5,2; 16,1; 18,5.
[68] S. Nr. 23.24.27.30.44.

Gegenstände benannt werden. (V. 4: goldene Lager, V. 5: Thron aus edlen Steinen; V. 8: Räucherwerk; V. 9: goldene Leuchter; V. 10: Harz aus Weihrauch).

41,3 verweist Elihu darauf, man habe viele Tage zugebracht und ertragen, 'wie Job sich rühmte, gerecht zu sein'. In all den Äußerungen, die Hiob vorher in den Mund gelegt worden sind, kommt dieses Motiv an keiner Stelle vor.

47,4–7 wird ausführlich von der Heilung Hiobs berichtet. Im Kapitel 44, das eigens der irdischen Wiederherstellung Hiobs gewidmet ist, findet sich davon keine Spur.

51,1 tritt unvermittelt ein bis dahin nicht erwähnter Bruder Hiobs mit Namen Nereus auf, der dann sogar als Erzähler fungiert.

2. Es finden sich aber umgekehrt auch Fälle, in denen ein vorhandener Erzählfaden nicht weitergesponnen wird.

7,12 droht der Satan dem Hiob: 'Wie dies Brot völlig verbrannt ist, ebenso will ich auch deinen Leib machen. Für eine Stunde gehe ich fort und (dann) werde ich dich zugrunde richten.' In der folgenden Erzählung kommt diese Androhung nicht zum Tragen. Die Zeitangabe 'eine Stunde' bleibt ohne Nachhall; die angekündigte Vernichtung 'verbrannt wie ein Brot' trifft nicht ein. Das anschließende Kapitel (8) berichtet, wie der Satan zu Gott geht und um Erlaubnis zur Vernichtung der Habe Hiobs bittet. Erst erheblich später (20) bittet der Satan um Macht über Hiob selbst.

27,6 heißt es vom Satan: 'Der Satan wandte sich dann betrübt von mir ab drei Jahre lang.' Der Satz erweckt die Erwartung, daß im weiteren Verlauf der Erzählung der Satan nochmals auftritt ('nach drei Jahren'). Aber das ist nicht der Fall. Der Satan wird im zweiten Teil der Erzählung zwar erneut erwähnt, aber nicht als unmittelbarer Gegenspieler Hiobs, sondern als die treibende Kraft, die hinter der gegen Hiob gerichteten Rede des Elihu steckt.[69]

3. Mehrfach stößt man auf Doppelungen in der Erzählung.

---

[69] Vgl. 41,5.

Zweimal wird erzählt, daß die Mitbürger Hiobs Vieh geraubt haben: 16,5f. wird der Raub festgestellt; 17,4 fordert der Satan zum Raub auf.

Auch das Kommen der Freunde Hiobs wird zweimal kurz hintereinander berichtet: 28,2–6 und 28,7ff.

Ähnlich gibt es zwei Szenen, in denen das Zusammentreffen der Freunde mit Hiob beschrieben wird: 29,1–4 und 31,1–7.

An zwei Stellen äußern die Freunde ihr Entsetzen und ihren Ärger über Hiob: 34,1–5 und 41,1–5.

4. Chronologische Angaben sind oft schwer auf einen Nenner zu bringen.

16,1 wird vermerkt, Hiob habe im Anschluß an die ihm zugekommene Offenbarung sieben Jahre lang seine Wohltätigkeit betrieben, danach habe der Satan begonnen, gegen ihn vorzugehen. Das paßt in keiner Weise zu dem Bericht in 5–8. Dieser setzt voraus, daß Hiob in der Nacht nach der Offenbarung durch den Engel den Götzentempel zerstört hat und sofort darauf, am folgenden Tag, vom Satan heimgesucht wird, diesen aber abweist. Der Satan verabschiedet sich daraufhin mit der Drohung, in 'einer Stunde'[70] wiederzukommen, eilt in den Himmel, bittet Gott um Macht über Hiob, erhält sie, raubt Hiobs ganzen Reichtum.[71] Schon Spitta hat mit Recht festgestellt, daß hier 'ein unauflöslicher Widerspruch besteht'.[72]

Ebenfalls Schwierigkeiten bereiten die Angaben über die Dauer der Leiden Hiobs.

21,1 werden 48 Jahre als Summe der Zeit genannt, die Hiob außerhalb der Stadt auf dem Misthaufen in seinen Plagen verbracht hat.

22,1 erwähnt, die Frau Hiobs habe nach 11 Jahren ihrem Mann kein Brot mehr bringen können.

26,1 spricht Hiob selbst zu seiner Frau von 17 Jahren, daß er von Würmern zerfressen seine Plagen ausgehalten habe.

28.1,8 schließlich wird vermerkt, Hiob sei nach 20 Jahren Leiden außerhalb der Stadt von den Mitkönigen besucht worden.

[70] Vgl. 7,12 – 'Eine Stunde' ist betonter Ausdruck kurzer Zeitspanne wie in Dan 4, 16 (19 Θ LXX); Apc 17,12; 18,10.17.19.

[71] Vgl. 8,1–3.

[72] Spitta (s. Anm. 11), 154.

Welchen Sinn haben diese Zahlenangaben? Daß ein Teil der Textüberlieferung andere oder gar keine Zeitangaben macht und die Leidenszeit Hiobs insgesamt auf 7 Jahre beziffert,[73] führt kaum weiter. Es
spricht alles dafür, daß es sich um sekundäre Lesarten handelt, mit
denen versucht wird, die chronologischen Ungereimtheiten zu besei-
tigen.[74] Zieht man die Zahlen zusammen, ergeben sich 96 Jahre
Leidenszeit. Das ist eine Zahl die sonst nirgendwo vorkommt. Im
Septuaginta-Zusatz zum Hiobbuch werden 170 (so S B) oder 178 (so
die meisten Handschriften) genannt. Geht man von der zuletzt
erwähnten Angabe von 20 Jahren Leidenszeit aus, so lassen sich die
vorhergehenden Angaben 'nach 11, 17 Jahren' damit in Einklang
bringen, die erste Angabe '48 Jahre' hängt aber in der Luft. Kurz:
die Angaben passen insgesamt schlecht zusammen.[75]

5. Wiederholt gibt es auch sonst sachliche Spannungen.
10,1 erzählt, Hiob habe in seiner Fürsorge 30 Tische für die Speisung
der Fremdlinge und 12 Tische zusätzlich für die Witwen aufstellen
lassen. In der hymnischen Beschreibung der Besitztümer Hiobs sind
es 60 (bzw. in der slawischen Textfassung 50) Tische.
42,3 erwähnt nach P (alle anderen Textzeugen weichen ab)[76] vier
Könige, die Hiob besuchen; offenkundig wird neben Eliphas, Baldad
und Sophar auch Elihu zu den Königen gezählt. Im ganzen übrigen
Testament Hiobs ist das nicht der Fall; es wird immer nur von drei
Königen (28,5; 30,2) oder einem König und seinen beiden Freunden
(39,4; 42,5) gesprochen.

1−45 verläuft die Erzählung abgesehen von der Einleitung gewöhnlich
in der Ich-Form, als Erzähler ist stets Hiob gedacht. In 46−53 ist nur
noch in der 3. Person von Hiob die Rede. Ein neuer Erzähler in der
Gestalt des Hiobbruders Nereus wird 51,1 unvermittelt eingeführt.
Derselbe Stilbruch begegnet auch in P zu 33,2.

6. Schließlich gibt es an einer Stelle einen merklichen literarischen
Einschnitt.

[73] Gegen P S überliefern V S1 in 21,1; 26,1; 28,1.8 jeweils die Zahl von 7 Jahren, in 22,1 nur eine allgemeine Zeitangabe.
[74] Gegen Spitta (s. Anm. 11), 145ff.; vgl. auch JSHRZ, III, 3, 342 zu TestHi 21,1a.
[75] Freilich: die Zahl von 48 Jahren ist die Summe der darauf folgenden Jahresangaben!
[76] In V fehlt der ganze Vers, in S S1 die Erwähnung der vier Könige.

Der Hymnus auf die Frau Hiobs (25, 1 – 8) unterbricht den Gang der Erzählung. Die Selbstdarstellung der Frau Hiobs endet nicht in 24, 10, sondern setzt in 25, 9ff. übergangslos fort. Der Hymnus läßt sich ohne Schwierigkeiten aus dem Text herausnehmen.

Diese Mängel und Fehler[77] lassen die kompositorischen Fähigkeiten des Verfassers in keinem besonders guten Licht erscheinen. Wie sind sie zu erklären? Wie weit geben sie nicht nur über das literarische Vermögen bzw. Unvermögen des Verfassers Aufschluß, sondern auch über möglicherweise von ihm herangezogene Quellen?

P. Nicholls[78] hat in seiner Arbeit letzteres zu zeigen versucht. Seine These, daß im Testament Hiobs vier Quellen verarbeitet sind, stützt sich wesentlich auf die literarischen Mängelerscheinungen im Text. Vom methodischen Ansatz her ist das durchaus sachgemäß. Ob die Durchführung und damit die Ergebnisse stichhaltig sind, bleibt zu prüfen.

Die vom Verfasser des Testaments Hiobs verarbeiteten Quellen stellen sich nach Nicholls wie folgt dar:
Die erste Quelle (J) ist in den Kapiteln 1 – 27 verarbeitet. Sie war eine im Ich-Stil abgefaßte Erzählung über Hiobs Leben. Das Original

---

[77] E. von Nordheim (s. Anm. 11) hat noch auf weitere Spannungen und Gegensätze verwiesen (131f.), dabei aber die Texte z. T. mißverstanden bzw. den Textbefund nicht genau beachtet. Der vermeintliche Gegensatz zwischen TestHi 1, 2 und 52, 1 besteht nur so lange, wie der genitivus absolutus in 52, 1 als Hauptsatz und nicht als Parenthese aufgefaßt wird (vgl. JSHRZ, III, 3, 371). – Daß das Thema der Erbverteilung in den Schlußkapiteln 'im Widerspruch zur Inhaltsangabe des Anfangsrahmens' steht, kann man nur behaupten, wenn die Bemerkung 'er wollte sein Haus bestellen' (1, 2) als textlich sekundär eingestuft wird. Das ist jedoch nach der Textüberlieferung (P und S stimmen hier überein gegen V; s. dazu JSHRZ, III, 3, 316f.) höchst zweifelhaft. Im übrigen kann man den letzten Satz der Schlußparänese 45, 4 nicht einfach textlich vom vorhergehenden Abschnitt abheben und dem folgenden zuweisen. – Daß die Episode der Töchter Hiobs thematisch nicht ganz in den Rahmen der vorhergehenden Erzählungen über Hiobs Leben und Leiden paßt, ist gewiß richtig, ebenso daß das vom Hiobbruder Nereus verfaßte Buch nicht das Testament Hiobs sein kann; fraglich bleibt jedoch, ob letzteres überhaupt so gemeint ist, vor allem aber ob auch die Kapitel 1 – 45 und 46 – 52 von der Form her nicht zusammen passen. Hier ist übersehen, daß die Einleitung TestHi 1, 2 – 4a nicht Hiob selbst zum Sprecher hat, sondern wie die Erzählung ab 46, 1 einen anderen Erzähler voraussetzt.

[78] S. Nicholls (s. Anm. 22), 57 – 82.

umfaßte vermutlich auch einen Dialog zwischen Hiob und seinen Freunden und schloß mit dem Bericht von Hiobs Triumph über den Satan und seine Heilung, Elemente, die aber nicht übernommen worden sind.[79]

Die zweite und dritte Quelle sind in den Kapiteln 28−45 enthalten. Sie kreisen beide thematisch um die mit Hiob befreundeten Könige und die Auseinandersetzungen zwischen ihnen und Hiob.
Die zweite Quelle (K) liegt in den Kapiteln 28−30; 34−40 sowie dem Schlußkapitel 53, ferner in Teilen der Kapitel 33 und 44 zugrunde. Es handelt sich vermutlich um einen in der 3. Person abgefaßten Bericht, der auch Erzählungen über das Leben der Freunde vor dem Besuch bei Hiob enthielt.

Die dritte Quelle (E) ist in den Kapiteln 31−2 und 41−3 sowie z. T. auch in den Kapiteln 33 und 44 enthalten. In ihrem Mittelpunkt steht die Gestalt Elihus, dessen letztes Geschick sie ursprünglich wohl auch beschrieben hat. Sie hängt möglicherweise mit den in 41, 6 erwähnten Denkwürdigkeiten des Elihu zusammen. Für diese Quelle gilt als bezeichnend, daß ihr die hymnischen Abschnitte des Testaments Hiobs angehören, ferner, daß ihr Text im Unterschied zu den anderen Quellen keinerlei klar erkennbare Verbindungen zum Text des biblischen Hiobbuches in Form von Zitaten oder Anspielungen aufweist.[80]

Die Vierte Quelle (D) umfaßt die Kapitel 46−52 mit den Erzählungen vom Wunder-Erbe der Töchter Hiobs und vom ebenso wundersamen Ende Hiobs. Ursprünglich handelt es sich um ein selbständiges Stück midraschartiger Ausmalung und Ausgestaltung der kurzen Notizen in Hi 38,2 und vor allem Hi 42,15.[81]

Mit dieser Quellenscheidungshypothese hat Nicholls fraglos nicht nur einen originellen, sondern auch einen wichtigen Forschungsbeitrag geleistet. Wenn sie zutreffen sollte, dann müßte man geradezu von dem gewichtigsten Beitrag in der neueren Forschung zum Testament

[79] Vgl. ebd., 82ff., 312f.
[80] Vgl. ebd., 84−104, 313ff.
[81] Vgl. ebd., 104−19, 315.

Hiob sprechen. Geht man die Beweisführung im einzelnen durch, so stellen sich freilich eine Reihe von Anfragen und Einwänden ein.

Zunächst fällt auf, daß Nicholls im Zusammenhang mit der Einleitung und dem ersten Hauptteil des Testaments Hiobs (1 – 27) nur von einer Quelle spricht und allein den Hymnus auf die Frau Hiobs (25, 1 – 8) ausgrenzt. Das ist nicht ohne weiteres einzusehen, denn es bestehen, wie bereits gezeigt, ja auch innerhalb dieser Kapitel z. T. nicht unerhebliche Sprünge und Spannungen. Überhaupt nicht stimmig sind die chronologischen Angaben zwischen der Erzählung in 5 – 8 und 16 – 20.[82] Zumindest im Hinblick darauf besteht durchaus Anlaß zu fragen, ob sich hier nicht die Verarbeitung zweier Quellenstücke ankündigt.

Eigentümlich ist im übrigen auch der Bericht über Hiobs Reichtum und Wohltätigkeit (9 – 15). Im Rahmen der Gesamterzählung handelt es sich um ein retrospektives Zwischenstück, das den Erzählfaden für längere Zeit unterbricht. Das wäre an sich noch kein Grund, hier eine eigene Quelle zu vermuten. Beachtet man jedoch, daß die Einbindung in den Kontext formal einiges zu wünschen übrig läßt und sachlich recht einseitig verläuft,[83] dann ist eine solche Vermutung durchaus naheliegend. Nicholls hätte dem allen zumindest nachgehen müssen.

Aber nicht nur das. Auch das quellenkritische Verfahren selbst, das Nicholls anwendet, wirft Fragen auf. Nicht wirklich zwingend ist einmal die Begründung, mit der der zweite Hauptteil der Hioberzählung quellenmäßig vom ersten Hauptteil abgehoben wird. Nicholls beruft sich auf die Schwierigkeiten in den chronologischen Angaben zwischen 21, 1; 22, 1; 26, 1 und 28, 1.8, auf die Unterschiede in den Leitmotiven sowie auf die Abwesenheit der Gestalt des Satans in den Kapiteln 28 – 45. Die genannten Befunde sind unstrittig, ihre Auswertung ist zumindest einseitig. Um die vorhandenen Schwierigkeiten zu erklären, wird nur die Möglichkeit der Benutzung unterschiedlicher Quellen bedacht. Daß der Verfasser möglicherweise eine

---

[82] S.o.S. 77f.

[83] Abgesehen von der kurzen Stichwortverknüpfung besteht mit dem vorhergehenden Erzählblock sachlich so gut wie keine Verbindung, in den verwendeten Motiven gibt es keine Überschneidung. Motive aus 9 – 15 werden hingegen im folgenden vielfach aufgenommen, abgesehen von Kapitel 16 allerdings überwiegend in den hymnischen Stücken, s.o. Nr. 23 – 30, ferner u.S. 83f.

vorhandene Erzählung nicht vollständig verarbeitet, sondern, kompositorisch nachlässig wie er ist, einiges ausgelassen haben könnte, wird gar nicht in Betracht gezogen. Im übrigen ist auch der Verweis auf die Unstimmigkeit der chronologischen Angaben in sich nicht durchschlagend. Denn sie setzt voraus, daß jemand den Text bearbeitet hat, unterstellt aber zugleich, daß er die dadurch entstandene Schwierigkeit nicht bemerkt hat.

Die These, im ersten Hauptteil der Hiobserzählung des Testaments Hiobs sei eine andere Quelle benutzt worden als im zweiten Hauptteil, läßt sich auf diese Weise allein wenigstens nicht belegen. Um sie abzustützen, müßten andere Befunde namhaft gemacht werden, z.B. besondere sprachliche und stilistische Eigenheiten. In dieser Hinsicht hat Nicholls aber so gut wie nichts angeführt, und es dürfte auch schwer fallen, solche Belege beizubringen.

Immerhin für Nicholls Annahme würde ins Gewicht fallen, wenn es stimmen sollte, daß im zweiten Haupterzählteil zwei quellenmäßig verschiedene Erzählfäden zusammengewoben sind. Auch diese These steht indes, so bemerkenswert manche Beobachtungen von Nicholls sind, genau besehen auf schwachen Füßen.
Schon die textliche Basis ist z. T. unsicher. An zwei Stellen stützt sich Nicholls auf Lesarten von zweifelhaftem Wert.
Die Zuweisung der Kapitel 32 und 33 zu Quelle E ist entscheidend bestimmt durch die Annahme, daß der Text ursprünglich von Elihu handelt[84] und nicht, wie bereits von Spitta[85] angenommen und neuerdings wenigstens teilweise durch die koptische Überlieferung erhärtet,[86] von Eliphas.
Die These von der Abfassung der Quelle K in der 3. Person steht und fällt mit der Lesart der Hs P in 33,2.[87] Eine weitere Schwachstelle enthält die Behauptung, die Quelle E sei frei von textlichen Bezügen auf das Hiobbuch. Für die Kapitel 31.32.43 trifft das zwar zu,

---

[84] Nicholls (s. Anm. 22), 94ff. zu 31,1.5; 32,1; 33,1.

[85] Spitta (s. Anm. 11), 150ff.; vgl. JSHRZ, III, 3, 350.

[86] Wie die neueren Untersuchungen der koptischen Fragmente durch H. Thissen und C. Römer gezeigt haben, ist entgegen meinen Angaben in JSHRZ, III, 3, die Lesart Eliphas dort nicht nur für 31,1 bezeugt, sondern auch für 33,1; in 31,5; 32,1 ist der Text defekt; vgl. den Beitrag von H. Thissen und C. Römer im vorliegenden Band.

[87] S.o.S. 78.

nicht hingegen für die Kapitel 41. 42. In ihnen finden sich sogar gehäuft biblische Zitate und Anspielungen.[88] Die eigentlichen Schwächen liegen aber nicht einmal hier. Sie bestehen wesentlich darin, daß Nicholls sich nicht darum gekümmert hat, ob und wie weit sich seine Quellenanalyse in den textlichen Gesamtbefund einfügt.

Die entscheidende Frage ist hier: kann man die Kapitel 31 – 2 und 41 – 3 so klar von den übrigen Texten abheben, wie das von der Quellenscheidung her der Fall sein müßte? Achtet man auf die sprachlichen und sachlichen Verzahnungen, dann kann davon keine Rede sein.

Es bestehen nicht nur Beziehungen unter den Texten der vermuteten Quelle E, sondern ebenso auch klare Bezüge zwischen diesen Texten und Texten der vermuteten Quelle K. An zwei Stellen kommt dies besonders deutlich zum Vorschein:

31, 2; 32, 8 ist als tragendes Motiv von der δυσωδία Hiobs die Rede. In den folgenden Kapiteln, die Nicholls quellenmäßig anders einstuft, kommt dasselbe Motiv vor, und zwar in einem Fall sogar im selben Wortlaut: 34, 4; 35, 1 (s. Nr. 47).

41, 4 wird von Elihu gesagt, er habe sich des 'früheren Glücks' des Hiob erinnert. Genau dieselbe Wendung findet sich im Munde des Baldad in dem zur Quelle K gezählten Kapitel 35 (V. 4; Nr. 56). Der Einwand, dies seien Einzelfälle, sticht kaum. Die Zahl läßt sich durchaus vermehren.[89]

Darüber hinaus läßt sich im Hinblick auf die für die Quelle E geltend gemachten Texte nicht übersehen, daß ein großer Teil von ihnen mit anderen Textteilen des Testaments Hiobs, vor allem auch mit Texten aus den Kapiteln des ersten Hauptteils verquickt sind. Das gilt insbesondere für die hymnisch geprägten Stücke. In ihnen finden sich, wie die folgende Übersicht zeigt, gehäuft Wendungen, die aus vorhergehenden Abschnitten stammen.

Hymnus Kapitel 32

(a) 32, 1 : 8, 3; 26, 3; 28, 5 (Nr. 23)
(b) 32, 1 : 9, 2f.; 16, 3; vgl. 44, 2.4; 45, 1; 53, 1.3.4 (Nr. 24)

---

[88] Vgl. JSHRZ, III, 3, 361f.
[89] S.o. Nr. 48. 49. 53.

(c) 32,2 : 9,4f.; 16,3; 25,4; 30,5 (Nr. 25)
(d) 32,7 : 10,1; 25,5 (Nr. 27)
(e) 32,3 : 10,5; 16,3 (Nr. 30)
(f) 32,10 : 24,9 (Nr. 40)
(g) 32,4 : 25,8 (Nr. 43)
(h) 32,8 : 31,2, vgl. 34,4; 35,1 (Nr. 46)

Hymnus Kapitel 43

(a) 43,13 : 4,8 (Nr. 17)
(b) 43,13 : 4,8 (Nr. 18)
(c) 43,3 : 31,8; 33,1; vgl. 44,1 (Nr. 48)
(d) 43,5 : 32,9 (Nr. 49)
(e) 43,7 : 33,4.9; 34,4 (Nr. 52)
(f) 43,3 : 34,2 (Nr. 54)

Eine Ausnahme bildet in diesem Zusammenhang nur der Hynmus in Kapitel 33, der selbst zwar im folgenden zitiert wird,[90] aber keine Bezüge zu vorhergehenden Texten aufweist.

Hingegen ist der Hymnus in Kapitel 25 in ähnlicher Weise wie die Hymnen in Kapitel 32 und 43 mit anderen Texten verzahnt.

Hymnus Kapitel 25

(a) 25,4 : 9,4f.; 16,3; vgl. 30,5; 32,2 (Nr. 25)
(b) 25,5 : 10,1; vgl. 32,7 (Nr. 27)
(c) 25,10 : 24,6; vgl. 26,2; 52,1 (Nr. 39)
(d) 25,1 : 35,5 (Nr. 41)
(e) 25,7 : 39,1 (Nr. 42)
(f) 25,8 : 32,4 (Nr. 43)

Die Verzahnung des Hymnus in Kapitel 25 mit weiteren Abschnitten des Testaments Hiobs ist bislang kaum wahrgenommen worden. Man hat gewöhnlich nur die Beziehung zum Hymnus in Kapitel 32 hervorgehoben.[91] Wie die Übersicht zeigt, gibt es daneben aber auch Querverbindungen zu anderen vorhergehenden und späteren Kapiteln.[92]

Für die Frage nach der Quellenbenutzung und einer möglichen Quellenzuordnung sowie darüber hinaus für die Einschätzung des

[90] S.o. Nr. 51–3.
[91] S.o. Nr. 44.
[92] S.o. Nr. 24.27.40.42.43.

kompositorischen Verfahrens im Testament Hiobs ist diese Verzahnung der Hymnen untereinander und mit dem weiteren Text des Testaments Hiobs von einiger Bedeutung. Daß selbst ein Text wie der Hymnus auf die Frau Hiobs (25, 1 – 8), der literarkritisch verdächtig ist, ein Einschub zu sein, offenkundige Verzahnungen mit dem engeren und weiteren Kontext aufweist, macht deutlich, auf welch unsicherem Boden die literarkritische Ausgrenzung und die quellenmäßige Identifizierung steht. In ihrer textlichen Einordnung und wohl auch in ihrer vorliegenden Gestalt sind die Hymnen dem Verfasser des Testaments Hiobs zuzuschreiben. Daß bei ihrer Gestaltung vorgegebenes Material benutzt wurde, ist zwar recht wahrscheinlich, läßt sich im einzelnen aber schwer belegen. Die Zuweisung zu einer bestimmten Quelle ist noch ungesicherter.

Was für die Hymnen gilt, dürfte für das Testament Hiobs insgesamt zutreffen. Der Versuch von Nicholls, den Erzählkern des Testaments Hiobs auf drei Quellen zurückzuführen, geht insgesamt am Befund in den Texten vorbei. Was vom Verfasser stammt, was ihm vorgegeben war, läßt sich überwiegend kaum mehr ermitteln.

Die einzige Quelle, deren Benutzung eindeutig feststeht, ist das biblische Hiobbuch selbst in seiner griechischen Übersetzung. Das läßt sich nicht nur an den über nahezu die ganze Schrift verstreuten Zitaten und Anspielungen ablesen,[93] das zeigt sich auch an einigen Stellen, in denen der Text kompositorisch unstimmig zu sein scheint.

Wenn in Kapitel 28 unvermittelt die mit Hiob befreundeten Könige auftreten, dann ist das im Rahmen der Anlage des Testaments Hiobs überraschend. Für den, der das biblische Hiobbuch kennt, wird aber nur Bekanntes ins Spiel gebracht. Wie sehr der Verfasser aus der biblischen Quelle schöpft, wird besonders deutlich in der Rede des Elihu in dem Vorwurf gegen Hiob, er habe sich gerühmt, 'gerecht zu sein' (41, 3). Davon ist im Testament Hiobs selbst vorher nichts zu finden. Die Annahme, hier komme die Spur eines ausgelassenen Abschnittes der 'Elihu-Quelle' zutage, könnte sich nahelegen, sie erübrigt sich aber, denn diese Aussage bezieht sich wörtlich auf eine

---

[93] Vgl. dazu B. Schaller, Das Testament Hiobs und die Septuaginta-Übersetzung des Buches Hiob, Biblica 61 (1980), 377–406.

Bemerkung, die am Anfang der Elihu-Kapitel im griechischen Hiobbuch steht. LXX Hi 32,2 heißt es: ὠργίσθη δὲ Ελιους ... ὠργίσθη δὲ τῷ Ιωβ σφόδρα, διότι ἀπέφηνεν ἑαυτὸν δίκαιον ἐνάντιον κυρίου.

Auch die unvermittelte Erwähnung des dritten Boten (19,1) läßt sich so leicht erklären. Der Erzähler nimmt aus der bekannten Hiobgeschichte nur diesen Zug auf, über die anderen Boten berichtet er nur mit einem Wort in einem Nebensatz.

Freilich lassen sich nicht alle Unstimmigkeiten im Text auf diese Weise erklären. Der Umgang mit der biblischen Vorlage belegt aber, daß der Verfasser nicht sonderlich auf kompositorische Abrundung aus war und geradezu etwas nachlässig gearbeitet hat. Wie weit ihm neben der Septuagintafassung des Hiobbuches noch andere literarische Quellen zur Verfügung standen, läßt sich kaum mehr genau festmachen. In zwei Fällen ist der Verdacht immerhin naheliegend: bei der Erzählung über die Hiob-Töchter in den Schlußkapiteln 46–52 sowie beim Bericht über Hiobs Reichtum und Wohltätigkeit in den Kapiteln 9–15.

Die Schlußkapitel sind thematisch und sprachlich besonders eigentümlich geprägt und heben sich dadurch vom übrigen Text des Testaments Hiobs ab. Das könnte auf eine eigene Quelle hinweisen. Aber selbst hier bleibt vieles offen. Handelt es sich wirklich um eine literarisch eigenständige Quelle? Wie weit gehört der Bericht über Hiobs Ende und Himmelfahrt dazu, wie weit die Schlußbemerkungen über Hiobs Begräbnis?

Was die Kapitel 9–15 anlangt, so hat zwar selbst Nicholls sie nicht als eigenes Quellenstück behandelt. Dennoch könnte es angebracht sein, hinter dem Text eine besondere Quelle zu vermuten. Es handelt sich um den einzigen Erzählblock, bei dem die Verklammerung mit dem Kontext zu wünschen übrig läßt und durch den der Erzählfaden sichtlich unterbrochen ist. Allein das ist schon auffällig. Nimmt man hinzu, daß der Block mit den vorhergehenden Blöcken keinerlei Verzahnung aufweist,[94] aber in den folgenden Abschnitten vielfach

[94] S.o. S. 56.

die Thematik bestimmt, und daß ferner zwischen dem vorhergehenden und dem folgenden Kapitel 8 und 16 auf der einen Seite die zeitlichen Angaben nicht zusammenpassen, auf der anderen Seite formale Verklammerungen bestehen, dann liegt es nahe, diese Befunde als Anzeichen für die Verarbeitung quellenmäßig verschiedener Überlieferung zu deuten. Aber selbst hier kann von einem gesicherten Ergebnis kaum die Rede sein. Im übrigen ist man völlig auf Mutmaßungen angewiesen. Daß in Kapitel 27 die Erzählung über das Auftreten des Satans abreißt, ist eigentümlich, ebenso das Vorkommen von Dubletten in der Erzählung über das Auftreten der Freunde Hiobs. Aber reicht das aus, um unterschiedliche Quellen zu erschließen? Kaum. Quellenkritisch gewiß nicht auswertbar ist das Auftreten der Frau Hiobs im ersten (21–6) und zweiten (39–40) Erzählteil. Zwischen beiden Erzählblöcken gibt es trotz unterschiedlicher Thematik der Episoden besondere Verzahnungen: im Motiv der δουλεία der Frau Hiobs 21,3; 39,2; 40,4 (Nr. 36), in der formelhaften Wendung ἀνακράζειν μετὰ κλαυθμοῦ: 24,1; 40,9 (Nr. 38) sowie in der Bezeichnung des Frauengewandes als ῥακκωδή: 25,7; 39,1 (Nr. 43).

Insgesamt wird man sich im Hinblick auf die hinter dem Testament Hiobs stehenden und in ihm verarbeiteten Materialien mit der Einsicht begnügen müssen, daß es im einzelnen nur noch begrenzt möglich ist, sie bestimmten Quellen zuzuschreiben. Daß der Verfasser aus dem reichen Arsenal der Hiob-Haggada des antiken Judentums geschöpft hat, ist offenkundig.[95] Was er benutzt hat, wie die ihm vorgegebenen Erzählstoffe beschaffen und wie umfangreich sie waren, bleibt überwiegend sein Geheimnis. Der Versuch von Nicholls, dieses Geheimnis zu lüften und das ganze Testament Hiobs auf vier Quellen zurückzuführen, kann kaum als gelungen bezeichnet werden.

Gewiß wäre es eindrücklicher und für das Verständnis des Testaments Hiobs auch ergiebiger, wenn sich die verarbeiteten Materialien genauer erfassen ließen. Aber auch ohne ein solches Ergebnis kommt man kaum darum herum, das Testament Hiobs auf Grund seiner Gestaltung als ein literarisch von einer Hand zusammengefügtes und geprägtes Werk zu bezeichnen. Die zahlreichen Verzahnungen und Verklammerungen der verschiedenen Erzählteile und -episoden weisen

---

[95] S. JSHRZ, III, 3, 306f., ferner Nicholls (s. Anm. 22), 201–60.

darauf hin, daß die erkennbare Disposition[96] einer durchgehenden Komposition zu verdanken ist. Trifft das zu, dann erhebt sich die für das Verständnis des Testaments Hiobs am Ende entscheidende Frage: Wie weit ist es möglich, die hinter der Komposition des Testaments Hiobs stehende sachliche Konzeption zu erfassen?

IV

Der Versuch, auf diese Frage eine Antwort zu finden, stößt freilich auf einige Schwierigkeiten.

Es gibt kein einheitliches Leitmotiv, das den ganzen Text durchzieht. Was an Grundmotiven vorhanden ist, bestimmt erkennbar nur einzelne Abschnitte.[97]

Dazu kommt — was noch schwerer wiegt —, daß die vorhandenen Aussagen und Vorstellungen sich theologisch oft nur gezwungen, z. T. gar nicht auf einen Nenner bringen lassen. Systematisch gesehen kann man das Werk in der Darstellung namentlich Hiobs zwei entgegengesetzten theologischen Grundentwürfen zuordnen. Auf der einen Seite finden sich Züge eines monistischen, auf der anderen Seite Züge eines dualistischen Welt- und Menschenbildes.

---

[96] Daß die Disposition auch die Schlußkapitel, insbesondere die Darstellung vom Erbe der Hiobtöchter, einschließt, wird meist übersehen. Das Motiv des Erbes ist einmal in der Schlußparänese (45, 4) der Haupterzählung verankert, darüberhinaus aber auch in der Einleitung bereits anvisiert. Die Wendung ἐξετέλει αὐτοῦ τὴν οἰκονομίαν (P S) impliziert, wie vor allem der Begriff οἰκονομία erweist, eine rechtliche Ordnung der Hinterlassenschaft; vgl. F. Preisigke, Wörterbuch der griechischen Papyrusurkunden, II (Berlin, 1927), 160f. Der Einwand, in den literarischen Testamenten komme das Erbmotiv sonst nicht vor, ist demgegenüber kaum stichhaltig. In den juristischen Testamenten der Zeit sind einschlägige Bestimmungen üblich (vgl. E. Lohmeyer, Diatheke, UNT, 2 (Leipzig, Hinrich 1913), 11–29). Daß sie auch in der literarischen Testamentengattung im Blick sein können, belegt neben TestHi das hebräische Testament Naphtali (I, 3), vgl. von Nordheim (s. Anm. 4), 110f., der dennoch formgeschichtlich puristisch 'der Test. Form ... jegliches juristische Interesse und Denken' abspricht.

[97] So ist z. B. das Motiv der Geduld wesentlich auf den ersten Hauptteil der Hioberzählung beschränkt, terminologisch dabei nicht einheitlich: ὑπομονή/ὑπομένειν 1, 5; 4, 6; 5, 1; 26, 4; μακροθυμία/μακροθυμεῖν/μακρόθυμος 21, 4; 26, 5; 27, 7; καρτερεῖν/καρτερία 4, 10; 27, 4; ὑφιστάναι 7, 13; 26, 1. — Im zweiten Hauptteil kommt das Motiv nur an zwei Stellen vor (μακροθυμεῖν 28, 5; 35, 4), aber ohne spezifische Betonung; statt dessen ist das Motiv der Erkenntnis verbreitet: γινώσκειν 35, 4.6; 36, 4.6; 38, 3.6; 40, 4; 43, 1; dies spielt freilich auch im ersten Hauptteil durchaus eine Rolle: 2, 4; 3, 2; 4, 8.11; 7, 6.7; 17, 1; 23, 1; s. ferner 49, 3.

Im ersten Erzählteil kreist alles um die irdische Bewährung und die innerweltliche Belohnung des frommen Hiobs. Der irdische Bereich ist nicht nur der Schauplatz der Wohltaten und der Leiden Hiobs, sondern auch seiner endlichen Wiederherstellung. Das sogenannte 'Tun-Ergehen-Schema' ist bestimmend.

Im zweiten Erzählteil und vor allem in den Schlußkapiteln ist davon kaum etwas zu greifen. Es herrscht eine andere Grundstimmung. Die Leiden werden nicht geduldig bestanden in der Hoffnung auf innerweltliche Belohnung, sondern sie gelten als unwesentlich, weil das Irdische schlechthin unwesentlich ist. Das Leitmotiv ist entsprechend nicht Geduld, sondern Einsicht, Erkenntnis.

Ist es angesichts dessen überhaupt sinnvoll, nach einer sachlichen Konzeption im Testament Hiobs zu suchen? Solange man das Werk mit einer systematisch theologischen Elle mißt, wird man das verneinen müssen. Die Frage ist nur, ob diese Elle angemessen ist. Hier sind durchaus Zweifel angebracht.

Das Testament Hiobs bietet sich formgeschichtlich als eine Mischung aus Testament und erzählerischem Midrasch dar.[98] Das läßt einige Schlüsse hinsichtlich seiner Funktion zu. Die Verquickung von Testament und Midrasch gibt zu erkennen, daß es sich um ein Stück Erbauungsliteratur handelt. Die Absicht des Textes ist es schwerlich, theologische Belehrung zu erteilen, sie will religiös unterhalten und erbauen. Für erbauliche Unterhaltung ist es kaum überraschend, sondern geradezu kennzeichnend, daß scheinbar Unvereinbares zusammengebunden wird. Auf diese Weise kommt ein durchaus eigenes Profil von Frömmigkeit zum Ausdruck.

Daß ein solches Profil auch dem Testament Hiobs nicht fehlt, wird deutlich, wenn man die Rollenverteilung und die Motivanordnung innerhalb des Werkes sich ansieht. Auf den ersten Blick gewinnt man den Eindruck eines schematischen Verfahrens. Sich ausschließende Gegensätze scheinen die Erzählung zu bestimmen. Der Hauptgegensatz Hiob–Satan setzt sich fort im Gegensatz Hiobs zu seiner Frau und zu seinen Freunden und im Ansatz auch im Gegensatz der Töchter Hiobs gegen seine Söhne. Genau besehen werden die Rollen-Verhältnisse aber nicht so einfach dargeboten. Die Frau Hiobs wird

---

[98] Vgl. JSHRZ, III, 3, 312ff.

keineswegs durchgehend als satanisch beeinflußt geschildert. Sie hat wie Hiob Taten der Wohltätigkeit vollbracht[99] und unterstützt nach dem Verlust der Besitztümer sich selbst aufopfernd ihren Mann.[100]

Und nicht nur das. Obgleich sie als 'eine der törichten Frauen'[101] gescholten wird, steht sie am Ende da mit dem Wissen, daß ihr Gedächtnis bei Gott liegt.[102] Auch die Freunde Hiobs erscheinen nicht nur als Handlanger des Satans. Am Ende wird nur Elihu als solcher angesprochen und verurteilt.[103] Die anderen gelangen zur wahren Einsicht[104] und haben vorher bereits durchaus der Geduld mit Hiob das Wort geredet.[105]
Kurz: keines der Grundmotive des Buches, Wohltätigkeit, Geduld, Erkenntnis, sind Hiob allein vorbehalten. Sie werden durchaus auch Gestalten zugeschrieben, die sonst gegen Hiob stehen. Das Gegensatz-Schema ist im Aufbau und der Durchführung nicht durchgehalten.

Für das Gesamtverständnis des Testaments Hiobs noch wichtiger als diese Verschränkung der Rollenverteilung ist der Umstand, daß die beiden oben genannten theologischen Grundrichtungen keineswegs getrennt voneinander auftreten. Sie sind durchaus miteinander verbunden und das an zentraler Stelle.

In dem als Schlüsseltext bereits erwähnten Abschnitt 4, 3–11 bezieht sich die für das ganze Testament Hiobs grundlegende Verheißung des Engels nicht einseitig auf eine innerweltliche oder auf eine endzeitlich-überweltliche Vergeltung. Beides ist miteinander verknüpft, beides wird als aufeinander folgend beschrieben: 'Doch wenn du ausharrst, mache ich deinen Namen berühmt unter allen Geschlechtern der Erde bis zum Ende der Welt. Und ich werde dir deinen Besitz wieder erstatten und es wird dir doppelt wiedergegeben werden, damit du erkennst: (Gott) sieht die Person nicht an, er vergilt Gutes jedem, der auf ihn hört. Du wirst auferweckt werden bei der Auferweckung.

[99] 25,4f.
[100] 21,1–23,11; 24,4–10.
[101] 26,6, nach LxxHi 2,10.
[102] 40,4.
[103] 43,1.
[104] Mit dem Motiv des Geistempfangs verbunden; 43,2.
[105] 35,4.

Du wirst sein wie ein Wettkämpfer, der Schläge austeilt und Schmerzen erträgt und (am Ende) den (Sieges) Kranz empfängt. Dann wirst du erkennen, gerecht und zuverlässig und mächtig ist der Herr, er gibt Kraft seinen Auserwählten' (4,6−11). Daß das himmlische Wesen das irdische überragt, versteht sich zwar von selbst. Aber das besagt nicht, daß das Irdische im Sinne einer dualistischen Weltsicht abgewertet wird.

Es ist wohl kaum ein Zufall, daß der wissende Hiob nicht nur vom Irdischen sagt, es sei unstet,[106] sondern auch betont, daß die Erkenntnis der Wahrheit durchaus bezogen ist auf die Kenntnis der irdischen Ordnung.[107] Und es ist ebensowenig kaum bloß Zufall, daß am Ende des ganzen Buches die Klage um Hiob laut wird unter Verweis auf seine irdischen Wohltaten an den Schwachen, Blinden, Waisen, Fremden, Witwen[108] und damit mittelbar die Mahnung des sterbenden Hiob an seine Kinder[109] wieder aufgenommen wird.

Theologisch gesehen enthält das Testament Hiobs geradezu ein Gemengsel unterschiedlicher, z. T. gegensätzlicher Anschauungen und Erwartungen,[110] dennoch ist es Ausdruck einer durchaus profilierten Frömmigkeit. Es spiegelt eine Frömmigkeit, die diesseits wie jenseits gerichtet ist, in der praktische Wohltätigkeit und Geduld im Leiden ebenso wie das Wissen um die Wirklichkeit der himmlischen Welt gepriesen wird. Es ist ein Zeugnis für die Verknüpfung von praktischer und spekulativer Frömmigkeit, die sich der Verheißung irdischen Wohlergehens in gleicher Weise erfreut wie der Verheißung des himmlischen Heils.[111]

Wenn nicht alles täuscht, ist es diese doppelte Ausrichtung, die in ihrer Verbindung die Konzeption des Testaments Hiobs prägt. Der Verfasser hat die Geschichte des Lebens und Leidens Hiobs mit dem Ausblick auf sein Erbe und Ende benutzt, um diese Art der

---

[106] 36,3; vgl. auch 33,4.6; 38,2.
[107] 38,5.
[108] 53,2f.
[109] 45,2.
[110] Vgl. JSHRZ, III, 3, 315f.
[111] Ein ähnlicher Frömmigkeitstyp meldet sich im 1 Timotheusbrief 4,7−8 zu Wort:
γύμναζε δὲ σεαυτὸν πρὸς εὐσέβειαν. ἡ γὰρ σωματικὴ γυμνασία πρὸς ὀλίγον ἐστὶν ὠφέλιμος, ἡ δὲ εὐσέβεια πρὸς πάντα ὠφέλιμός ἐστιν, ἐπαγγελίαν ἔχουσα ζωῆς τῆς νῦν καὶ τῆς μελλούσης.

Frömmigkeit seinen Lesern[112] vor Augen zu führen und sie damit zu erbauen und anzuspornen.

[112] Im Unterschied zu C. Haas, Job's perseverance in the Testament of Job, s.u. S. 117ff. vermag ich im TestHi keine spezielle Ausrichtung auf Proselyten und deren Ermahnung erkennen; zur weiteren Begründung vgl. auch JSHRZ, III, 3, 314.

5

IMAGES OF WOMEN IN THE TESTAMENT OF JOB

Pieter W. van der Horst
Rijksuniversiteit te Utrecht

The Testament of Job has the characteristics of other Jewish 'testaments' of the Hellenistic and Roman periods: a deathbed-scene, a retrospective view of his life by the dying protagonist followed by ethical admonitions that derive from this life-story, and finally death, burial and lamentation.[1] This retrospect with admonitions occupies the greatest part of the treatise and makes extensive use of biblical material. So, as might be expected, T. Job is based on the biblical book of Job, but it should be added immediately that it uses little more than the framework of the biblical story; and much of the story is not used at all. Little of the many long speeches in particular is used, even of God's speech in chapters 38–41, whereas motifs that play only a minor role in the biblical story are heavily emphasized or are strongly expanded in a haggadic way.[2] For instance, it is striking that the theme of the rebellious Job who protests against his sorry fate recedes completely to the background (and with it the question of the theodicy) and gives way to that of Job as a paragon of ὑπομονή, of patience and longsuffering, an image of Job that we know also from the New Testament, which is roughly contemporaneous with T. Job, when

---

[1] See E. von Nordheim, *Die Lehre der Alten* I. *Das Testament als Literaturgattung im Judentum der hellenistisch-römischen Zeit* (Leiden, 1980), 119–35. J.J. Collins, 'Structure and Meaning in the Testament of Job', *SBL Seminar Papers 1974*, I, 37–9.

[2] A survey of the deviations of T. Job from the biblical story of Job can be found in D. Rahnenführer, 'Das Testament des Hiob und das Neue Testament'. *ZNW* 62 (1971), 68–93, on p. 70.

A discussion of some of these motifs can be found in I. Jacobs, 'Literary Motifs in the Testament of Job', *JJS* 21 (1970), 1–10. See also E. Schürer, *The History of the Jewish People in the Age of Jesus Christ, A New English Version*, revised and edited by G. Vermes, F. Millar and M. Goodman, vol. III, 1 (Edinburgh, 1986), 552–4.

93

in James 5.11 Job's ὑπομονή is held up as an example to be imitated by the readers.[3]

It should not be forgotten that the great differences between T. Job and the biblical story of Job are partly due to the fact that the author uses not the MT but the LXX,[4] and the LXX version of Job is no less than 15 to 20 per cent shorter than MT. Yet the changes made in the Job story by the LXX translator are mostly quite different from those in T. Job.[5] The LXX abbreviates often and expands only in some places (2.9 and 42.17), whereas the author of T. Job not only abbreviates but completely rewrites the whole story and does not shrink from drastic changes. Several examples could be given of this drastic rewriting, one of the most striking being the much-expanded role of Satan, especially in chapters 2–27. In this chapter, however, I want to focus on one specimen of this haggadic procedure, the role of women.

The role of women in the Testament of Job

As is well known, in the biblical book of Job women definitely do not play a prominent role. In 1.2, 4, 13, 18 the mere existence of Job's daughters is mentioned; in 2.9 his wife summons him to speak a word against God (lit. to bless God = to curse God) and die, and in 19.17 she is mentioned in passing; in 31.9–10 Job says that if another man's wife should succeed in seducing him, his own wife would have to perform a slave's labour for others; in 42.13–15 his three daughters are mentioned by name (Jemimah, Keziah and Keren-happuch) and they are said to be the most beautiful girls in the country and, remarkably enough, to share with their brothers in the inheritance. Apart from a couple of traditional phrases like 'widows and orphans' or 'who is born from a woman', not even 1 per cent of the verses of the book of Job speak of women, his wife and his daughters.

[3] See the contribution by C. Haas in this volume.
[4] B. Schaller, 'Das Testament Hiobs und die Septuaginta-Übersetzung des Buches Hiob', *Biblica* 61 (1980), 377–406.
[5] For the LXX see G. Gerleman, *Studies in the Septuagint*, I, *The Book of Job* (Lund, 1946); D. H. Gard, *The Exegetical Method of the Greek Translator of the Book of Job* (Philadelphia, 1952); H. M. Orlinsky, 'Studies in the Septuagint of the Book of Job', *HUCA* 28 (1957), 53–74; 29 (1958), 229–71; 30 (1959), 153–67; 32 (1961), 239–68; 33 (1962), 119–51; 35 (1964), 57–78; 36 (1965), 37–47; H. Heater, *A Septuagint Translation Technique in the Book of Job* (Washington, 1982).

In the LXX this percentage is somewhat higher, of course, but in essence the situation is the same. In contrast, no fewer than 107 out of 388 verses in T. Job deal with women, i.e., almost thirty times as much space as in the biblical book. What could be the reason for this, and what image of women results? Let us first make an inventory of the data.

In 1.3 we read, besides the names of the seven sons (which do not figure in either MT or LXX),[6] those of the three daughters from his second wife. These names are given in conformity with the LXX: Hemera, as a translation of Jemimah,[7] Kasia, as a transliteration of Keziah,[8] and Amaltheias Keras, as a very free rendering of Keren-happuch;[9] Keren-happuch means 'horn (i.e. box) of mascara', Amaltheias Keras means 'horn of Amaltheia', who was the goat that nurtured the infant Zeus on Crete and whose horn became a symbol of abundance (*cornucopia*).[10] In 1.6 the mother of these children is mentioned, namely Job's second wife, Dinah, the only daughter of the patriarch Jacob. This tradition was already adumbrated in 1.1, where it is said that Job is also called Jobab, the second king of Edom (Gen. 36.33; cf. LXX Job 42.17d), which immediately gives the whole story a setting in the time of the patriarchs and makes Job, as a descendant of Esau, a descendant of Abraham as well. The tradition that Dinah is Job's wife is also known from Ps-Philo, LAB 8.7−8, Gen. Rabba 57.4, 76.9, Targ. Job 2.9, and elsewhere.[11] The name of Job's first wife we will discuss presently.

---

[6] On the tendency to give names to nameless persons in the Bible see B. Heller, 'Die Scheu vor Unbekanntem, Unbenanntem in Agada und Apokryphen', *MGWJ* 83 (1939), 170−84; cf. B.M. Metzger, 'Names for the Nameless in the New Testament', in his *New Testament Studies, Philological, Versional and Patristic* (Leiden, 1980), 23−45.

[7] W. Pape and G. Benseler, *Wörterbuch der griechischen Eigennamen*, I, 3rd edn (Braunschweig, 1911; repr. Graz, 1959), 459 mentions Hemera as a feminine proper name.

[8] *Ibid.*, I, 631 does mention Kasia as a topographical name (of a mountain and an island), not as a feminine proper name, but Kasios as a masculine proper name is common. There is a ninth-century Byzantine poetess called Kasia; see I. Rochow, *Studien zu der Person, den Werken und dem Nachleben der Dichterin Kasia* (Berlin, 1967).

[9] Further only attested as a toponym according to Pape and Benseler, I, 69.

[10] On the names of the daughters see also K. Kohler, 'The Testament of Job', in *Semitic Studies in Memory of A. Kohut* (Berlin, 1897), 288ff.

[11] This and other Job-haggada has been collected by L. Ginzberg in *The Legends of*

In 7.5−11, in the framework of the story of Satan's repeated attempts to bring Job to apostasy, it is a significant feature that Job's true-hearted slave-girl does not recognize Satan in the beggar at the gate. In her kindness she gives Satan *not* the burnt loaf that Job had ordered her to give him − Job, of course, had seen through his disguise − but a good loaf of her own. When Satan criticizes her for her disobedience, she declares that he is right and gives him the charred loaf (a salient feature to which we will return). It is striking too that, where the LXX in 31.13 makes Job's slave-*girls* complain, 'who will provide for us from his meats that we may be filled?', T. Job puts these words in the mouths of his *slaves*, and adds a curse (13.4−5); at first sight this seems to be a change that favours women, but it is neutralized in the next chapter (14.4−5), which speaks about the (δια) γογγύζειν, the murmuring, of his female slaves, to which Job reacts by singing songs about the payment of recompense, accompanying himself on the harp.

Sitidos

These passages, however, are insignificant when compared to the extensive chapters devoted to Job's first wife, Sitidos. Let us begin with her name. Some translators call her Sitis, following their feeling for the Greek language that Sitidos must be the genitive of Sitis.[12] But in the MSS there is considerable confusion about the correct spelling of her name. Some read Sigidos, others Sitodos, or Sitida, or Sites, or Site, or Sitis, whilst some omit the name altogether. The reading 'Sitidos' is more obviously the *lectio difficilior*, for copyists would have been more inclined to change this apparant genitive into the required nominative (Sitis) than the other way round. The other forms are all variations upon these two alternatives. The reading 'Sitis' is probably based upon the thought that this name must have

the Jews, II (Philadelphia, 1920), 225−42, and V (Philadelphia, 1925), 381−90. Much of it can be found in a long passage in the Babylonian Talmud, Bava Bathra, 15a−16b, where *inter alia* there is much discussion of the question in which period Job had lived, the answers varying from patriarchal to post-exilic times. Quite interesting is the remark by an anonymous rabbi (BB 15a) that in his view Job had never existed (*lo haya welo nibra*) but was only a *mashal*, a parabolic type, an acute remark which his colleagues do not appreciate.

[12] So e.g. R. P. Spittler in J. H. Charlesworth (ed.), *The Old Testament Pseudepigrapha* (*OTP*), I (New York, 1983), 848ff.

been derived from Ausitis, the name of the country that Job came from (mentioned in LXX Job 1.1, 42.17b, as a translation of Uz). Even some modern scholars support this derivation,[13] but it is unnecessary and improbable. Although the name Sitidos (or Sitis) does not occur elsewhere, the *Wörterbuch der griechischen Eigennamen* by Pape-Benseler (see n. 7) mentions quite a number of masculine proper names and toponyms beginning with Σιτ- or Σιτι-, all of them deriving from σίτος, 'bread', or σιτίζω, 'to give bread, to feed'. In view of the fact that in the story about Job's wife it is a dominant theme that she does every possible thing in order to be able to give bread to Job daily, I presume that this unusual name has some connection with this motif.[14]

In chs. 21–5, the author states that since Job is sitting on the dungheap, Sitidos has been working as the slave of a rich man (cf. Job 31.9–10) in order to earn bread for Job and herself. When after some time her master withholds Job's share of the bread, she shares her own meagre portion with her husband and goes to the market in order to beg for the bread she wants to give to Job. When Satan disguises himself as a breadseller, Sitidos does not recognize him and begs him for bread. He first asks her for money, which she does not possess; then he asks for her hair in exchange for the bread. She thinks: 'What value to me is the hair of my head as compared to my hungry husband?' (23.9), so she allows Satan to cut off her hair.[15] When she has delivered the loaves to Job, she bursts into a bitter and desperate lamentation about herself. What is conspicuous in this lament (ch. 25) is that there is a sudden transition from the first to the third person in 25.1 and again from the third to the first person in 25.9. Verses 1–8 are thought by some scholars to be a later interpolated lament *about* Job's wife. It has a poetic structure in which six times, after descriptions of her former wealth and happiness, there is the refrain, 'but now she sells her hair for loaves' (with minor variations).

---

[13] *Ibid.*, *ad* 25.1, and B. Schaller *ad* 25.1 in JSHRZ, III, 3 (Gütersloh, 1979).

[14] My colleague Prof. T. Baarda suggests that Sitidos might be a corruption of the Hebrew *'ishto*, 'his wife'.

[15] Several texts show clearly that being shorn was the utmost disgrace to a woman: e.g. Aristophanes, *Thesm.* 830f.; Paul, 1 Cor. 11.6; Tacitus, *Germ.* 19; Apuleius, *Met.* 7.6.3.; Lucian, *Dial. meretr.* 5.3. See also S. Lieberman, 'Shaving of the Hair and Uncovering of the Face Among Jewish Women', in his *Texts and Studies* (New York, 1974), 52ff. and M. Küchler, *Schweigen, Schmuck und Schleier* (Freiburg/Göttingen, 1986), 79–82.

The fact that this 'hymn' is thematically related to the immediately preceding chapters and structurally related to a similar hymn on Job's fate by one of his friends (ch. 32, with the refrain 'Where now is the glory of your throne?') seems to me to plead against this interpolation-hypothesis. Sitidos' lamentation ends with the words 'Speak a word against the Lord and die', the only thing we hear her saying in the biblical book of Job (2.9), directly followed (and somewhat mitigated) by the remark 'Then I too shall at last be freed from the despair about your bodily sufferings' (25.10). This remark emphasizes that even her call to speak a word against God arises from good intentions and from sheer despair about Job's misery. Then Job reveals to her that these words had been delivered to her by Satan, who at that very moment stood behind her in disguise (and about whom the author had said in 23.11 that he led her heart astray). It is he, says Job, who confuses her thoughts and wishes her to behave like a foolish woman who deceives her husband's integrity. So Job's wife is a victim rather than an agent in this first long passage devoted to her.

She returns in chs. 39–40, after Job's confrontation with his friends, who are called kings here (cf. LXX Job 42.17e; in T. Job 28.7 Job himself is called king of Egypt). There we read that Sitidos has run away from slavery because she had even been prevented from going out of the house. She prostrates herself before the kings, and crying, points out to them her bitter poverty, whereupon one of them drapes his purple robe around her shoulders. She asks them to have their soldiers remove the ruins of the house that had collapsed on top of her children, so that she can bury their bones. Then Job intervenes by saying that such an action would be in vain since they would not find his children, for they have been taken up into the heavens by their creator (ἀνελήφθησαν, 39.12, an idea of bodily assumption into heaven which contrasts with that of Job's own death when only his soul is taken up into heaven in ch. 52). The kings declare him to be mad, but Job rises and prays to 'the Father' and then says 'Look towards the east and see my children crowned alongside the *doxa* of the Heavenly One' (40.3). Sitidos sees it, falls to the ground, and says, 'Now I know that I have a memorial with the Lord' (40.4). Then she goes to the stall of cows that her masters had stolen from Job, lies down in one of the mangers, and dies cheerfully. When she is found dead, all the animals start weeping so loudly over her that the entire town comes to see what has happened. She is buried near the dilapidated house, and the poor of the city sing a lamentation over her of which the author says that it has been written down in the *Paralipomena*,[16] almost certainly a fictitious piece of writing.

What is the picture that the author wishes to draw of this woman? There is little doubt that at first sight she is a sympathetic woman. With never-failing loyalty and sincere love she exerts herself to the utmost on behalf of her husband. She undergoes the greatest possible humiliation, i.e. having her head shorn, rather than letting him go hungry. Also her great care to have the bones of her children buried is a testimony that she lives up to the standards of Israel's piety. It is, therefore, not without reason that both men and animals burst into lament when this noble woman is found dead.

But there is another side to the picture, namely her 'lack of perception'.[17] The whole of T. Job is imbued with the contrast between the supramundane reality and this world where Satan is active. Job has insight into this distinction and he is contrasted with those who do not. This is done in ch. 7, where his female slave does not recognize Satan in the beggar at the gate, whereas Job knew beforehand that it was Satan. A second contrast that is much elaborated is that between Job and the kings. Time and again they wonder whether Job has gone insane. When Job says that his own throne is in heaven, and that his kingdom will last for ever, Eliphaz and the others think that his mental faculties are no longer intact (ch. 33). And when he says that his children have been taken up into heaven, they are convinced that he has gone mad. Their spiritual blindness and lack of insight, by which they become an easy prey for Satan, is a recurring theme in the episode of Job and the kings.[18] Although Job's wife is presented as a more sympathetic personality than the kings, it is in the final analysis also true of her that, in spite of her good intentions, she does not have awareness of and insight into the invisible background of the things that happen. She has no spiritual intelligence and in spite of her virtues she errs repeatedly.

---

[16] Probably the *Paralipomena of Eliphaz*, which are mentioned in 41.6. The name of Eliphaz has probably dropped out by haplography since the first word of the next sentence is Eliphaz.

[17] G. W. E. Nickelsburg, *Jewish Literature between the Bible and the Mishnah* (London, 1981), 245.

[18] See Collins, 'Structure', 42: 'The real issue between Job and his friends is awareness of heavenly reality.'

She does not perceive that she is led astray by Satan. It is Job who
has to reveal that to her. She does not know that her children need
not be buried. It is Job who has to disclose that to her. It is therefore
not without reason that she is not, like Job, reinstated into her former
splendour; unlike Job's wife in the biblical story, she dies before the
deliverance out of the misery has arrived, and so she makes way for
no less a person than Dinah, Jacob's only daughter.

One could ask why she is assigned such a significant role in
comparison to her role in the biblical story. The reason is that only
in that way can she serve as a foil to show off Job's superior handling
of the situation.[19] Athalya Brenner makes the following pertinent
comments:

> She is used in order to create a symmetry in the plot, so that
> two mirror images complement each other. Job and God are
> on the one side. Job is aware of the significance of the
> proceedings, because God has alerted him beforehand. Satan
> and the wife are on the other side. The wife, however (like
> the servant girl earlier, a nice anticipatory touch), joins the
> side she is on unwittingly. A nice comment on religious
> awareness of males and females respectively, of the 'wise'
> and 'foolish' of wisdom literature in general. Again this is
> hardly complimentary towards women.[20]

However well and properly Sitidos fulfils her role as spouse of Job
and as mother of her children, finally she belongs to the category of
the ignorant and the foolish whom Satan can easily get into his grip.
This is an image of women that is well known to us from many other
Jewish writings of the Hellenistic and Roman periods. Not only
Philo and Josephus, who are notorious in this respect,[21] but also
Ecclesiastes, Ecclesiasticus, the Testament of Reuben, the Mishnah
and a great number of other sources present women as creatures who
can easily be misled and seduced (and themselves easily seduce), who

---

[19] *Ibid.*, 40.
[20] Dr Brenner wrote this to me in a letter of 20 April 1986. I am very grateful to her for
several valuable insights.
[21] On Philo see, e.g., I. Heinemann, *Philons griechische und jüdische Bildung*
(Breslau, 1932; repr. Hildesheim, 1962), 231–41; on Josephus, e.g. A. Schlatter,
Die Theologie des Judentums nach dem Bericht des Josephus (Gütersloh, 1932),
148–9, 163–9.

need to be protected against themselves and are best kept inside the home as much as possible.[22] So we see that although the author of T. Job has an open mind for the excellent qualities women can have as spouses and mothers (cf. Prov. 31), he combines that with a low opinion of women as far as their spiritual abilities are concerned. Sitidos does not see where evil powers lie in wait, nor does she see what God is doing; she is spiritually blind. Kind though she may be, she is dull, and it is only fitting that it is the cows that are the first to bewail her death.

Job's daughters

Sitidos, however, is not the only woman who plays a prominent role in T. Job. There are also Job's daughters, not his daughters from Sitidos, but those from his second wife, Dinah. In chs. 46–53 they are the protagonists. There we read that Job divides his inheritance among his seven sons, whereas his daughters receive nothing (in conformity with Num. 27; cf. mBB 9.1). When the girls raise a sad protest: 'Are we not also your children? Why then did you not give us some of your goods?' (46.2), Job answers: 'I have not forgotten you; I have designated for you an inheritance that is better than that of your brothers' (46.3–4). It is clear that the fact that in the biblical book of Job 42.15 his daughters are explicitly said to be the co-heiresses of their brothers is the starting-point of this passage. Job then asks his first daughter, Hemera, to get three golden boxes (or gold boxes, i.e. boxes with gold – see below, p. 104) out of the treasury or crypt. Out of these boxes Job takes three girdles or sashes which

---

[22] See *inter alia* L. Swidler, *Women in Judaism. The Status of Women in Formative Judaism* (Metuchen, 1976); L. J. Archer, 'The Role of Jewish Women in the Religion, Ritual and Cult of Graeco-Roman Palestine', in A. Cameron and A. Kuhrt (eds.), *Images of Women in Antiquity* (Kent, 1983), 273–87; L. J. Archer, *Her Price is Beyond Rubies* (Sheffield, 1989); J. Leipoldt, *Die Frau in der antiken Welt und im Urchristentum* (Gütersloh, 1962), 49–79. It is striking to see that in the Greek and Roman world there was a gradual movement from an inferior position of women towards a position of equality, whereas in Judaism the development was the other way round. See K. Thraede, 'Frau', *RAC*, 8 (1972), 197–269; C. Schneider, *Kulturgeschichte des Hellenismus*, I (München, 1967), 78–117; L. Bringmann, *Die Frau im ptolemäisch-kaiserlichen Aegypten* (Bonn, 1939), now superseded in many respects by S. B. Pomeroy, *Women in Hellenistic Egypt* (New York, 1984). See also the collection of material in C. Spicq, *Les Epitres pastorales*, I (Paris, 1969), 385–425, and esp. in Küchler, *Schweigen, Schmuck und Schleier, passim*.

the three daughters have to wear about their breasts. (It is very difficult to get a clear image of these girdles since the author uses a different word every time for them, except the word one would expect, sc. ζώνη. In 46.6 he uses χορδή = string, cord; in 48.1 σπάρτη = rope, cord; in 52.1 περίζωσις = belt, girdle; in 47.11 φυλακτήριον = amulet. In view of the fact that the objects designated are placed over the breast, for which elsewhere the term ζωνή is used (see e.g. Rev. 1.13 and 15.6), I use the translation 'girdle'.[23]) These girdles are so radiant that no one can describe them, because they are not from the earth but from heaven, and sparks shoot from them like rays of the sun. Job tells his daughters to wear them over their breasts so that it may go well with them all the days of their life (46.9). Then his second daughter, Kasia, remarks that although Job had said that this inheritance was better than that of their brothers, yet to her mind they cannot possibly make a living from these strange girdles. Job answers: These girdles will not only enable you to live but will also lead you into 'the greater world', i.e. to live in the heavens. For these are the girdles that God himself had given to Job when he said to him: 'Arise, gird your loins like a man' (Job 38.3, 40.7).[24] Job put them on and immediately he was healed in body and soul and God revealed to him the past and the future (a formula describing prophecy[25]). These girdles, Job now says, will make you immune to the enemy (Satan), for it is a φυλακτήριον τοῦ πατρός (47.11), probably not 'an amulet of your father', but 'an amulet given by your Heavenly Father'.[26] 'Gird yourselves with them in order that you may be able to see those who are coming to take my soul to heaven' (47.11).

---

[23] On girdles in antiquity in general see W. Speyer, 'Gürtel', *RAC*, 12 (1983), 1232–66; for different types of girdles used by Jews see esp. S. Krauss, *Talmudische Archäologie*, I (Leipzig, 1910), 172–5, 613–18.

[24] In the biblical text, the quotation continues, 'I shall question you, and you should answer me.' This second part of the quotation is in all the MSS of T. Job, but does not make any sense in the context. It may be a later addition. See Schaller *ad* 47.5 in JSHRZ, III, 3, 368. On Job 38.3 in post-biblical literature see H. Kosmala, *Hebräer-Essener-Christen* (Leiden, 1959), 217f.

[25] See W.C. van Unnik, 'A Formula Describing Prophecy', in his *Sparsa collecta*, II (Leiden, 1980), 183–93.

[26] For the apotropaic powers of magic girdles in many cultures see I. Scheftelowitz, *Die altpersische Religion und das Judentum* (Giessen, 1920), 77ff; also Speyer, 'Gürtel', 1234ff.

When Hemera puts on her girdle, she receives another heart,[27] so that she is no longer mindful of earthly things, and she sings a hymn to God in the language of the angels and in accord with the way the angels sing hymns (τῇ ἀγγελικῇ διαλέκτῳ and κατὰ τὴν τῶν ἀγγέλων ὑμνολογίαν). The Spirit lets her songs be inscribed on her garment (or rather on her *stele*, since I prefer to read στήλη instead of στόλη).[28] When Kasia binds on her girdle, her heart changes as well, so that she no longer regards worldly things. She too becomes ecstatic and sings of the work of the exalted τόπος (= *maqom*, a well-known periphrasis for 'God') in the language of the ἀρχαί, a class of angels (cf. Rom. 8.38; 1 Cor. 15.24; Eph. 1.21, etc.; Col. 1.16, etc.). If anyone wishes to know the work of the οὐρανοί (= *shamayim*, another periphrasis for 'God'), it can be found in the Hymns of Kasia, obviously another fictitious composition. When Amaltheias Keras binds on her girdle, her heart is changed as well, so that she keeps aloof from worldly matters, and she sings of the δεσπότης τῶν ἀρετῶν, 'Master of virtues' or 'Master of mighty deeds', in the language of the cherubim. The author concludes this scene by saying that whoever wants to see a trace of the *doxa* of the Father[29] will find it written down in the Prayers of Amaltheias Keras.[30]

Quite unexpectedly, in the three final chapters (chs. 51–3) the 'I' is no longer Job but his brother, Nereus. He describes Job's final hours and burial. He says that together with God and the Holy Spirit he has been present at the angelic vocal performance of the daughters and that he has written down all the hymns on the basis of the notes, i.e. probably the translations, that the sisters made for one another (cf. 1 Cor. 14.27–8). These are the great acts of God, he says,

[27] The expression 'another heart' derives from 1 Sam. 10.9, where it is said of Saul at the moment he becomes ecstatic.

[28] See the discussions of this problem in Schaller and Spittler. R. Reitzenstein, *Poimandres. Studien zur griechisch-ägyptischen und frühchristlichen Literatur* (Leipzig, 1904), 57, n. 9 mentions a late Graeco-Egyptian parallel to the motif of a holy text being inscribed upon a garment; see also Apoc. Pauli 12. But I suspect that *stélé* is the correct reading. There are examples of writings called 'The Stélé of ...' (e.g. in the Nag Hammadi Library), and in view of the fact that the words of the second and third daughters are said to have been recorded in a book, it is very likely that here too there is a reference to a piece of writing.

[29] The MSS read λοιπὸν ἴχνος ἡμέρας καταλαβεῖν τῆς πατρικῆς δόξης. The meaning of this, esp. of ἡμέρας (om. V), is far from clear.

[30] The references to fictitious writings are modelled upon OT passages like 1 Kings 14.29; 2 Chron. 35.25, *et al.*

τὰ μεγαλεῖα τοῦ θεοῦ = *magnalia dei*. Three days later Job falls ill and he sees the angels who come for his soul. He gives a lyre to Hemera, a censer to Kasia and a kettle-drum to Amaltheias Keras, so that they may praise the angels who are coming to bring Job's soul to heaven. The three daughters see the gleaming chariots with the angels and they glorify them, each in her own heavenly tongue. Only the daughters, no one else, see how Job's soul is taken up and ascends to the east by chariot. Job's body is buried, and at the burial the daughters lead the way, girded with their heavenly sashes and singing hymns to God. Job's brother and his sons raise a lament.

In my opinion we have here an image of women that is markedly different from that of Sitidos in the preceding chapters. John Collins remarks that what holds good for Job's wife and his servant also applies to his daughters, sc. that they, in contrast to Job himself, only receive insight into the heavenly reality after Job has pointed out this reality to them or, in the case of the daughters, has given them the means to gain that insight. Collins says: 'Womankind in *Test. Job* symbolizes ... the human state of ignorance'.[31] But this is too general a statement in my opinion. The agreement or similarity between the two groups of women goes no further than the motif that Job's intervention is needed in order to help the women to gain insight. But Job's servant and his wife are enlightened only incidentally and momentarily; it is not a lasting insight which they obtain. Their heart is not changed, to put it in the terms of chs. 48–50. For this is the crucial factor with the daughters: they undergo a radical and lasting change; in fact they become virtually heavenly beings. A number of elements in the story are indicative of this. Firstly there are the girdles. In my opinion these are golden girdles. For in 46.5 it is stated that these three girdles are kept in τρία σκευάρια τοῦ χρυσοῦ, which, it is true, one might translate as 'the three golden boxes'; but since one rather expects then τρία σκευάρια χρυσᾶ, one may equally well translate 'the three boxes with gold', i.e. the three receptacles of golden objects. This fits in perfectly with the fact that in 46.6–7 it is said that sparks shoot from the girdles like rays from the sun and that no one could describe their beauty. This detail, combined with

[31] J. J. Collins, 'Testaments', in M. E. Stone (ed.), *Jewish Writings of the Second Temple Period* (CRINT, II, 2) (Assen/Philadelphia, 1984), 352–3; J. J. Collins, *Between Athens and Jerusalem* (New York, 1983), 223.

the fact that the girls have to wear these girdles around their breasts, makes one immediately think of two passages in the Apocalypse of John, 1.13, where it is said of the heavenly Christ that he wears a golden girdle round his breast, and 15.6, where it is said of the seven angels that they had girdles of gold round their breasts. These two texts do not stand isolated; there are several other Jewish and Christian texts that speak of the golden girdles of heavenly beings.[32] This would seem to me, therefore, to be an indication that the 'changed heart' here means that their whole being has been transmuted from an earthly into a heavenly one, and that it is for that reason that it is said so explicitly three times that τὰ τῆς γῆς or τὰ κοσμικά are no longer live options for them.[33]

Their heavenly status becomes still more evident by their newly acquired ability to speak in the languages of the angels. We meet here a Jewish notion, known also from 1 Cor. 13.1, that the angels speak their own language and that the diverse classes of angels each speak their own dialect or tongue.[34] Almost superfluously it is added that the three sisters sing in accordance with the *hymnologia* of the angels.[35] Their ability to praise God in the language and in the way of the angels[36] actually indicates that they have already ascended from the earth and that they have their *politeuma* in heaven, to put it in a Pauline way (Phil. 3.20). The fact that in the final chapter (53) it is said that after Job's death his brother and his sons do nothing but raise a lament together with the widows and orphans, whereas the three daughters cheerfully lead the burial singing hymns to God, indicates a radical reversal of the usual roles: whereas giving utterance to laments was usually the role of women,[37] here it is the men who

---

[32] See Speyer, *RAC*, 12 (1982), 1251, 1253; e.g. Apoc. Zeph. 6.12; Apoc. Pauli 12.

[33] Interesting in this connection is the interpolation of MS. V at 48.1 where it is said of Hemera: καὶ παράχρημα ἔξω γέγονε τῆς ἑαυτῆς σαρκός.

[34] See 1 En. 40; Asc. Is. 7.15; Apoc. Abr. 15.7; 17.1ff.; and elsewhere. P. Billerbeck, *Kommentar zum Neuen Testament aus Talmud und Midrasch*, III (München, 1926), 449; J. Michl, 'Engel', *RAC*, 5 (1962), 69; S. D. Currie, 'Speaking in Tongues. Early Evidence outside the New Testament bearing on "Glossais Lalein"', *Interpretation* 19 (1965), 274–94, esp. 281ff. (now reprinted in the volume mentioned in n. 47 below).

[35] I. Gruenwald, 'Angelic Song', *EncJud.*, 15 (1971), 144.

[36] That it is praise of God that all is about is clear from the use of δοξολογεῖν in 49.2 and 30.2 and of τὰ μεγαλεῖα τοῦ θεοῦ in 51.4.

[37] M. Alexiou, *The Ritual Lament in Greek Tradition* (Cambridge, 1974), 10–18.

play this role. In fact by doing so they betray a 'female' 'lack of perception', since they do not share in the joyful insight of their sisters into the glorious fate of their father's soul. And, it should be stressed, besides Job it is only the daughters who are able to see how their father's soul is brought to heaven by heavenly figures in gleaming chariots. Emphatically it is stated that no one else could see that (52.9), Nereus and Job's sons included. Nothing of this applies to Sitidos. And this essential difference makes it impossible, in my opinion, to speak in a generalizing way of women as symbols of ignorance in T. Job. In chs. 46–53 women play an extraordinarily positive role; in fact they play the leading part instead of Job, who is in these chapters no more than a supernumerary actor. It is not the sons but the daughters who rise to an almost superhuman spiritual level by means of the God-given magic belts, and it is they and not the men who gain insight therefore, and a permanent one at that, into the heavenly reality that is the background of the earthly one. One must say that this is an image of women that is extremely unusual in early Jewish literature.

The Jewish character of T. Job 46–53

It is for precisely this reason that some scholars have contested both the authenticity and the Jewish character of these chapters. Various arguments have been put forward against their authenticity.[38] These chapters could not have been written by the original author of T. Job for the following reasons: 1. In 1.2 Job wants to address his children because he has fallen ill, whereas in 52.1 he falls ill only three days *after* his address. 2. In 1.4–6 the author presents a concise summary of the chapters that will follow, approximately in these words: 'I will tell you all that the Lord has done to me and everything that has happened to me'; this is out of tune with chs. 46–53, in which Job plays only a very insignificant role. 3. In ch. 51, where Nereus represents himself as the author of the book, he reports as the book's contents especially the translation of the hymns of the three daughters, in which they sang of the *magnalia dei*; this does not fit in with the contents of chs. 1–45.4. In 45.1–3 Job draws the most important conclusions from the story of his life in the form of ethical admonitions:

---

[38] See most recently von Nordheim, *Die Lehre der Alten*, I, 131f.

to do well to the poor, not to neglect the helpless, not to take foreign wives. These conclusions do not suit the contents of chs. 46–53. As a matter of fact one does not expect these chapters at all; one expects a short report of Job's death, not a long report of his daughters' ecstasy. 5. The *ego* in chs. 1–45 is Job himself, but the *ego* in chs. 51–3 is his brother, a quite unexpected turn. This cannot come from the same writer.

Not all these arguments are equally convincing. But it is clear that in 46.1 there occurs a *metabasis*, especially in view of the other *ego* in chs. 51–3. The differences, however, can also be explained from the fact that the author has joined different sources in a rather maladroit way.[39] In the same way the fact that a summary of one part of the book does not agree with the contents of the other part can be explained as well. There certainly is a clear tension between chs. 1–45 on the one hand and 46–53 on the other, and especially in view of the very different images of women in both parts it seems to be indubitable that both parts cannot have come from the same source. But one may assume that the Jewish redactor has used various haggadic traditions about Job and his family and has not ironed out the discrepancies everywhere. The fact that in Job 42.15 there is such an explicit mention of the exceptional fact that the daughters were fellow-heirs with their brothers could not fail to evoke haggadic elaboration of this motif. And the author/redactor did not let the opportunity slip to adopt such a piece of haggada in his *Testament*.

But, as has already been said, there are scholars who do not regard chs. 46–53 as Jewish at all, but as Christian.[40] The one who has defended this position most recently is Russell Spittler.[41] His line of argument is as follows: the phenomenon of Jewish or Christian ecstatic women has its closest parallel in Montanism in the second

---

[39] That the author used diverse sources is also clear from a comparison of chs. 2–27 on the one hand and 28–45 on the other; see Collins, 'Structure and Meaning', 46–7, and especially the (not always convincing) discussion of T. Job's sources in P. Nicholl's 'The Structure and Purpose of the Testament of Job', unpublished dissertation, Jerusalem, 1982.

[40] Names of scholars who see these chapters or the whole T. Job as a Christian document can be found in Schaller, JSHRZ, III, 3, 308, n. 43, and Rahnenführer, *ZNW* 62 (1971), 70–2.

[41] R. P. Spittler, 'The Testament of Job. Introduction, Translation, and Notes', unpublished dissertation, Harvard University, 1971. A summary by Spittler in *OTP*, I, 834.

half of the second century. The only allusion to T. Job in the first five centuries of our era is to be found in the *De patientia* (14.5) of Tertullian, an author who went over to Montanism, though only after he had written that treatise. Josephine M. Ford's thesis that Montanism was originally a Jewish-Christian sect makes it very probable that Montanists were interested in the possibility of inserting Montanist interpolations into Jewish writings.[42] In his *Hist. eccl.* V.17, 1–4 Eusebius gives a quotation from an anti-Montanist writing in which the author asks where in the Bible prophets behave ecstatically; according to him, nowhere. In this situation of polemics in the last decade of the second century a Montanist author would have reacted to this by adding to T. Job a passage that gave the required biblical model for ecstatic prophecy. All these data taken together add up to the thesis that chs. 46–53 are a piece of Montanist propaganda.

This theory seems to me to be untenable for the following reasons: 1. The fact that in his pre-Montanist period Tertullian perhaps gives evidence of a knowledge of T. Job is obviously no proof whatsoever that chs. 46–53 are Montanist. 2. Ecstatic prophecy, also by women, did not only occur in Montanism.[43] 3. Ford's theory of the Jewish-Christian character of Montanism has found little positive response.[44] 4. The biblical precedent for ecstatic prophecy required by the anti-Montanist author could not, of course, be created by interpolating ecstatic women into a non-biblical text. At the end of the second century almost everyone, anti-Montanists too, knew how to distinguish between the Bible and post-biblical stories as far as the Old Testament was concerned.[45] If a Montanist had wanted to react adequately to this challenge, he would have done better, for instance, to put upon the stage in a pseudepigraphon the four daughters of Philip, who in Acts 21.9 are explicitly called prophetesses. That would have had much more cogency than such a procedure with Job's daughters, for whom the biblical tradition did not yield such a

[42] J.M. Ford, 'Was Montanism a Jewish-Christian Heresy?', *JEH* 17 (1966), 145–58.

[43] See F. Pfister, 'Ekstase', *RAC*, 4 (1959), 944ff.

[44] See, e.g., W.H.C. Frend, 'Montanism: Research and Problems', *Rivista di storia e letteratura religiosa* 20 (1984), 521–37, esp. 533.

[45] See R.T. Beckwith, *The Old Testament Canon of the New Testament Church* (London, 1985), *passim*.

starting-point. 5. Apart from the daughters' ecstasy there is not the slightest reason to think of a Montanist origin for chs. 46–53, for nothing that was characteristic for Montanism is to be found there; no prohibition of a second marriage, no emphasis on strict fasting-rules, no warning against fleeing in times of persecution, no descent of the heavenly Jerusalem in Pepuza in Phrygia, etc. We have to conclude that this original and bold hypothesis cannot be maintained.

It has to be added that a number of striking points of agreement with the New Testament should not tempt us to assume a Christian origin for these chapters. Of course, the glossolalia of the daughters reminds one of 1 Cor. 12 and 14, the languages of the angels of 1 Cor. 13.1, the μεγαλεῖα τοῦ θεοῦ of Acts 2.11 (there, too, used in a context of ecstatic speech; note also the use of ἀποφθέγγεσθαι and διάλεκτος in Acts 2.4, 6 and T. Job 48.3), the renouncing of τὰ κοσμικά of Titus 2.12 (ἀρνήσασθαι ... τὰς κοσμικάς ἐπιθυμίας), and the μηκέτι τὰ τῆς γῆς φρονεῖν (48.2) of Col. 3.2. One should not misjudge these similarities in terminology and motives, for to the majority of them Jewish parallels can be adduced. To the renouncing of worldly affairs there are, of course, Jewish analogies, for even if one can probably find only Christian parallels to this pejorative use of κοσμικός, the idea is to be found in Jewish writings, certainly in an apocalyptic context (cf. in T. Job itself 36.1!). The same applies to the idea of keeping your thoughts no longer fixed on earthly things: the most literal parallels are Christian, but the idea is definitely not exclusively Christian. As to the *magnalia dei*, there is a parallel in T. Job itself when Job says in 38.1 'why should I not speak of the μεγαλεῖα τοῦ κυρίου?'. But especially in the book of Ben Sira the author/translator often mentions the *megaleia* of God (17.9, 18.4, 33.8, etc.), a term that, incidentally, was already used by the LXX translators of Deut. 11.2 for God's great deeds (cf. Ps.104.1 *v.1.*, and 3 Macc. 7.22). As to the languages of the angels, it has already been said above that this is a Jewish conception (see p.105 with n.34). What remains, however, is the glossolalia.

In his *Religion des Judentums*, Bousset remarked on our passage: 'Stände der jüdische Charakter des betreffenden Abschnittes fest, so wäre damit bewiesen, dass die eigentümliche Erscheinung des

Zungenredens im Judentum ihre Heimat habe.'[46] That is the problem
we have to deal with now. So far there have been found no other
indisputable testimonies to the existence of glossolalia in early
Judaism. Do we have to conclude, therefore, that a text in which this
ecstatic phenomenon is described cannot be Jewish? Gerhard
Dautzenberg denies this in his article 'Glossolalie' in the *Reallexikon
für Antike und Christentum*.[47] He points out that the earliest reports
on Christian glossolalia, 1 Cor. 12–14 and Acts 2, contain several
Jewish elements and that one may assume, therefore, that it is a
phenomenon that has its roots in Jewish religiosity: there is the motif
of the language of the angels (1 Cor. 13.1), the speaking about God's
great acts (Acts 2.11), the fact that the earliest manifestations of this
phenomenon occur in Jerusalem; all this is indicative of Jewish roots.
Obviously this is not a compelling proof. But Dautzenberg adds the
following considerations. From the beginning there have been ecstatic
components in ancient Israelite prophecy. Especially in the early
period of biblical prophecy the ecstatic element is prominent (1 Sam.
10.5–11; 19.18–24; 1 Kings 18.22–9; Num. 11.25–7; 24.3–9,
15–19). But in the classical and later periods too this element is not
absent (e.g. Ezek. 1.28; 3.15,23,26; 24.27; 33.22; Jer. 23.9; 29.26;
Zech. 13.2–6; Dan. 10.9–11). And some texts seem to indicate that
in ecstasy sometimes unintelligible language was spoken (see esp. Isa.
28:10).[48] In post-biblical times too unintelligible, ecstatic speech by
charismatics was not unknown.[49] This is indicated, for instance,

[46] W. Bousset and H. Gressmann, *Die Religion des Judentums im späthellenistischen
Zeitalter*, 3rd edn (Tübingen, 1926), 396.

[47] *RAC* 11 (1981), 226–46. We now have an excellent survey of research on
glossolalia in W. E. Mills (ed.), *Speaking in Tongues. A Guide to Research on
Glossolalia* (Grand Rapids, 1986), especially Mills' own introductory chapters
and bibliography (1–31 and 493–528).

[48] See W. Jacobi, *Die Ekstase der alttestamentlichen Propheten* (München/
Wiesbaden, 1920); J. Lindblom, *Prophecy in Ancient Israel* (Oxford, 1962),
47–65, 122–37; C. G. Williams, 'Ecstaticism in Hebrew Prophecy and Christian
Glossolalia', *Studies in Religion*, 3 (1973/1974), 320–38; D. E. Aune, *Prophecy
in Early Christianity and the Ancient Mediterranean World* (Grand Rapids, 1983),
86–7 with notes on 370.

[49] See, e.g., P. Volz, *Der Geist Gottes und die verwandten Erscheinungen im Alten
Testament und im anschliessenden Judentum* (Tübingen, 1910), 78ff.; E. Mosiman,
Das Zungenreden geschichtlich und psychologisch untersucht (Tübingen, 1911), 39f.;
Dautzenberg, 232f.; S. D. Currie, 'Speaking in Tongues. Early Evidence Outside
the New Testament Bearing on "Glossais Lalein"', *Interpretation* 19 (1965),
274–94 (now reprinted in Mills' volume: see n. 47).

by the fact that Philo and Josephus deal extensively with prophetic ecstasy, especially with immediate speech by God or his Spirit through a person in ecstasy, including in their own time.[50] And even if the expression 'speaking in tongues' is used nowhere, in this line of development (or 'trajectory') T. Job 48–50 finds its natural place. This impression is confirmed when one sees that in the probably first-century Jewish Apocalypse of Zephaniah the visionary author reports an experience that comes very close to what we read in T. Job 48–50. In a vision he has been taken up into heaven and he sees myriads of angels in prayer. He puts on an angelic dress and joins them in their prayers in their own language, which he says he knew because they spoke to him in that language (Apoc. Zeph. 8.1–5).[51] Praying in the language of the angels is, as appears from 1 Cor. 14.14–17 and probably Rom. 8.26–7, a glossolalic activity, and therefore most likely identical to the speaking or singing in angelic languages, the glossolalia, in T. Job 48–50 (even though, strikingly enough, the expression γλώσσαις λαλεῖν is lacking in T. Job). In my opinion, therefore, David Flusser very properly remarks that the mystical hymns and praises in T. Job possibly reflect the liturgy of a Jewish mystical group, which he then, to be true, without cogent arguments identifies as a second-century AD Egyptian Jewish group.[52] An earlier dating and another provenance are equally possible. The fact that Flusser himself points out the affinity with the so-called 'angelic liturgy' in 4Q Serekh Shirot 'Olat ha-Shabbat from the first century BC[53] demonstrates that a Palestinian origin about the beginning of the Common Era can certainly not be excluded.

In a recent investigation into the origin of the expression 'speaking in tongues', Harrisville comes to the confident conclusion that it lies in pre-Christian Judaism, possibly even in Qumran. He points to passages like 1 Enoch 71.11 and Martyrdom of Isaiah 5.14 as instances of incomprehensible ecstatic speech (see also perhaps 4 Ezra 14.37ff.),

---

[50] See Dautzenberg, 232 for references.

[51] See O. S. Wintermute's translation in *OTP*, I, 514. Cf. perhaps also 1QH 6.13.

[52] D. Flusser, 'Psalms, Hymns and Prayers', in Stone, *Jewish Writings*, 564.

[53] See J. Strugnell, 'The Angelic Liturgy at Qumran – 4Q Serek Shirot 'Olat Hashshabbat', in *Congress Volume Oxford 1959* (Suppl. to Vet. Test., 7) (Leiden, 1960), 318–45. See now Carol Newsom, *Songs of the Sabbath Sacrifice: A Critical Edition* (Atlanta, 1986). Newsom does not believe there is such an affinity (oral communication).

but also to other material that makes clear that the Jews of the Hellenistic period did not regard glossolalia as 'a category separate from the ecstatic *per se*'.[54] Ecstasy could express itself, as with the biblical prophets, in language varying from intelligible through hardly understandable to totally inarticulate and incomprehensible. In this connection it is very interesting to note that Lucian, in his portrait of Alexander the false prophet, says that at his first appearance this man girded himself with a gilded girdle and then uttered in ecstasy unintelligible sounds, such as may also be heard among Hebrews and Phoenicians (*Alex.* 12–13).[55] Be that as it may, we can agree with Schaller that, although T. Job cannot easily be attributed to any of the Jewish groups or movements known to us, there is no doubt that we have to do with a completely Jewish, non-Christian composition[56] in which we find a melange of Jewish wisdom and mysticism and of Hellenistic magic.[57] Although the Hellenistic world probably offered enough examples of ecstatic speech in general, for glossolalia we need not seek a Hellenistic origin.[58] We can state fairly confidently that, as regards glossolalia, the early Christians adopted a Jewish form of religious experience.

As corroborative evidence we could point to an interesting passage in Ps-Philo where, it is true, nothing is said about ecstasy, but where all the other elements of T. Job 48–50 appear in an undeniably

---

[54] R. A. Harrisville, 'Speaking in Tongues: A Lexicographical Study', *CBQ* 38 (1976), 35–48, see here 47 (now reprinted in Mills' volume); see also Bousset and Gressmann, *Religion des Judentums*, 394ff.

[55] The motif of a golden or gilded girdle recurs time and again in a context of magic: golden girdles were worn by Kirke, Kalypso, Abaris, Empedocles; see Speyer, 'Gürtel', 1238f., 1243f.

[56] Schaller, JSHRZ, III, 3, 314–16.

[57] See n. 55. H. C. Kee, 'Satan, Magic, and Salvation in the Testament of Job', *SBL Seminar Papers 1974* (Missoula, 1974), I, 53–76, sees the origin of T. Job in a circle of Judaeo-Greek merkavah mystics, but the element of 'throne-vision' does not at all play a prominent role in T. Job. Nicholls, 'The Structure and Purpose of the Testament of Job', 258 aptly remarks: 'There are no points of contact between it [T. Job] and the wide range of texts which deal with speculation about the merkabah. What evidence there is would suggest that the circle in which Test. Job arose had little interest in this form of mysticism'.

[58] For ecstatic speech in Hellenistic religiosity see W. Bousset in *GGA*, 163 (1901), 762f.; F. Pfister, Ekstase, *RAC*, 4 (1959), 944–87; E. Rohde, *Psyche*, II (Leizig/ Tübingen, 1898; repr. Darmstadt, 1961), 18–22; Reitzenstein, *Poimandres*, 55–9. Note also the restrictions made by C. Forbes, 'Early Christian Inspired Speech and Hellenistic Popular Religion', *Nov. Test.* 28 (1986), 257–70.

Jewish context. In LAB 20.2–3 God appoints Joshua as the prophetic successor of Moses and says to him,

> '(Since Moses has died), take his garments of wisdom and clothe yourself, and with his belt of knowledge gird your loins, and you will be changed and become another man' ... And Joshua took the garments of wisdom and clothed himself and girded his loins with the belt of understanding. And when he clothed himself with it, his mind was afire and his spirit was moved, and he said to the people ...

This combination of the reception of a girdle from or of a person who had been endowed with God's Spirit and the ensuing inner change is found here again, now related to the prophetic figure of Joshua. It seems to me very improbable that one of these writings is dependent upon the other. Rather we have here a case of a non-interdependent use of this motif. One can imagine that the motif strongly appealed to our author, who was heavily inclined to spiritualization, the more so since it offered him the opportunity to spiritualize the biblical remarks about the extraordinarily beautiful outer appearance of Job's daughters (42.15) by altering that into a beautiful inner self, a 'changed heart', as the author puts it in the words of 1 Sam. 10.9, where the expression is used of Saul becoming ecstatic. So we may conclude that in the somewhat clumsily appended chs. 46–53 the author has adopted a piece of haggada in which Job 42.15 (on the exceptional inheritance of Job's exceptionally beautiful daughters) was the starting-point for the depiction of a scene in which, exceptionally too, women take the spiritual lead and become superior to men.[59] It is probable that this haggada originated in ecstatic-mystical circles of early Judaism from about the beginning of the Common Era, very probably also in a group in which women played a leading role by their greater ecstatic gifts and their superior spiritual insight into heavenly reality. Other Jewish literature from antiquity does not give us much cause to think of women as leaders in Jewish circles. Nevertheless, we can assume, on the basis of epigraphic materials studied by Bernadette Brooten in her *Women Leaders in the Ancient*

---

[59] Nickelsburg, *Jewish Literature*, 246, rightly says that Job's gift to his daughters 'ascribes a higher religious status to women than to men, surely a reversal of values in the contemporary world'.

Synagogue (Chico, 1982),[60] that there were certain religious circles
in which women played a or the leading part. It is thinkable or
even feasible that such women often saw their position assailed
and that hence they tried to strengthen it by creating haggada
that legitimated their leading role. In this connection it is vital
to notice that this whole section begins with an explicit request
for equal rights. In 46.2 the daughters say, 'Are we not also your
children?' etc. Female authorship of the source adopted in chs.
46–53 cannot, therefore, be excluded.[61]

The attempts made so far to locate this image of women in
early Judaism have yielded nothing but the theory of Therapeutic
origin.[62] The Therapeutae are described by Philo in his *De vita
contemplativa* as a Jewish monastic group in Egypt, the members
of which, both men and women, are wholly devoted to ascesis,
meditation and religious meetings of which the central parts are
allegorical interpretation of Scripture and community singing.
It is conspicuous that women play a greater role in this than one
would expect on the basis of other data on the position of Jewish
women. Philo speaks of ecstatic experiences that occur in both
groups and of alternate and combined singing by them during
their meetings. Many of these women are widows, and widows
are mentioned several times in T. Job, once even as a singing
group (14.2–3). It is my opinion that these agreements and similarities are too small to base upon them a theory of the Therapeutic

[60] To Brooten's dossier may now be added two new items: the Jewish *presbyterissa*
in an inscription in Tripoli: see Y. le Bohec, 'Inscriptions juives et judaïsantes de
l'Afrique Romaine', *Antiquités Africaines* 17 (1981), 173, no. 4; and the *presbytera*
discussed by R. S. Kraemer, 'A New Inscription from Malta and the Question of
Women Elders in the Diaspora Jewish Communities', *HTR* 78 (1985), 431–8.

[61] Compare Athalya Brenner's suggestion of female authorship of parts of the Song
of Songs in her *The Israelite Woman* (Sheffield, 1985), 49f., and for other parts
of the Old Testament her article 'Female Social Behaviour: Two Descriptive
Patterns within the "Birth of the Hero" Paradigm', *VT* 36 (1986), 273. Because
of their position, women who wanted to publish a book probably had to write
under male pseudonyms. See also R. S. Kraemer, 'Hellenistic Jewish Women:
The Epigraphical Evidence', *SBL 1986 Seminar Papers* (Atlanta, 1986), 185.
(183–200).

[62] Defended by Kohler, Spittler, 'The Testament of Job', and M. Philonenko,
'Le *Testament de Job* et les Thérapeutes', *Semitica* 8 (1958), 41–53; M. Philonenko,
'Le Testament de Job. Introduction, Traduction et Notes', *Semitica* 18 (1968),
1–75, esp. 15ff.

origin of T. Job.[63] Firstly, the agreements are only partial. For instance, as regards ecstasy and hymnic singing, T. Job ascribes these only to women, not to both men and women. However conspicuous the position of women in the Therapeutic community may have been as compared to that in other Jewish circles, in the final analysis these women remain in a subordinate position; it is men who lead the community, it is men who read and expound Scripture, not women.[64] Secondly, most other characteristics of this community are lacking in T. Job, namely praise of poverty, community of goods, frequent fasting, plain clothing, rejection of slavery, emphasis on virginity, etc. One should also take into consideration the fact that Philo's description of this group is of dubious historical quality, since it is one of those well-known idealizing pictures of religious groups we meet so often in Hellenistic literature.[65]

For the motif of enhancing the role of a biblical woman in a positive sense one could also refer to the role of Rebecca in Jubilees.[66] In Genesis, Abraham is already dead when Rebecca gives birth to Jacob and Esau, but in Jubilees he is still living at that moment, and the author then explicitly says: 'Abraham loved Jacob, and Isaac loved Esau' (19.13), thus giving a patriarchal legitimation to Rebecca's love for Jacob. Her wile (Gen. 27) is legitimated theologically not only by Abraham's preference for Jacob, but also by God himself, who sees to it that everything escapes Isaac's notice by his blindness (Jub. 26.18). The culminating-point of this long story, in which Rebecca is so prominent (Jub. 19–35), is the passage in which the Spirit descends upon her and she praises God, places her hands upon the head of Jacob and gives her matriarchal blessing both to him and to his posterity (Jub. 25.11–23), all this after Abraham and Isaac had

---

[63] See Collins, 'Testaments', 354, and esp. Schaller, JSHRZ, III, 3; Flusser, 'Psalms', 564, n. 46, incorrectly states that Schaller *defends* the Therapeutic thesis.

[64] It has to be conceded that during the week these women led a separate, autonomous life.

[65] See A.-J. Festugière, 'Sur une nouvelle édition du "Da Vita Pythagorica" de Jamblique', *Revue des études grecques* 50 (1937), 470–94, and P. W. van der Horst, *Chaeremon, Egyptian Priest and Stoic Philosopher. The Fragments collected and translated with explanatory notes* (Leiden, 1984), 56–61. However, Philo's image of the Therapeutrides is at variance with the picture of womankind he draws otherwise, which might plead for a real historical kernel in his presentation.

[66] P. W. van Boxel, 'The God of Rebekah', *Service d'information et documentation judéo-chrétienne*, ix (1976), 14–18.

already blessed Jacob (19.29; 22.11–13)! Finally, it is she who knows how to reconcile Isaac, Esau and Jacob to one another (Jub. 35). Here, too, we see a biblical woman who, by the Spirit of God, comes to truly matriarchal deeds. In spite of the great differences between these two writings in many other respects, there is a strong affinity on this point.[67]

Finally, we will probably have to reconcile ourselves to the fact that for the time being we will not be able to situate T. Job more precisely within early Judaism. Perhaps so much the better, because that broadens our vista on the pluriformity and multicoloured character of Judaism at the turn of our era. In this writing we see juxtaposed, but not without tension and discrepancy, on the one hand an image of women as creatures easy to lead astray and without insight, and on the other hand, a picture in which women are endowed with the highest imaginable spiritual qualities, are sharing in the heavenly reality, and are taking the lead self-consciously thanks to this endowment. We know from early Christian history that charismatic gifts could create strong emancipatory tendencies. It is instructive to see that, in this respect too, Christianity could draw on Judaism.

---

[67] One could also compare Judith's 'feminism', on which see G. W. E. Nickelsburg in Stone, *Jewish Writings*, 46–52, esp. 49f.

6

JOB'S PERSEVERANCE IN THE TESTAMENT OF JOB

Cees Haas
Vlaardingen

Introduction

Job's perseverance in the sufferings that Satan inflicts upon him is the main theme in chapters 1–27 of the Testament of Job. This is shown immediately in ch. 1: Job, just before his death as he looks back upon all the things he has gone through, says to his children that he has exhibited complete perseverance (1.5: ...ἐν πάσῃ ὑπομονῇ γενόμενος). Apparently perseverance in suffering is Job's most characteristic quality. It is also mentioned in 4.6, 10, 5.1, 21.4, 26.4, 5 and 27.4, 7. These passages show that not only ὑπομονή and ὑπομένω, but also καρτερία and καρτερέω as well as μακροθυμία, μακρόθυμος and μακροθυμέω are important words to denote Job's virtue.[1] The last word occurs also in 11.10, 28.5 and 35.4, but in these passages it has a different meaning (see p. 129 below).

The purpose of this chapter is to investigate what perseverance in suffering in T. Job implies and against what background it has to be understood.

The vocabulary of perseverance in the Testament of Job

The three words for perseverance in T. Job are largely synonymous. Often two words are found side by side, and several times one word is taken up by another: see 26.4, 5, where Job uses μακροθυμέω immediately after ὑπομένω; and also 27.4, where Job's καρτερία is

---

[1] I use the text edition of S. P. Brock, *Testamentum Iobi*, PsVTG, 2 (Leiden, Brill, 1967). It is based on MS P and gives the variants of MSS S and V together with a number of important variants of the Slavonic version of the document. The text edition of R. A. Kraft and others, *The Testament of Job according to the SV Text*, SBL Texts and Translations, 5, Pseudepigrapha Series, 4 (Missoula, Montana, 1974) is based on MSS S and V. Kraft as well as Brock gives a survey of the available witnesses to the text and of the textual history of T. Job.

mentioned, whereas in 27.7 he summons his children to μακροθυμία. This summons is based on the example of Job, who in 1.5 again calls himself a model of ὑπομονή.² Apparently in this passage ὑπομονή is the general term that covers the other two words, for in this saying of Job about himself it is used as a key word for all that he is about to tell his children in chs. 2–27.

Though largely synonymous, the words for perseverance in T. Job are not used arbitrarily. It will appear that each of them occurs in a specific context and is connected with a specific idea of suffering; this applies to ὑπομονή as well, though it is also used as a general term.

Therefore, this section will analyse what these notions are, where they are found in T. Job, with which word for perseverance they are connected and which aspect of perseverance they represent.

Perseverance as standing firm in battle

In 4.6, where the angel is speaking to Job, and in 5.1, Job's answer, the verb ὑπομένω occurs in connection with a specific idea of Job's suffering.

In both passages ὑπομένω is linked with the coming battle of Satan with Job. See 4.4a: 'he [Satan] will angrily rise against you for battle [πόλεμον]'. In 5.1 ὑπομένω has as its opposite ἀναποδίζω, used likewise in connection with a battle. In 2 Macc 14.44 it means to retreat, step back, used of soldiers in a battle (here not as a first step to surrender, as in T. Job, but for other reasons).

From the opposite word it is obvious that ὑπομένω means to stand firm (literally: to stay in the same position), of Job under the heavy

---

² In other documents also, both Jewish and Christian, these words are closely related. One finds the following combinations:

> Ὑπομονή κτλ. and καρτερία κτλ. in Philo, *Cherub.* 78; *Deus Imm.* 13 (plus ἀνδρεία); *Omn. Prob. Lib.* 24; 4 Macc 6.9; 15.30. (In 4 Maccabees ὑπομονή κτλ., mentioned twenty-three times, and καρτερία κτλ., mentioned twelve times (plus καρτερός (three times), and καρτερῶς, διακαρτερέω, ἐγκαρτερέω and καρτεροψυχία (once each)) are virtually interchangeable.)
> Ὑπομονή κτλ. and μακροθυμία κτλ. in T. Jos 2.7 and 17.2, Col 1.11, Jas 5.7–11, 1 Clem 64.1, Barn 2.2, Ign. Eph. 3.1. See also 1 Cor 13.4 and 7; 2 Cor 6.4 and 5; 2 Tim 3.10; 1 Clem 62.2; Ign. Pol. 6.2. However, in these passages μακροθυμία κτλ. may have the meaning of 'long-suffering'. In Sir. 2.1–18, in a context of suffering as a temptation, the three words are found together as in T. Job. See verses 2, 4 and 14 respectively.

pressure of Satan's attacks, because, as soon as he retreats only one step, he is irretrievably lost. Satan is very powerful[3] and at that moment he will force a definitive breakthrough. So ὑπομένω in T. Job is much more than 'to endure' or 'to bear passively'. It is a very active reaction of Job to what is threatening him and requires all his strength.[4]

> For ὑπομένω as 'standing firm' in a battle against an all powerful enemy see, e.g., Herod., *Hist.* VI. 96: πρὸς τὰ ὅρια οἴχοντο φεύγοντες οὐδὲ ὑπέμειναν, as the reaction of the inhabitants of the city of Naxos to the onrushing Persian armies.[5] Cf. Wisd Sol 16.22, 17.5 and Sir 22.18.

The reason for Satan's battle with Job is described in chs. 2−4. Job, in this document a heathen king (3.7; 28.7; 29.3),[6] lives quite near an idol's temple and constantly sees whole-burnt sacrifices being offered up there (2.2, 3; according to the Slavonic version Job himself worshipped idols before his call). At a certain moment he starts doubting. He wonders whether the god venerated in the temple is the true God, who made heaven and earth, sea and man (2.4).[7] Then, at night, an angel appears to him in a bright light (3.1, 5.2), who calls him and informs him about the true nature of the idol. He is not (the true) God, but the power of the devil, by whom human nature will be deceived (3.3).[8] Then Job begs the angel to grant him authority

---

[3] For the superior strength of Satan see 27.2: Satan is a spirit and therefore disposes of superhuman power, whereas Job is flesh and has human power only.

[4] See also F. Hauck, 'ὑπομένω, ὑπομονή', *TWNT*, 4 (1942), 585−93; M. Spanneut, 'Geduld', *RAC*, 9 (1976), 243−94, esp. 256−60; and H.-H. Schrey, 'Geduld', *TRE*, 12 (1984), 139−44, esp. 141.

[5] For more examples see Hauck, 'ὑπομένω', 585, 13−18.

[6] Job, named Jobab before his call (1.1, 2.1), is identified here, as in Job 42.17b,d LXX, with Jobab, king of Edom, mentioned in Gen. 36.33−4 and 1 Chron. 1.44. See also Aristeas historicus, 'Concerning the Jews', in Eusebius, *Praeparatio evangelica* 9.25.3. Nevertheless, in T. Job 28.7 Job is called King of all Egypt.

[7] Cf. Abraham's doubt in Jub. 11.16−17 and 12.1−5; Apoc. Abr. 3 and 4. See also Jos., *Ant.* I.154−6 and Philo, *Abr.* 70.

[8] For the devil and demons and their identification or close connection with the idols, see also Pass. Andr. 2 (II.1, 4, 12−14 and 22−4); Act. Andr. et Matt. 26 (II. 1, 104, 13−14); Pass. Bart. 1 (II. 1, 129, 1−2); 5 (139, 6 and 32−3; 140, 6, 11, 20 and 24), 6 (141, 33). See also Jos. As. 12.9. For the apocryphal acts, martyrdoms and passion narratives of the apostles the edition of R. A. Lipsius and M. Bonnet, *Acta Apostolorum Apocrypha* (Lipsiae, 1891 (I), 1898 (II.1), 1903 (II.2), reprinted Darmstadt, Wissenschaftliche Buchgesellschaft, 1959), is used. As the chapters are

to purge this place of Satan (i.e. to destroy the temple),[9] so that sacrifices will no longer be offered to him. He is not the true God and therefore is no longer entitled to be venerated.

The angel replies that the angry Satan will then rise up against him for battle (4.4a), during which he will bring on him one plague after another. He will take away his goods and carry off his children (4.4c, 5); he will, however, be unable to bring death upon Job himself (4.4b). If Job stands firm, his name will be renowned in all generations of the earth till the consummation of the age,[10] and the Lord will repay his goods to him twice over (4.7).[11]

In ch. 5 Job affirms that he will stand firm till death in his battle with Satan (verse 1), after which the angel seals him for protection and leaves him.[12] The following night Job, taking fifty youths with him, goes to the idol's temple and levels it to the ground (verse 2b).[13] After that he returns to his house and, like someone expecting an attack, orders the doors to be secured (verse 3).

So Job has to suffer, because he bids Satan farewell and acknowledges him no longer as a god (see 7.4 and 10: ἀπαλλοτριόομαι[14]),

mostly large, the part that is referred to is, if necessary, indicated by the number of the page of the volume concerned followed by the number(s) of the line(s). So, e.g., Pass. Andr. 2 (II. 1,4,12–14 and 22–4) means: Passio Andreae, chapter 2, volume II. 1, page 4, lines 12–14 and 22–4. For the remaining Christian martyria the edition of H. Musurillo, *The Acts of the Christian Martyrs* (Oxford, Clarendon Press, 1972, reprinted 1979) was consulted.

[9] For the purification of the place where an idol's temple stands by destroying it, see, e.g., 2 Chron 34.3, 5, 8.

[10] See also 53.8. For the motif of universal or/and long-lasting renown see the examples given by D. Rahnenführer, 'Das Testament des Hiob und das Neue Testament', *ZNW* 62 (1971), 23; and B. Schaller, *Das Testament Hiobs*, JSHRZ, III, 3 (Gütersloh, Gütersloher, 1979), 329.

[11] See also 44.5. For the reward mentioned in 4.9 see p. 127 below.

[12] For the meaning of the seal see Schaller, *Testament Hiobs*, 330. Also the following texts, not mentioned by him, are of importance: Act. Pli. et Thecl. 25 (I, 253,7–8): the seal in Christ (baptism) protects against temptation; Act. Andr. et Matt. 27 (II. 1, 105,8–106,2): the devil sends seven demons to Andrew in order to kill him. When they see the seal on his forehead that the Lord has given him, they take fright, are not able to come near him and flee; Pass. Bart. 7 (II. 1, 146, 4–5 and 20–2): the sealing of the forehead with one's own finger, then the evil will flee.

[13] Cf. Judg. 6.25–7 (Gideon; here also the assistance of (ten) servants); Jub. 12.12 (Abraham); Apoc. Abr. 5.6–17 (Abraham); Jos. As. 10.12–13 (Aseneth grinds her idols to pieces and throws them out; she does the same with the sacrifices and the vessels of libation).

[14] See on the meaning of this word Schaller, *Testament Hiobs*, 331.

of which he gives proof by the destruction of his temple. Positively: he has to suffer for the sake of his faith in the true God like other proselytes.[15]

The taking away of Job's goods by Satan, the carrying off of his children and the protection of his life from on high are elements borrowed from the biblical book of Job.[16] His being repaid twice over as a compensation for his sufferings is found there too (Job 42.10; cf. 12). Here, however, it receives much more emphasis; in the book of Job it is a rather loose statement at the end, but in T. Job it is found in the opening chapters of the book in a promise of reward uttered by an angel to incite Job to stand firm in the coming battle. The author of T. Job (or the tradition he makes use of) evidently has geared this element of the book of Job to the main theme of chs. 1–27.

> The call vision in 3.1–5.2a is not a real one. The introduction in 3.1–2 shows great resemblance to the call vision of Abraham in Apoc. Abr. 8.1,2. It is, with reference to Job's question in 2.4, followed by a disclosure of the true nature of the idol in the temple (3.3). Immediately after that Job begs to be granted authority to purge Satan's place (i.e. sanctuary) (3.5–7). Henceforth the angel is only speaking about the coming battle of Satan with Job: Job is informed about it (4.4–5), hears of the rewards he will receive if he stands firm (4.6–7), declares himself ready to it (5.1) and is sealed (5.2). So a very essential part of the call vision is lacking: the revelation of the true God, to be expected after the disclosure of the idol's true nature.
>
> In short: this vision starts as a call vision, but very soon turns into a vision that prepares Job for his coming suffering.[17] In this respect it resembles the type of vision

---

[15] For suffering as a result of conversion to the faith in the God of Israel see also the prayer of Aseneth in Jos. As. 12.9–11; Jos., *Ant.* I.157; Mark 10.29–30; Act. Phil. 64–73 (II.2, 94,4).

[16] See Job 1.13–18 and 2.6. T. Job presupposes the existence of the biblical book of Job and draws much from the narrative framework (Job 1 and 2, 42.7–17), but only very little from the main part of the book (e.g. remarks on Job's wealth, piety and generosity in T. Job 9–16, cf. Job 29–31). Without any doubt T. Job makes use of the LXX version of the book. See, e.g., Schaller, *Testament Hiobs*, 306.

[17] The combination of a call and an announcement of suffering is also found in the account of the calling of Paul in Acts 9.1–19, with the difference that the announcement of suffering is not made to Paul himself, but to Ananias, the disciple who is sent to him by the Lord in order to open his eyes and to baptize him (see verse 16).

that is found at the beginning of Christian martyria. By means of these visions martyrs are prepared for their coming suffering and death. No revelation of the true God is found, because the martyrs already know Him.[18]

Even in the use of words there is a resemblance. In 5.1 Job declares that he will stand firm until death against Satan, though in 4.4 the angel has told him that Satan will not be able to bring death upon him. Job is speaking here as a martyr, who knows that his suffering will end with his death.[19]

After Satan has given Job an indication of what is to come (chs. 6 and 7; see especially 7.12),[20] the first phase of their battle is related in ch. 16: Satan burns up his herds, and what is left of them is confiscated by his fellow countrymen (this element is not found in the book of Job). The second phase follows in chs. 17 and 18 (with ἐπέστη in 17.2 compare ἐπαναστήσεται in 4.4; in 18.5 the word πόλεμος returns): now Satan kills Job's children, and his fellow countrymen pursue him (διώκω) and snatch up everything in his house at the instigation of Satan (this element is also not in the book of Job). The end of the battle is reached in 27.1, where Job, who has stood firm in an exemplary fashion, challenges Satan to fight (πολέμησόν με). At this Satan has to confess that he is no longer able to accept the challenge, because Job has brought him into deep distress, even though as a spirit Satan is much stronger than Job. He even states that he is at the end of his strength (διαφωνέω)[21]

---

[18] See the examples mentioned on pp. 152–3 below.

[19] For Job as a martyr see I. Jacobs, 'Literary Motifs in the Testament of Job', *JJS* 21 (1970), 1–3; Schaller, *Testament Hiobs*, 303; and E. Noort, *Een duister duel, Over de theologie van het boek Job*, Kamper Cahiers, 59 (Kampen, Kok, 1986), 19–23.

[20] For the magic meaning of the burnt loaf in these chapters see H. C. Kee, 'Satan, Magic and Salvation in the Testament of Job', *Society of Biblical Literature 1974 Seminar Papers*, I (Cambridge, Massachusetts, 1974), 56–7. The burning of Job's body as a loaf that is announced by Satan in this passage is not mentioned again in the document. Here we find one of the numerous compositional failures in T. Job. See on this section III of B. Schaller's chapter 'Zur Komposition und Konzeption des Testaments Hiobs' elsewhere in this volume (pp. 46–92 above).

[21] Literally: to fail to answer roll-call, because one has perished in battle (see, e.g., Num. 31.49), then with the more general meaning to perish (in battle) (see, e.g., Jdt 10.13), to be at the end of one's strength (this meaning in T. Job 13.1, cf. 13.4, ἀπέκαμνον), to be despondent or to be finished (e.g. Ezek. 37.11) and as a consequence to give in or to give up (cf. Schaller's translation 'ich gebe auf').

and that he withdraws (ὑποχωρέω, a synonym of ἀναποδίζω in 5.1)[22] (27.2).

Satan's angry attacks are intended as a retaliatory action against Job. Just as Job has destroyed the house of the god (or: the temple of the great god[23]) (17.4), Satan in return assails his 'house' (see 17.4: ἀνταποδώσω αὐτῷ ...).

In 8.1b–3a, cf. 16.2,4, we read that before his attack on Job, Satan ascends to heaven in order to implore the Lord that he may receive authority to destroy Job's goods (and kill his children).[24] Such a request is not mentioned in chs. 2–7 and not suggested either. There Satan is depicted as the anti-divine power, who is not on speaking terms with God and will come into action against Job on his own authority. God only knows beforehand what Satan will do to Job and discloses it to him through his angel (see 4.3).

It is obvious that the image of Satan in 8.1b–3a and 16.2,4 differs from that in chs. 2–7. In these passages we recognize the figure of the Satan of the book of Job, who acts as a servant of God and does not bring misery on Job in order to take revenge, but in order to try him in God's name by means of temptations and therefore requests permission of God (see Job 1.6–12, cf. 2.1–6).

The author of T. Job has apparently adapted the image of Satan of chs. 2–7 to that in the book of Job. The result is the image of a Satan whose fight with the believers because of their faith functions as a means of temptation of them in God's hand.

As Job has promised in 5.1, he does not retreat under the pressure of Satan's attacks. After the first one, he does not utter blasphemous words against God because of the hardship he must undergo for His sake, but glorifies Him (16.7)[25] as a sign that he stands firm with all his heart, out of true love for God (see 5.1 MS V), and that his conversion is genuine.

To the robbery of his house, however, he at first reacts by being confused (18.4). He is unable to utter a word, like a woman exhausted

---

[22] See e.g. Homer, *Iliad* 4.505, 6.107, 22.96.

[23] See on the expression 'the great god' Schaller, *Testament Hiobs*, 339.

[24] Neither in T. Job nor in the book of Job is there mention of a separate permission to kill Job's children. Apparently Job's children fall into the category of his goods.

[25] Schaller, *Testament Hiobs*, 338, refers at 16.7 to Job 1.21–2 LXX. However, the words 'blaspheme' and 'glorify' do not occur in this passage or elsewhere in Job LXX.

by birth pangs. Here Job reacts in the same way as in the main
section of the book of Job (3.1–42.6).[26] He resembles the righteous
sufferers in the Psalms of the Bible and of the Qumran community.[27]
They too cannot utter a word (see Ps 76 (77).5, also: being disturbed)
and feel themselves like a woman exhausted by birth pangs (1QH
III.6–7, cf. Ps 17 (18).5, 6 and 114 (116).3). After his initial reaction
of confusion, however, Job remembers the battle foretold by the Lord
through his angel (and the panegyrics which had been told to him[28])
(18.5) and takes courage again. He becomes like one wishing to enter
a city (the heavenly Jerusalem)[29] in order to discover its wealth and
inherit a portion of its splendour (verse 6), and who, sailing to it,[30]
is overtaken in mid-ocean by a threefold wave and the opposition of
the wind and subsequently throws the cargo into the sea in the
conviction that the entering of the city and the inheriting of 'the better
things', i.e. the heavenly salvation (see T. Job 46.4a and Heb 6.9;
10.34; 11.16, 35, 40), is worth the loss of everything (verse 7). Thus
Job considers his goods as nothing compared to the heavenly city[31]
about which the angel spoke to him[32] (verse 8).

[26] We may note there his sighing, groaning and moaning (3.24, 23.2, 10.1, 30.28, 19.7,
30.20, 28), being disturbed (37.1; cf. 19.6), being embittered (7.11, 9.18, 10.1),
weeping (3.24), being weary (10.1, 17.2).

[27] See for the reactions of the righteous to the suffering they have to undergo in the
Old Testament and in Qumran literature L. Ruppert, *Der leidende Gerechte und
seine Feinde* (Echter Verlag, 1973), 208.

[28] See on this p. 120 above.

[29] Cf. Heb. 11.10, 16, 12.22, Act. Phil. 140 (II.2, 74, 3) and 148 (90, 3) and the texts
mentioned by Schaller, *Testament Hiobs*, 340.

[30] It is not clear whether 18.6–7 must be considered as one parable or as two, the first
in verse 6, the second in verse 7. In favour of the latter view is the fact that verse 7
starts with a new καὶ ὡς. However, the first view is adopted here because εἰς τὴν
πόλιν ταύτην and κληρονομήσω in verse 7 refer back to εἰς πόλιν τινὰ and
κληρονομεῖν in verse 6. So also the translations of R. A. Kraft, *Testament of Job*,
41, and Schaller, *Testament Hiobs*, 340. R. P. Spittler, 'Testament of Job', in: J. H.
Charlesworth (ed.), *The Old Testament Pseudepigrapha*, vol. I (London, Darton,
Longman and Todd, 1983), 846–7, thinks of two parables.

[31] It is uncertain whether the heavenly Jerusalem is entered immediately after suffering
and death or only in the eschatological future, though one is inclined to think of the
first possibility. The conceptions of ultimate salvation of the believers in T. Job are
too diverse to justify a choice for one or the other. See on this subject Schaller,
Testament Hiobs, 315–16.

[32] Actually the angel does not speak about this city in chs. 3–5. This is again one of the
passages in T. Job where compositional failure is evident. See on this section III of
Schaller's chapter in this volume.

The image of the battle changes here to a different one expressing the same idea. The waves and the opposition of the wind that afflict the ship also represent the suffering by which Satan afflicts Job and illustrate Job's perseverance, though the word is not mentioned: Job keeps setting course for the city to reach it in spite of wind and waves.

The book of Job gives a completely different picture of Job's suffering. There Job does not suffer for God's sake as a consequence of his conversion (see pp.120–1 above), but is tried in the name of God, while Satan, at least in chs. 1 and 2, acts as a mediator. Moreover, Job is not informed beforehand about his suffering; it takes him by surprise as a dark mystery.

In Job 1 and 2 LXX ὑπομονή κτλ. does not occur. It does occur frequently in the main part of the book (3.1–42.6) but not with the particular meaning it has in T. Job 4.6 and 5.1: standing firm in the battle with Satan.[33] In the book of Job Satan is no longer playing any part from ch. 3 onwards but Job is fighting with God and with his friends. The word ὑπομονή κτλ. in T. Job may have been borrowed from the book of Job, but if so, its meaning has been changed totally.

Perseverance as stubbornness or toughness

Καρτερία κτλ. is found in 4.10 and 27.4. It is connected with a different image of Job's confrontation with Satan, that of a wrestling match, or more precisely, a *pancration*, i.e. a man-to-man fight in the arena, in which all means and tricks are allowed except biting and scratching. This fight took place without an arbitrator. One of the fighters had to indicate surrender by a gesture or a shout (see 27.4: ἐφώνησεν).[34] The word denotes the tirelessness, stamina, stubbornness or toughness by which Job as an athlete (ἀθλητής; see 4.10 and 27.3) takes the blows etc. of his opponent, Satan (the παλαιστρικά in 27.5, for the content of which see 27.3,4 and πυκτεύων in 4.10), in order to hold out against him. And this with success, for, though he is underneath (27.4), he is nevertheless victorious (27.5).

[33] In the book of Job ὑπομονή κτλ. means to wait for, await, wait before doing something (3.9, 7.3, 14.14,19, 17.13, 20.26, 32.4,16), stand or endure (misery) (6.11, beside ἀνέχομαι), hold out (esp. not holding out of the sinner against God) (9.4, 15.31, 22.21, 41.3; cf. 8.15), hold out (against a human opponent in an argument) (33.5).

[34] See on this Schaller, *Testament Hiobs*, 347.

The opposite word is διαφωνέω (27:4): to be at the end of one's strength, to be despondent and so give in or give up (see n. 21). It is also used in connection with the battle of Satan with Job (see 27.2). Since καρτερία κτλ. in T. Job is the ability to take a lot, it is hardly surprising that it is found close to μακροθυμέω (see 27.4 and 27.7), which, as will appear later, means 'to bear, endure patiently'.

> Καρτερία κτλ. means the stubbornness, toughness by which one stands firm; ὑπομονή is the standing firm itself. So the latter word encompasses more than the former one.[35] Because of this it can be used in T. Job as the general term too.
>
> In Greek thinking, notably in Stoicism, followed by Philo, καρτερία κτλ. is an important word to denote the attitude of the wise man in all that happens to him.[36] This too can be compared with that of a fighter towards his opponent in the match in the arena (see Philo, *Omn. Prob. Lib.* 24–6 – there also the image of a *pancration*). The struggle of the wise man with the passions too, can only be accomplished successfully if he possesss καρτερία (e.g. Philo, *Deus Imm.* 13 (beside ἀνδρεία and ὑπομονή), *Agric.* 152, *Somn.* I.120[37]). Just as in the case of ὑπομονή, the opponent is very powerful.[38] Apart from Philo the word occurs many times in 4 Maccabees (the stubbornness of the believers in martyrdom).[39] In the remaining Jewish literature it does not occur frequently. The same applies to early Christian literature. There is a strong preference for ὑπομονή κτλ.

[35] For more on this see Spanneut, 'Geduld', 252. See also Philo, *Omn. Prob. Lib.* 26: τῷ καρτερικῷ καὶ παγίῳ [stubborn] τῆς ὑπομονῆς; 4 Macc 15.31: καρτερῶς ὑπέμεινεν.

[36] See Spanneut, 'Geduld', 245–53. See also Philo, *Cherub.* 78 (besides ὑπομονή) and *Omn. Prob. Lib.* 24 (ἐγκαρτερέω besides ὑπομένω).

[37] Καρτερία as firmness against the allurements of desire (cf. Philo, *Agric.* 97 and 105: the καρτερία blocks the way of the ἡδονή) can have the meaning of 'self-control'; see Philo, *Vit. Mos.* I.25.

[38] See Spanneut, 'Geduld' 245, speaking of the works of Plato: 'Unter καρτερία wird eine Art der ἀνδρεία verstanden, die mit φρόνησις verbunden ist. Sie ist also eine Kraft der vernünftigen Seele, die den Menschen instandsetzt, einem stärkeren Feind zu widerstehen (Lach 190e/193e).'

[39] See n. 2.

In 4.9 we are told that Job will be raised up to take part in the resurrection (cf. 53.8 MS V) and will then receive the crown, the prize for the winner in the *pancration*.[40] So in addition to the earthly reward, connected with the battle with Satan, he will receive a heavenly one.[41] This stems from Job 42.17a LXX, where it is said about Job that he, clearly as a compensation for his suffering, will rise again with those whom the Lord will raise up.[42] In T. Job, however, the promise concerned is not a rather loose statement at the end, as in the biblical book, but a solemn declaration in the opening chapters that is placed in the mouth of an angel who incites Job to toughness. Again the author of T. Job (or the tradition he makes use of) has geared an element of the book of Job to the main theme of chs. 1–27. Also in 18.5 one reads about a reward for Job as one for the winner in the match in the arena. Here the word 'crown' is not mentioned, but the passage refers to the 'panegyrics' (ἐγκώμια)[43] with which the crown is presented.

The images of the battle and of the *pancration* of Satan with Job always follow each other immediately (see 4.4–8 and 9–11, 27.1–2 and 3–5, also 18.5: πόλεμος and ἐγκώμια) and consequently are closely connected. They have to be considered as variations of the theme of the suffering for the Lord's sake as a combat with Satan; both are very suitable for making clear what perseverance in suffering means.

---

[40] The moment of the receiving or taking (ἐκδεχόμενος) the crown out of God's hand and that of the resurrection are linked by means of γὰρ in 4.10. In 40.3 we find the idea that one will receive a crown immediately after death. The conceptions of the ultimate salvation of the believers in T. Job are diverse. See also n. 31.

[41] For the combination of an earthly and a heavenly reward for suffering for the Lord's sake see further Mark 10.29–30 and parallels. Also Apoc. Pauli 51 (transl. H. Duensing, in: E. Hennecke and W. Schneemelcher, *Neutestamentliche Apokryphen*, II, 3rd edn (Tübingen, Mohr, 1964), 565) may be explained in this way: 'Die Leiden, welche ein jeder erduldet um Gottes willen, wird Gott ihm vergelten zwiefach ... Die Leiden, welche der Mensch um Gottes willen erträgt, Gott betrübt ihn nicht, wenn er aus der Welt geht.'

[42] This 'is written', but it is not said where.

[43] See H. S. Liddell, H. Scott, H. S. Jones and R. McKenzie, *A Greek–English Lexicon* (Oxford, Clarendon Press, 1966), s.v. ἐγκώμιος II. Schaller, *Testament Hiobs*, 340, wrongly translates by 'Verheissungen'. Actually the angel does not speak about panegyrics for Job in chs. 3–5, just as he says nothing about the heavenly city (see 18.8). However, the panegyrics belong to the imagery of the *pancration* and the receiving of the crown found in 4.10.

There is only a difference in the purpose Satan wishes to achieve. In the battle, it is to do Job as much harm as possible, while in the *pancration* it is to extract from Job the admission that he is the stronger party; see 27.5, where Satan has to admit that Job is the winner, though he had expected to win the match.

In Job LXX too we hear about Job's καρτερέω: see 2.9. Here it means 'to maintain (saying)'. So it has not the specific meaning it has in T. Job. Here too the conclusion must be: if the word is borrowed from the book of Job, its meaning has been changed.

Perseverance as patience

If ὑπομονή κτλ. means 'standing firm', and καρτερία κτλ. the stubbornness or toughness by which one does so, μακροθυμία κτλ. means the patience by which one perseveres and endures all things. Patience is an important aspect of perseverance in T. Job since Job's suffering takes a long time − forty-eight years according to 21.1, the sum of the eleven years, seventeen years and twenty years in 22.1, 26.1 and 28.1 respectively.[44]

The opposite words are ἐκκακέω (S and V: ἐγκακέω), which means to become despondent, remiss (24.10), and ἀκηδία, i.e. melancholy, weariness, despair (25.10), which are characteristic of Job's wife.[45] It is caused by the weakness of her heart (25.10).

For μακροθυμία κτλ. see 26.5. Job says to his wife, who has lost patience (see her reproach in 24.1), 'Let us be patient, till the Lord in compassion shows his mercy' (σπλαγχνισθεὶς ἐλεήσῃ ἡμᾶς). Job's patience is no passive resignation, but implies waiting intently for God's saving intervention founded on one's hope in God (see also 24.1).[46]

---

[44] According to 21.1 MS V and Slav Job's suffering takes only seven years. On the problem of the duration of Job's suffering in T. Job see section III of Schaller's chapter.

[45] See on the contrast between Job's attitude in suffering and that of his wife further the contribution of P. W. van der Horst, 'Images of Women in the Testament of Job', pp. 93–116 above. This paper was first published in *NedThT* 40 (1986), 273–89.

[46] For God's ἐλέειν as salvation from distress see, e.g., Ps. 6.3; 24(25).16; 26(27).7, etc. For God's σπλαγχνίζεσθαι as salvation from distress, cf. Mark 1.41, 9.22, Luke 7.13, 10.33. For both words together in connection with salvation see Luke 1.78.

In the Greek Bible μακροθυμία κτλ. is predominantly used of God's long-suffering, the delaying of his wrath or judgement, either to give the sinners time to convert (e.g. Ps 7.12, Rom 2.4, 1 Tim 1.16) or to let them reach the full extent of their sins (2 Macc 6.14, Rom 9.22). It is also used of men to denote their long-suffering, i.e. the restraining of feelings of anger and wrath, not being carried away by these feelings (e.g. Prov 14.29, 15.18, 17.27, 25.15).[47]

The meaning the word has in T. Job is typically a Greek and Hellenistic one[48] and is found only in a limited number of cases. See Sir 2.4; Bar 4.25a. In 1 Macc 8.4 μακροθυμία means 'steadfastness' (or determination), as in Jos., *Bell.* 6.37. In Matt 18.26, 29 μακροθυμέω means to be patient with a person, until he has paid his debt: cf. T. Job 11.10. In Heb 6.12, 15 the word means the patience by which one expects the fulfilment of God's promises, while in Jas 5.7, 10−11 waiting patiently for the coming of the Lord (verse 7), who is at the door (verse 9), is compared with the waiting of the farmer looking for the crop (verse 7: ἐκδέχεται ... μακροθυμῶν).

In T. Job 28.5 and 35.4 μακροθυμέω means to be patient with a person who has suffered a loss and therefore to be silent.

In 27.7, at the end of Job's account of his struggle with Satan, the word has the same meaning. Job, as a person who has suffered much himself and has been patient, summons his children to exercise patience too, in everything that happens to them, 'for patience is better than anything'. Also in ch. 21 Job's patience in his suffering is mentioned. In this chapter Job reports how he witnessed with his own eyes how his wife was compelled to hire herself out as a maidservant to the rich people of his city in order to earn bread for herself and her husband (verse 2). By this pretension (ἀλαζονεία) of his former subjects Job is stunned (κατανενυγμένος) (verse 3). He cannot stand the abuse of his wife. But after this, Job says, 'I

---

[47] See J. Horst, 'μακροθυμία κτλ.', *TWNT*, 4 (1942), 377−90, H. W. Hollander, 'μακροθυμέω κτλ.', *EWNT*, 2 (1981), 935−8.

[48] See J. Horst, 'μακροθυμία', 377−8.

resumed a patient reason' (ἀνελάμβανον λογισμὸν μακρόθυμον),[49]
i.e. Job accepts and bears patiently the injustice done to his wife.

Μακροθυμία κτλ. only occurs in the later chapters of the account
of Job's suffering, and in these chapters, apart from ch. 27, it is the
only word for perseverance. The one exception to this is ὑπομένω
in 26.4, which here means almost the same as μακροθυμέω (see
pp. 134–5 below). The two other words, and the images of Job's
suffering connected with them, occur, again apart from ch. 27, only
in the earlier chapters.

This later part of the account of Job's suffering starts rather
abruptly in 19.1,[50] shortly after 18.5, where the 'battle' and the
'panegyrics' are still mentioned, and it continues till ch. 26. These
chapters are in much closer agreement with Job 1 and 2 LXX than
the preceding ones: Job accepts as coming from God the loss of his
children (19.1) that Satan inflicts upon him (see 19.4, a literal
quotation of the last part of Job 1.21 LXX[51]). Also the worms and
the ulcers with which Satan smites Job (20.6, 7)[52] he accepts as
coming from God (see his reaction in 20.9, not found in Job LXX,
and his reaction to his suffering in 26.4, an almost verbatim quotation
of a part of Job 2.10 LXX).

Here the suffering of Job is not a suffering for God's sake, like
that in chs. 2–7 and 16–18, but – as in the book of Job – a suffering caused by God, who puts Job to the trial.[53] And, as in 8.1b–3a

---

[49] For this expression cf. 2 Macc. 6.23: ὁ δὲ λογισμὸν ἀστεῖον ἀναλαβών, said of
the martyr Eleazar. By means of the λογισμός one controls the passions; see 4 Macc.
1.1,7,9,13 etc.. For the opposite expression see Mart. Lugd. 35: μηδὲ ἔννοιαν
ἔχοντες διαβολικοῦ λογισμοῦ.

[50] In 19.1 we unexpectedly meet 'the last messenger' (MS V: 'another messenger'),
evidently derived from Job 1.18 LXX, where the last of three messengers is
mentioned, whereas in T. Job preceding messengers are not found. Cf. 16.7,
where it is only said that 'they' report to Job the destruction of his goods.
Another compositional failure in T. Job. See again Schaller's chapter.

[51] In Job 1.21 LXX Job's words are a reaction to the loss both of his goods and his
children; in T. Job 19.4, however, a reaction to the loss of his children only.

[52] Is this a matter of one disease, with worms creeping out of Job's body causing
festering wounds? Or has one to think of two separate diseases, worms and ulcers?
Neither T. Job nor Job LXX (see 2.9c and 7.5: worms; 2.7: ulcers) is clear on
this point.

[53] So T. Job deals with suffering for the Lord's sake, inflicted on Job by Satan as
God's enemy as well as with suffering as temptation and trial, inflicted on Job by
Satan as God's servant. This contra Schaller, *Testament Hiobs*, 315, where
he argues: 'Leiden gilt als Folge der Umkehr vom Götzendienst zum wahren

and 16.2, 4 (see p. 123 above), Satan is not the anti-divine power who takes action against Job on his own authority, but a servant of God who begs his permission to do this (20.2, 3; cf. Job 2.6 LXX).[54]

In chs. 19–26, as in chs. 16–18 (see especially 16.7), Job does not utter a single improper word against God, again showing his patience and the genuineness of his conversion. See 20.1, where Job declares that Satan was unable to provoke him to contempt (ὀλιγωρία, i.e. speaking contemptuously against God[55]) because of the loss of his goods and his children. This refers back to Job's reaction in 19.4: he blesses the name of the Lord.

Speaking contemptuously against God implies cursing of God and murmuring against Him. See 13.5 and 14.5, the two other passages in T. Job where ὀλιγωρία and the verb ὀλιγωρέω occur; these passages belong in that part of chs. 1–27 where Job's wealth, generosity to the needy and piety in the period before his suffering are described (chs. 9–15).

> In 13.4, 5, at least according to the text of MSS S and V, that is here to be preferred to that of P,[56] it is said that the servants of Job who prepare the meals for the many widows and poor grow weary (ἀπέκαμνον, cf. διεφώνουν in verse 1, i.e. they are at the end of their strength; see note 21).[57] They curse Job in contempt (ὀλιγωροῦντες κατηρῶντο), asking him to feed them so that they can eat their fill at long last (cf. Job 31.31 LXX). Ὀλιγωρέω means here contempt for Job expressing itself in curses against him.

Gottesdienst. Es wird daher nicht als Versuchung dargestellt, sondern als Ausdruck des Kampfes, den der Satan gegen die Frommen führt', and contra K. Berger, 'Abraham', *TRE*, I (1977), 373, who considers Job's suffering only as temptation and trial. Anyway, Schaller's statement on p. 315 is contradictory to that on p. 303, where he speaks of Job as one who 'allen Versuchungen seiner vom Satan beeinflussten Frau und Freunde überlegen entgegentritt'.

[54] With regard to 20.9 R. P. Spittler, *Testament of Job*, 848, remarks: 'Curiously, while the "commander" is in the author's mind assuredly God (cf. 26.4; Job 2.10), it is nevertheless Satan to whom Job's plague was just attributed (20.6).' This is not strange at all, if one realizes that Satan acts here as God's servant.

[55] Schaller's translation of ὀλιγωρία by 'Nachgeben' (*Testament Hiobs*, 341) is not correct.

[56] The text of P does not make good sense. See also the opinion of Brock, *Testamentum Iobi*, 15.

[57] Schaller, *Testament Hiobs*, 336, translates διεφώνουν in verse 1 by 'wurden unwillig' and ἀπέκαμνον by 'wurden verdrossen'; this is not impossible.

In 14.4–5 Job's maidservants, apparently just as tired by
their many tasks, murmur among themselves against Job
(διεγόγγυζον).⁵⁸ Then Job takes up his psaltery and sings
for them about the payment of recompense (for their
murmuring, or for the good works they do to the needy?).
Thus he makes them stop murmuring in contempt of him
(τῆς ὀλιγωρίας τοῦ γογγυσμοῦ). Here too the contempt for
Job is expressed in speaking against him, this time not
described as cursing, but as murmuring.⁵⁹

The use of ὀλιγωρία and ὀλιγωρέω in these passages proves that in
20.1 also contempt, but here of God,⁶⁰ is referred to.

This motif also stems from the book of Job. There Satan tries to
provoke Job to curse the Lord (1.11, 2.5 LXX, described euphemisti-
cally by εὐλογέω). He does not succeed here either: Job does not sin
– with his lips – against the Lord (1.22 and 2.10 end LXX), i.e. he
does not curse Him. The word 'murmur' does not occur in the book
of Job.

After Satan has tried in vain to incite Job to show contempt for
God by causing the loss of his goods and his children, he aggravates
his suffering by smiting him with the worms and ulcers (20.6,7) in
order to achieve his goal. But this time too without success, as appears
from Job's reaction in 20.9.

Then Satan plays his trump card. He approaches Job through his
wife, whom he manages to get into his power by disguising himself
as a bread seller on the market and taking possession of her hair (chs.
22,23) as a means of leading her heart astray (23.11).⁶¹

⁵⁸ Schaller, 367, translates διεγόγγυζον by 'mit einander stritten'. That is not correct.
Διαγογγύζω does not mean 'to murmur against each other', but 'to murmur among
themselves', sc. against someone else. Apparently Schaller has chosen this translation
because the text does not specify against whom the maidservants murmur.

⁵⁹ Cf. Philo, *Vit. Mos.* I, 181–7, a passage in which he discusses the event at Mara
in the desert (Ex. 15.22–6). There ὀλιγωρία and ὀλίγωρος (183, 184) are connected
with μεμψιμοιρεῖν (181, i.e. to grumble at or complain about one's lot), a verb closely
related to διαγογγύζειν in the biblical passage (see Ex. 15.24).

⁶⁰ Compare ὀλιγωρία and the grumbling ensuing from it in the passage of Philo's
Vit. Mos. mentioned in n. 59; here it is directed against Moses as God's representative,
at least according to the biblical passage discussed here (see Ex. 15.24). For
murmuring immediately directed against God see Ex. 16.7,8; Num. 14.27,29;
Ps. 105 (106).25 and Wisd Sol 1.11.

⁶¹ Satan gets Job's wife in his power through her hair – a magical conception.
See Kee, 'Satan', 59.

This does not give him much trouble, for Job's wife, though very caring for her husband (22.2, 24.4), has lost the patience that is typical of Job (see 24.10 and 25.10). Thus controlled by Satan she summons Job to eat the bread she has acquired, to speak a word against the Lord (i.e. to curse God or murmur against Him in contempt) and to die (see Job 2.9e LXX; also 1 Kings 17.2 for eating bread and dying afterwards as a sign of despair and being at a dead end). In utmost despair she bewails again his and her misery at great length (see 24.1–4; cf. Job 2.9–9d LXX).

But once again Satan fails. Job replies to his wife that he is not depressed by his pains so much as by her statement (26.1–2).[62] He refuses to utter a word against the Lord and is willing to endure all his sufferings in order not to be alienated from the truly great wealth (cf. 18.6) (26.3). After that he speaks to his wife words of patient acceptance (26.4; cf. Job 2.10 LXX), summons her to be patient together with himself (26.5), and utters his amazement at the fact she does not realize that the devil unsettles her reasoning,[63] so that he might deceive him too (cf. 3.3,6) and make an exhibition of her as one of the senseless women who misguide their husbands' simplicity (26.6).

Apparently 'simplicity'[64] is a condition for patience in temptation and trial. It must be the opposite of the 'weakness of the heart' (25.10) of Job's wife that brings her to despair.

At this moment Job has shown his patience sufficiently. Even through his wife Satan gets no access to him. Therefore there is nothing left that Satan can do; he departs ashamed (καταισχυνθεὶς ἀνεχώρησεν) (P and S: for three years; V has no time limit) (27.6). As in 18.4 (see pp. 123–4 above) Job is initially very perturbed

---

[62] Job repeats here his wife's words in 25.10 in order to express his aversion the more strongly. See also verse 3.

[63] Cf. T. Sim. 4.9; T. Zeb. 8.6; T. Dan. 4.2,7; T. Gad. 6.2; T. Asher 6.5 etc.

[64] The simplicity or single-mindedness of Job, his complete devotion to the Lord, is not mentioned in Job LXX, but see ἀκακία in 2.3, a closely related word (see, e.g., Past. Herm. Vis. I.2.4; III.8.7; Mand. II, 1 and 7). See on simplicity J. Amstutz, ΑΠΛΟΤΗΣ, *Eine begriffsgeschichtliche Studie zum jüdisch-hellenistischen Griechisch*, Theophaneia, 19 (Bonn, Hanstein, 1968), esp. 118, n. 6 (why the word is used here 'im abschätzigen Sinne von "Einfältigkeit"' is not explained; in my opinion this is not correct); see also H. W. Hollander and M. de Jonge, *The Testaments of the Twelve Patriarchs, A Commentary*, PsVTG, 8 (Leiden, Brill, 1985), 233–4.

when Satan strikes him (see 19.1, 20.7, 21.3). After that, however, he accepts it – just as in 18.5; see 19.4, 20.9, 21.4 and also 26.4,5. Again Job reacts, at least initially, as in the main part of the book of Job; again he may be compared with the righteous sufferers in the Psalms of the Bible and of the Qumran community.[65]

All three ideas of suffering come together in ch. 27. In verses 1–2 Satan as Job's enemy admits that he is at the end of his strength (because of Job's standing firm) and withdraws from the battle. In verses 3–5 he admits as Job's opponent in the *pancration* that Job is the winner because of his stubbornness or toughness. In verse 6 Satan, as Job's tempter, who wished to provoke him to speak in contempt against God, leaves him ashamed because of Job's patience (see verse 7). So Job is the winner on all fronts by his perseverance, and can justly call himself a model of perseverance (1.5). By combining so neatly the main motifs of chs. 1–26 in this chapter, which closes the first part of this composition, the author shows himself to be a conscious and skilful redactor. The compositional failures we noticed earlier are therefore all the more striking. Here we meet one of the problems in the investigation of the document that have not yet been solved adequately.[66]

Μακροθυμία κτλ. is found in Job 7.16 LXX, where Job in utmost distress declares that he no longer has the patience to endure what has befallen him and wants to die. This is an attitude completely different from that found in T. Job and consequently the image of Job as a patient sufferer cannot have been borrowed from this passage. The latter picture of Job may, however, be understood as an interpretation of Job's attitude to his suffering as it is described in Job 1 and 2 LXX, though the word μακροθυμία is not found there.

Endurance of evil

In 26.4b, a part of Job's reaction to the summons of his wife to utter a contemptuous word against the Lord and found almost verbatim

---

[65] For his disturbance (19.1 and 20.7), see, e.g., Ps. 41 (42).6, 11 and 42 (43).5, further Ps. 6.3–4; 30 (31).10; 37 (38).10. For his being stunned by his misery (21.3) see Ps. 59 (60).5. 'Αδημονία (distress, 20.7) only occurs in Symmachus in Ps. 60 (61).3. See further Ruppert, *Der leidende Gerechte*, 208ff., where many passages from Qumran Psalms are quoted.

[66] For a fresh approach see Schaller's chapter in this volume.

in Job 2.10 LXX, the verb ὑπομένω is found once more. In this context, however, it does not mean 'to stand firm' as in 4.6 and 5.1, but 'to bear, endure' with inward acceptance. The ὑπομένω of the evil things is found here beside the δεχέσθαι of the good things. The meaning of ὑπομένω in this passage comes very close, then, to that of μακροθυμέω (see 26.5).

This meaning fits very well in the context as a whole, in which both ὑφίσταμαι (verse 1), i.e. to undergo, to submit to[67] (the worms in Job's body), and ὑποφέρω (verse 3), i.e. to bear, endure,[68] are also used. This meaning of the word is also suggested by Job 2.10 LXX, which has ὑποίσομεν instead of ὑπομένομεν.

Why does the author use ὑπομένομεν in this passage instead of ὑποίσομεν as in Job 2.10 LXX? He may have borrowed it from an LXX-text of Job different from that known to us. It is also possible that the author has deliberately substituted the one word for the other in order to link the passage closely to the main theme, i.e. ὑπομονή (1.5).

Variations in the manuscripts

From this study it has appeared that the author of T. Job consistently connects each of the three words for perseverance with a specific idea of suffering: in the battle with Satan ὑπομονή κτλ. is used, in the *pancration* with Satan καρτερία κτλ., and for suffering as a temptation μακροθυμία κτλ.

As to the occurrence of these terms in MSS other than P, which has so far formed the basis of the discussion, we may remark that V deviates considerably as to the use of καρτερία κτλ. In 17.1 it reads καρτερίαν instead of καρδίαν in P (and S). This variant may be due to a reading error on the part of the copyist. If not, καρτερία is not used consistently as in P, the image of Job's suffering in this chapter being that of the battle with Satan and not that of the *pancration*.

Next V uses the composite verb προσκαρτερέω (with the same meaning as the simple verb) in 4.5, where it gives a somewhat altered version (μισθόν instead of στέφανον) of the text found in P in 4.10 and adds the following: καὶ τοὺς πειρασμοὺς προσκαρτερῶν καὶ

---

[67] See Liddell and Scott, *Greek–English Lexicon*, s.v. ὑφίστημι (B.II.3). The verb also occurs in T. Job 7.13.
[68] See Hauck, 'ὑπομένω', 585, 41–3.

τὰς θλίψεις. So here the verb is connected with suffering as temptation and trial (apparently all Job's suffering may be characterized as such according to this manuscript; see also 2.2 according to MS V), whereas the simple verb in the text of P is connected consistently with the image of the *pancration*.

So in V καρτερία κτλ. is not used as consistently as in P. This is another indication that V is further removed from the original text of T. Job than P;[69] the development of consistent to less consistent use of a word is more probable than the other way round.

> With regard to the use of ὑπομονή κτλ. V does not deviate vis-à-vis P: cf. 20.2, where ὑπομονή, just as in 4.6 and 5.1, means standing firm in the battle with Satan. By the addition which V has made to the text of 20.2 a link has been formed between the account of Job's suffering in chs. 2−7 and 16−18 and that in chs. 19−26. In 26.3 ὑπομένω means the same as the same word in 26.4.

S does not deviate from P in its use of the three words. In this respect too it appears to be a reliable manuscript.[70]

Job as a proselyte

In 4.6,7 and 9,10 the Lord through his angel holds out to Job the prospect of earthly and heavenly rewards in order to encourage him to persevere in his confrontation with Satan. This motivation is, however, connected with another one: by these rewards, he will gain insight into God's nature (see 4.8,11). So Job is addressed here as a proselyte, who will still have to learn many things about God.

After God has made Job's name renowned everywhere and has repaid him twice over because of his perseverance, Job will know 'that the Lord is impartial [ἀπροσωπόληπτος] rendering good things to each one [ἑκάστῳ] who obeys (Him)'.

[69] See on the lesser value of V the judgement of Brock, *Testamentum Iobi*, 9; M. Philonenko, 'Le Testament de Job, Introduction, traduction et notes', *Semitica*, 18 (1968), 9; Kraft, *Testament of Job*, 5; Schaller, *Testament Hiobs*, 317−18; and Spittler, *Testament of Job*, 830.

[70] See the judgement of Brock, *Testamentum Iobi*, 8 ('equal in value, and indeed incidentally superior, to that of P') and Schaller, *Testament Hiobs*, 317−18.

God's impartiality, literally His being without respect of persons, implies that he judges people exclusively with regard to their obedience to Him and repays them accordingly, either good things like Job or bad things (cf. Col 3.25 and 1 Pet 1.17), without favouring one person above the other, for instance because he is a Jew. Job and every gentile who like him comes to the God of Israel should know this. God does not discriminate against non-Jews.[71] Job will also know that the Lord is just, true (i.e. trustworthy) and strong, giving strength (ἐνισχύων) to his elect (cf. Hag 2.22 LXX MS A), again without regard to their being Jews or gentiles.

The moment Job will see this is in the eschatological future just as in the case of the heavenly reward (τότε in 4.11 refers back to the moment of the resurrection). Then Job, and all who are like him, will recognize God's justice, truth and strength in his raising his elect from the dead and giving to them the crown in heavenly glory. Nevertheless, Job already receives a foretaste of this future in his earthly life. Firstly, immediately after his suffering he experiences God's strength. See 47.7: his body receives strength (ἐνίσχυσεν, the same verb as in 4.11) through the Lord as if it had not suffered (see also 47.6, 8). Secondly, in His judgement on Elihu, who, inspired by Satan (see 41.5 and 42.2), has uttered arrogant words against Job, God's justice and truth are already demonstrated with respect to the sinner. See 43.13. At the same time this judgement demonstrates God's impartiality.

So in T. Job Job is the gentile convert, who through many sufferings will see that the God whom he has chosen is the only true One. He may know this partially in this earthly life and fully in the eschatological future. In Job all proselytes are encouraged to persevere in their sufferings in order that they too may experience this.[72]

By his perseverance Job will also show himself as a true proselyte, who may rightly call himself a 'servant' of God (4.2). The term 'servant' of God (θεράπων, see Job 2.3 and 42.7 LXX, cf. 1.8, παῖς)

---

[71] Cf. Rom. 2.11 and Acts 10.34–5, where Peter, in connection with the entry of gentiles into the Christian Church, at that time consisting of Jews only, says: 'I see now how true it is that God is not a respecter of persons [οὐκ ... προσωπολήμπτης], but that in every nation the man who is God-fearing and does what is right is acceptable to Him.'

[72] This does not imply, however, that the document as a whole was addressed to proselytes or that it should be regarded as a Hellenistic Jewish 'Missionsschrift' (see Rahnenführer, 'Testament des Hiob', 88–93). Job is speaking to his children, who are Jews by birth (see T. Job 1.5).

is in T. Job the indication of the new status Job has received by his conversion. It occurs twice more in T. Job. The first time is in 37.8 (only P and Copt). In this passage the friends of Job through Baldad (36.4) throw doubt upon his being a servant of God and even take him for an insane person on account of his hope in Him (see 37.1–6, 8).

The second occurrence of the term 'servant' is found in a statement of God, by which He vindicates Job over against his friends (see 42.5). God enters into the discussion between Job and his friends and says: 'You there, Eliphaz – you and your two friends – why did you sin?' (cf. Job 42.7 LXX). 'You have not spoken truly regarding my servant Job' (cf. Job 42.8 LXX). Here God himself confirms publicly that Job rightly calls himself His 'servant' and that by his perseverance after his conversion he has shown himself a true believer.

Job accepts the suffering Satan brings upon him after his conversion. Nevertheless he generally reacts first by being distressed (see pp. 123–4 and 133–4 above). T. Job gives a lifelike portrait of Job; he is a person who is deeply moved by what happens to him, but perseveres in spite of this. This portrait agrees with his status of a proselyte, who still has to learn many things.

The background to the theme of perseverance

This section will analyse the background of perseverance in T. Job with its three aspects of standing firm, stubbornness or toughness, and patience, and of the ideas of suffering connected with them. Special attention will be paid to texts in which, as in T. Job, perseverance is found in a context of conversion.

Standing firm in the battle with Satan

For the notion of perseverance as 'standing firm' in the battle with Satan, the following texts may be compared:

(1) Eph 6.10–20. The believers are summoned to be strong in the Lord and in the might of his power (verse 10) and to put on the armour of God (see verses 14–17) in order to be able to stand firm (στῆναι) against the devices of the devil, by which he tries to overthrow them (verse 11). They have to take up the armour of God in order to be able to stand their ground (ἀντιστῆναι) in the evil day and, fully

equipped, to stand (στῆναι) (verse 13). This particular armour coming from God is indispensable, because their fight (πάλη, here not the wrestling match, the original meaning of the word, but the man-to-man fight in battle[73]) is not against flesh and blood, but against the principalities, the powers, the rulers of this dark world and the spiritual forces of evil in the heavens (verse 12), all of them to be considered as representatives of the devil. Keeping watch with all perseverance is also mentioned (verse 18) beside praying (verses 18, 19).

Here the words στῆναι and ἀντιστῆναι denote the same attitude towards the devil as ὑπομένω in T. Job. Just as in T. Job 27.2, the devil is called stronger than a human enemy (the fight is not against blood and flesh, but against ...). For that reason the believers can stand firm against him only if they are equipped with the more than earthly armour from God and let themselves be strengthened by the Lord and the might of his power. In verse 13 (the evil day) the fight against the devil is connected with the end of days.

(2) In Apoc. Sedr. 5.3–8[74] Sedrach complains to God about the outcome of the transgression of Adam (4.5):

> If you loved man, why did not you kill the devil, the artificer of all iniquity? Who can fight against an invisible spirit [πολεμεῖν, cf. T. Job 4.3]? He enters the hearts of men like a smoke and teaches them all kinds of sin. He even fights [πολεμεῖ] against you, the immortal God, and so what can pitiful man do against him? Yet have mercy, Master ...

Here too the devil is stronger than man and therefore very difficult to resist, not only because he is a spirit, but also because he is invisible, as a result of which he is able to obtain free access to a man's heart in order to deceive him (ἀπατάω 4.5, 5.1; cf. T. Job 3.3, 6, 26.6) and cause him to sin.

This view of man is, unlike that in T. Job and Eph., very pessimistic: resistance against the devil is considered hardly possible.

(3) Also the Revelation of John knows of the battle of Satan with the believers. Satan acts here together with his creature Antichrist, embodied in the Roman empire. In ch. 13 it is described as the beast

---

[73] See A. Oepke, 'ὅπλον, κτλ.', *TWNT* 5 (1954), 300, 30.
[74] O. Wahl (ed.), *Apocalypsis Esdrae, Apocalypsis Sedrach, Visio beati Esdrae*, PsVTG, 4 (Leiden, Brill, 1977).

from the sea (cf. Dan. 7), on which the dragon (i.e. devil, Satan, see 12.9) confers his power and rule and great authority (verses 1,2). The whole world follows it (verse 3) and worships it because of its power (see verse 4: 'Who is like the beast? Who can fight [πολεμῆσαι] against it?' Cf. the superhuman power of Satan in T. Job, Eph. and Apoc. Sedr.). The beast receives (from God, cf. T. Job 8.3 etc.) the right to reign for forty-two months (verse 5). It is also allowed to wage war (ποιῆσαι πόλεμον) on the saints and to defeat them (verse 7). In this battle they will have to show their perseverance (ὑπομονή) and faith (verse 10b, cf. 14.12).

The battle of the beast from the sea with the believers is part of an eschatological war encompassing heaven and earth, in which the powers of evil set out to wipe out completely the Church and its Lord, albeit without success, because they will taste defeat in the end (see 11.7, 12.7, 16.14, 17.14, 19.19, 20.7–10; see also the battle of the sons of light with the sons of darkness in 1QM).

(4) In the so-called 'synoptic apocalypse' the fight against the believers also belongs to the events of the last days (see Mark 13.9–13): the believers will be handed over to the courts etc. (verse 9; in the parallel passage Luke 21.12 also: 'they will ... persecute you' (διώξουσιν); cf. T. Job 18.2. Persecution is one of the means used by Satan in his battle with the believers). Even a brother will hand over his brother to death and a father his child; and children will rise up against their parents (ἐπαναστήσονται, cf. T. Job 4.4) and send them to their death (verse 12). 'But he who holds out [ὁ δὲ ὑπομείνας] to the end will be saved' (verse 13). Cf. Matt 24.13 (and 10.22) and Luke 21.19: 'By standing firm [ὑπομονή] you will win your life.'

Satan is not mentioned here, but as in the Revelation of John, he is the source of inspiration of those who do harm to the believers.[75]

(5) For the attack of Satan especially on the proselyte see Jos. As. 12.9–10. Aseneth is pursued (καταδιώκει με) by the wild lion of old, the father of the Egyptian idols. He is furious (cf. T. Job 4.4), because, as a sign of her conversion to the God of Israel, she has broken her idols to pieces and thrown them out together with offerings and vessels of libation (10.12–13; cf. T. Job 5.2).

---

[75] For Satan as the inspiration of the persecutors of the believers see, e.g., Asc. Is. 5.1,15; Mart. Pol. 2.4 (cf. 17.1); Pass. St Pauli Apost. 7 (I,30,21): 'nero diaboli exagitatus'; Mart. Petr. et Pauli 61 (I,170,1–14).

In 16.7 it is said that Job does not utter blasphemous words (βλασφημέω) because of the sufferings he has to go through for God's sake, but glorifies (δοξάζω) Him. By this he shows that he stands firm in the battle against Satan out of true love for God, and that he sticks to his conversion, since it is characteristic for converts to glorify God.

For glorifying God or giving glory to Him (δίδωμι δόξαν) as a sign of conversion see:

(1) Dan. 4.34 LXX. After his recovery Nebuchadnezzar hears an angel speaking to him: 'Serve the God of heaven, the Holy One [i.e. be converted] and give glory to the Most High' (cf. 4.34 Theod.: 'and I blessed [εὐλόγησα] the Most High and I praised [ἤνεσα] Him that lives for ever and glorified (Him), for ...'). See also 4.37 LXX: 'Now I return thanks (to God) [ἀνθομολογοῦμαι] and I praise Him who ... I give thanks [ἐξομολογοῦμαι] and praise, for ...' (cf. 4.37 Theod.: 'Now I, Nebuchadnezzar, praise and exalt [ὑπερυψῶ] and glorify the King of heaven, for ...').

(2) Rev. 16.9. This verse speaks about the unbelieving people who do not convert to God, who inflicts plagues upon them, and do not give Him glory. In fact, they blaspheme God's name.

(3) Act. Phil. 63 (II.2, 26,13–14). People who have become believers are said to praise God and glorify Him. In Past. Herm. Sim. VI.3.6 and VIII.6.3 those who seize the opportunity offered once more for conversion glorify God. Sometimes we hear that the word of God is glorified at the conversion. See Acts 13.48; cf. 2 Thess 3.1. Glorifying God in misery as a sign of adherence to Him occurs many times in martyria. See, e.g., Dan. 3.26,51, 52–90 LXX and Theod.; Mart. Justini c.s. 6 rec. A and B: 'The holy martyrs glorifying God'; Mart. Agape c.s. 7.2: 'And the holy woman Irene, singing and glorifying God ...', cf. Acts 5.41 and Heb. 10.34.

For blaspheming God as a sign that one does not (want to) convert to Him, see Rev. 16.9 mentioned above, together with 16.11,21. It is also characteristic of gentiles. See Tob. 1.18 (MS S); Dan. 7.8,20, cf. 15 LXX; 2 Macc. 10.4,34; 12.14; Jos. *Ant.* 6.183. For blaspheming God as a sign of apostasy (i.e relapse into paganism), in T. Job abandoning conversion, see Past. Herm., Sim. IX.19.1: 'apostates and blasphemers against the Lord (and betrayers of the servants of God)'. See also Vis II.2.2: '... have set God at naught [ἠθέτησαν εἰς τὸν θεόν], and have blasphemed the Lord'.[76]

With the image of Job's suffering and his perseverance as a dangerous voyage to a city (18.6, 7) may be compared 4 Macc. 7.1−3, where the epilogue to the martyrdom of Eleazar declares that his reason as an excellent helmsman kept the ship of piety on a straight course on the sea of passions, with the storm of the threats of the tyrant around him and swamped by the threefold waves (τρικυμία, as in T. Job 18.7) of tortures, until it arrived in the harbour of the immortal victory[77] (in verses 4 and 5 other comparisons follow). This is stated as a demonstration of his ὑπομονή (and καρτερία) mentioned in 7.9, 22 and in 6.9, 13, where his martyrdom is related.

Stubbornness or toughness

For perseverance as stubbornness or toughness in the *pancration* with Satan most parallels are found in martyriological literature. In addition to the image of a *pancration* that of a man-to-man struggle (ἄθλησις) or of a fighting contest (ἀγών) in the arena is used, while the martyr is called 'athlete' (ἀθλήτης, cf. T. Job 4.10) or 'combatant, competitor' (ἀγωνιστής).

The word καρτερία κτλ. no longer plays an important part here, except in 4 Maccabees, where it occurs next to ὑπομονή κτλ. Furthermore it occurs only twice in martyria. See Mart. Apollonii 27 and Ep. Phileae 9. The word occurring most frequently here is ὑπομονή κτλ. See, e.g., Mart. Pol. and Mart. Lugd. (seven and twelve times respectively).

In the following texts Satan is not always mentioned, yet in the last resort it is he with whom the believer is fighting:

(1) Heb. 10.32−6: here the believers who are in danger of losing heart are reminded of the struggle of suffering they endured in earlier

---

[76] Ἀθετέω εἰς τὸν θεόν, literally to act faithlessly towards God: see Jer. 5.11 LXX, where it is connected with forsaking God, swearing by other gods (verse 7) and denying Him (verse 12). So it is another expression for abandoning God.

[77] Philo too makes use of this image, in connection with the combat of the wise man with the passions. See *Somn.* II.225, mentioned by Schaller, *Testament Hiobs*, 340, and *Sacr. AC* 90. For the opposite, with regard to people who are carried away by the passions see *Post. C.* 22 and *Deus Imm.* 98. See also E. Peterson, 'Die "Taufe" im Acherusischen See', in: *Frühkirche, Judentum und Gnosis* (Freiburg, Herder, 1959), 317−18, esp. his n. 29.

days (πολλὴν ἄθλησιν ὑπεμείνατε παθημάτων). With 'the better and more lasting possession' (heavenly salvation) (verse 34) compare the 'better things' that Job wants to inherit in T. Job 18.7. In verse 36 it is said to the believers that they need ὑπομονή. Through that they will win what God has promised (cf. T. Job 4.6–11; see also verse 35).

(2) For suffering as an athletic match or a contest in the arena in martyriological literature see, e.g., 4 Macc. 6.10; 9.23–4; 11.20; 12.14 (the martyrs as combatants of virtue); 16.16; 17.11–16; Mart. Carpi c.s. 35: 'like a noble athlete he received the angry onslaught of his adversary'; Mart. Lugd. 1.36: 'Surely it behoved these noble athletes, after sustaining [ὑπομείναντες] a brilliant contest and a glorious victory, to win the crown of immortality.'[78]

(3) In the contest the martyr wins by his tough or stubborn perseverance (T. Job 27.5). See 4 Macc. 1.11: 'having overcome the tyrant by ὑπομονή'; 16.14 (here καρτερία); cf. 9.18,30; 11.20–1; 11.24–5; 17.2; Mart. Pol. 19.2: 'By his perseverance [ὑπομονή] he overcame the unjust governor and so won the crown of immortality'; Mart. Lugd. 1.18: the martyr Blandina is filled with such power that those who torture her grow weary and exhausted (cf. T. Job 27.2 of Satan). They must admit that they are beaten (compare T. Job 27.5, where Satan admits this to Job); 1.36 (see above); 1.42: '... and had overcome the Adversary [Satan] in many contests ...'; Mart. Dasii 8.2: 'So now by this triple formula I confess my faith in the holy Trinity, for strengthened by it I can quickly conquer and overthrow the Devil's madness'; Mart. Agape c.s. 2.4: '... in order that thus by a short time in the fire they might overcome those that are devoted to fire, that is, the devil and all his heavenly host of demons, and, attaining the incorruptible crown of glory, they might endlessly praise along with the angels the God who had showered this grace upon them'.

(4) Just as in T. Job (see 4.10) the reward for stubborn perseverance is the receiving of the crown in God's glory, called 'incorruptible crown, crown of [eternal] life, unfading crown of glory' and the like (1 Cor. 9.25; Jas 1.12; 1 Pet. 5.4; Rev. 2.10, 3.11, 4.4, 10; also 'crown of righteousness', 2 Tim. 4.8). See in martyria 4 Macc. 17.15: 'piety won, crowning her athletes'; Mart. Pol. 19.2 (see above); Mart.

---

[78] See further V.C. Pfitzner, *Paul and the Agon Motif, Traditional Athletic Imagery in the Pauline Literature*, Suppl. Nov. Test., 16 (Leiden, Brill, 1967).

Matt. 4 (II.1, 221, 10–11): 'Your crown of perseverance' (ὑπομονή); Act. Phil. 144 (II.2, 86, 1): 'the eternal crown of victory'; Mart. Lugd. 1.36 (see above); 1.42: 'and through her contest was crowned with the incorruptible crown'; Mart. Agape c.s. 2.4 (see above); Act. Eupli 2.3: 'So it was that the blessed Euplus received the unfading crown from Christ our God.' For panegyrics (ἐγκώμια) as a reward (see T. Job 18.5) there are no parallels outside T. Job.

(5) For the resurrection from the dead as a reward for perseverance in suffering (see T. Job 4.9) we also find many examples in martyria. In addition to this, assumption or ascension to heaven immediately after death are mentioned. See, e.g., 2 Macc. 7.9, 14, 23, 29, 36; 4 Macc. 7.3, 19; 9.8: 'For by this suffering and by this perseverance [ὑπομονή] we will receive the prizes of virtue and we will be with God, for whose sake we suffer'; 13.17 etc.; Mart. Pol. 2.3; 14.2; Mart. Pauli 4 (I,112, 14–16); 5 (115, 6–7); 6 (116, 7–8); Pass. Andr. 7 (II.1,18,15–16); 11 (27, 18–19); Act. Justini c.s. 5.1 rec. A: the prefect asks Justinus: 'Do you believe that you will ascend to heaven?' Thereupon he replies: 'I have confidence from my perseverance [ὑπομονή], if I endure [ὑπομείνω]'; cf. rec. B; Mart. Lugd. 1.41 and 63; Mart. Pionii 21.4; Mart. Conon 6.4 etc.

(6) The particulars of Job's combat with Satan as a *pancration* show close resemblance with Philo, *Omn. Prob. Lib.* 24–6.[79] In this passage Philo speaks about the truly wise man who 'willingly and patiently endures [ἑκουσιῶς ἅμα καὶ τλητικῶς ἐγκαρτερῶν] the blows of fortune' (verse 24) and who 'will not obey just anyone who gives him orders, even though he menaces him with outrage and tortures and threats however dreadful' (verse 25). In verse 26 he compares him with the pancratiast:

> I have observed in a contest of pancratiasts how one of the combatants will strike blow after blow both with hands and feet, every one of them well aimed, and leave nothing undone that might secure his victory, and yet he will finally quit the arena without a crown [ἀστεφάνωτον] in a state of exhaustion and collapse [cf. T. Job 27.4], while the object of his attack ... will yield not a whit to the blows, but by his stark and stubborn endurance [τῷ καρτερικῷ καὶ παγίῳ

[79] F. H. Colson (ed. and transl.), *Philo*, IX (London, Cambridge, Massachusetts, Heinemann/Harvard, 4th reprint, 1967).

τῆς ὑπομονῆς] will break down utterly the strength of his adversary and end by winning a complete victory.

Patience

For perseverance as patience in temptation and trial the following texts may be compared:

(1) Sir. 2.1–18. Here the teacher says to a pupil who aspires to be a servant of the Lord (comparable with Job as a proselyte) that he must prepare himself for temptation and trial (πειρασμόν) (verse 1; cf. the preparation of Job for the coming suffering by the angel in T. Job 3–4), that he must make his heart straight (cf. verse 17) and have stamina (καρτερέω) (in the coming trial), and must not hasten (to give in) when it comes (verse 2). He must hold fast to the Lord and not desert Him (cf. Job's simplicity, his complete devotion to God as a condition for patience in T. Job 26.6), so that he finally grows up (verse 3), i.e. reaches the full measure of insight in God's nature (cf. T. Job 4.8, 11). Further he must accept and bear every hardship that is sent to him (δέξαι, cf. T. Job 26.4), and be patient (μακροθύμησον) in all vicissitudes of the humiliation that result from trial (verse 4). Cf. T. Job 26.5.

In verse 6 the pupil is summoned to trust the Lord and set his hope on Him (see: 'and He will help you'). The same is said in verse 7: 'You who fear the Lord, wait for his mercy' (ἔλεος). See also verses 9, 11 (18). The trust in God's mercy, pity and help is also characteristic for the patient Job (see T. Job 24.1 and 26.5). In verse 8 those who fear the Lord are encouraged to trust in Him, for then they will not miss their reward (cf. T. Job 4.6, 7 and 9, 10). In verse 10 the trust in God of the believer is strengthened by referring to the past generations, who trusted the Lord without being disappointed. In verses 12–14 the summons turns to a threefold 'woe' addressed to those who do not persevere. Verse 12 says: 'Woe to faint hearts (cf. the weakness of heart of Job's wife in T. Job 25.10) and nerveless hands and to the sinner who goes on two paths' (i.e. who is devoted not only to the Lord, but also to other gods and powers, the opposite of Job's simplicity), and verse 14: 'Woe to you who have given up perseverance' (ὑπομονή). For only perseverance makes a man trust in God in suffering. In the closing part of the summons in verses 15–18 again those who fear the Lord are addressed. Here all three words for perseverance occur as in T. Job, but only in the context of suffering as temptation and trial.

(2) Wis. 3.1–9. Here we find a description of the blessed portion of the pious, who on earth had much to suffer from the foolish and godless men. After their death their souls are in God's hand and torment will not touch them any more. The foolish and godless think they are dead and reckon their departure as defeat and disaster, but actually they are at peace (verses 1–3; here assumption to heaven occurs immediately after death as in martyria). In their misery their hope was full of immortality (verse 4) (cf. Job in T. Job 18, who in his misery hopes for the heavenly glory). By means of their misery God tried them (πειράζω) and thus after a little chastisement they received great blessings (i.e. the ascension to heaven after death) (verse 5). In the moment of their visitation (in the eschatological future) they will flame up and be like sparks that sweep through the stubble (the godless) (verse 7). Then they will judge the gentiles and rule over the nations (cf. Dan. 7.22) and the Lord will be their King for ever and ever (verse 8). And those who have put their trust in Him will understand the truth, i.e. the truth that He is the only true God (cf. T. Job 4.11), and attend upon Him, for grace and mercy will be for His elect (verse 9).

(3) Ps. Sol. 16. This is a psalm of thanksgiving of a pious man who nearly succumbed to a temptation, but was saved by God in his mercy (verses 1–5). His near fall was caused by his moving away from the Lord, the God of Israel (verse 3) (the opposite of simplicity). Therefore he prays to God that henceforth He will not remove his mercy from him, or his remembrance from his heart until his death (verse 6, comparable with simplicity).

In verses 10–14 the psalmist asks God to clothe his tongue and lips with truth, to put away from him wrath and unfounded anger (that express themselves via tongue and lips) and to remove from him murmuring (γογγυσμός) and pusillanimity ($\dot{\delta}$λιγοψυχία), when he chastises him as a correction (i.e. trial, see verse 14). He requests the Lord to support his soul with pleasure together with cheerfulness. For who will be able to endure chastisement in poverty, if the Lord does not strengthen him?

Speaking in wrath and unfounded anger is to be considered as directed to God: one shows that one does not accept one's suffering. The same applies to murmuring. Cf. T. Job 20.1, where it is said of Job that Satan is not able to provoke him to contempt for God, i.e. a contempt that receives expression in murmuring against God and cursing of Him. So here too murmuring against God is the typical sin, to which the believer may be driven by the severity of the temptation. It is caused by pusillanimity or discouragement,[80] comparable with the despondency (ἐκκακέω, T. Job 24.10) and melancholy, weariness or despair (ἀκηδία, T. Job 25.10) of Job's wife, who has given up patience.

The psalm ends with the statement (verse 15): 'When the just perseveres [ὑπομεῖναι] therein [in trial], God will show him his mercy.' Cf. T. Job 26.5.

(4) Just as Job is in T. Job so Joseph is a model of perseverance in the Testament of Joseph.[81] See 2.7, where Joseph says to his children and brothers: 'in ten temptations (πειρασμοῖς) He [God] showed that I was approved, and in all of them I was patient [ἐμακροθύμησα]; for patience is a mighty remedy, and endurance [ὑπομονή] gives many good things' (cf. T. Job 27.7). As in T. Job, μακροθυμία and ὑπομονή are largely synonymous.

Two examples of Joseph's temptations are given: the account of Joseph and the Egyptian woman (3.1–9.5 together with the paraenetical teaching in 10.1–4) and that of Joseph and his envious brothers (10.5–16.6 combined with the paraenetical teaching in 17.1–18.4).[82]

In the first story, in which Joseph's perseverance (and chastity) is demonstrated by his not giving in to the advances of the Egyptian woman, through which Satan besets him (see 7.4; cf. Job in T. Job), the patient Joseph continually prays to the Lord to be delivered from her. His prayer is accompanied by fasting (see 3.3, 4.3, 8, 7.4, 8.1, 9.4, 3.4, 5, 4.8; cf. 9.2. See the paraenetical teaching on 10.1: 'You

---

[80] For ὀλιγοψυχία as pusillanimity or discouragement see, e.g., Jdt 7.19 (being discouraged by the superior power of a surrounding army); 8.9 (being discouraged by lack of water); cf. Sir. 4.9. The word can also mean 'impatience/being impatient'. See, e.g., Num. 21.4; Judg. 16.16; Ex. 6.9.

[81] *The Testaments of the Twelve Patriarchs*, ed. M. de Jonge in cooperation with H. W. Hollander, H. J. de Jonge and Th. Korteweg, PsVTG, I, 2 (Leiden, Brill, 1978).

[82] For the two accounts as illustrations of Joseph's perseverance and patience and the division in the text, see H. W. Hollander, *Joseph as an Ethical Model in the Testaments of the Twelve Patriarchs* (Leiden, Brill, 1981), 16 and 39–49, and Hollander and de Jonge, *The Testaments*, 363–5.

see, therefore, my children, what great things endurance works, and prayer with fasting'). This is not said of Job; the only time he prays is in T. Job 40.2,3, but in a completely different context. Praying and fasting are to be considered as signs of Joseph's devotion to the Lord; cf. the simplicity of Job.

Further Joseph's weeping and his sadness are mentioned (3.6,9, 6.3, 8.1). Just like Job, Joseph is deeply distressed by what happens to him, but nevertheless does not give in. Next to Joseph's patience, his humility of heart is mentioned (10.2); cf. Sir. 2.17. Because of his patience Joseph is delivered from his misery by God like Job in T. Job. See 1.7, 9.5, 10.3 (also: being exalted and magnified).

In the second story Joseph shows his perseverance by keeping silent about his origin before those who bought him as a slave in order to save the reputation of his brothers (see 10.6, 11.2–3, 14.2, 15.3, 17.1). He does so out of respect and love for them (10.6, 11.1, 17.2), even though he must suffer much because of it. Joseph too does not 'sin' with his lips, but the background of it is completely different from that in T. Job (and Ps. Sal. 16).

In 18.1–4 Joseph relates how for patience's sake he was delivered by the Lord from the evil things that were done to him. The Lord exalted him and blessed him with good things for ever. For he took the daughter of his masters as his wife, and a hundred talents of gold were given him with her, and the Lord made them (i.e. his masters) his servants. Also the Lord gave him beauty and strength unto old age. Like Job Joseph receives in this life a reward for his patience (see T. Job 4.6,7).

(5) In Jub. 17.15–19.9[83] Abraham is the example of patience in temptation and trial. Like Job he is tried as a proselyte. This part of Jub. contains an account of the last two of the ten temptations of Abraham (see 19.8; cf. the ten temptations of Joseph in T. Jos. 2.7), i.e. the offering of his son Isaac (17.15–18.19) and the purchase of a burial place for Sarah (19.1–9). Seven of them, already past, are mentioned in 17.17. The eighth was probably Sarah's barrenness (14.21).[84] In 17.18 Abraham is characterized as follows: 'And in everything in which He tested him, he was found faithful. And his soul

[83] Jubilees, transl. O.S. Wintermute, Charlesworth (ed.), *The Old Testament Pseudepigrapha*, II, 35–142.
[84] See on this K. Berger, *Das Buch der Jubiläen*, JSHRZ, II, 3 (Gütersloh, Gütersloher, 1981), 418.

was not impatient. And he was not slow to act because he was faithful and a lover of the LORD.' Like Job Abraham is patient in his temptations and thus demonstrates the genuineness of his faith and love for God (cf. T. Job 5.1 MS V).

The introduction to the temptation of Abraham by means of the offering of Isaac (17.15, 16) resembles Job 1.8–11 and 2.4–5. After a voice in heaven has witnessed to Abraham's faith and love for God, Mastema (Satan) comes before God and suggests to Him that he order Abraham to offer up his son Isaac, whom he loves above all things. If Abraham obeys, then God will know whether he is truly faithful and is serious about his conversion.

In ch. 18 there follows the account of the offering of Isaac. This temptation too Abraham endures with patience. He does obediently what God has ordered. See verse 11, where the angel of the presence says to Abraham at the moment he is about to slaughter his son: 'Do not put forth your hand against the child and do not do anything to him because now I know that you are one who fears the LORD and you did not deny your firstborn son to me.' By Abraham's obedience and his patience, Mastema, who proposed this temptation, is ashamed like Satan by Job's patience (T. Job 27.6); see verse 12.

Just like Job in T. Job, Abraham receives an earthly reward because of his attitude in temptations: the Lord will surely bless him and multiply his seed and it will inherit the cities of their enemies (verse 15). And by his seed all nations of the earth will be blessed. Furthermore the Lord has made known his faithfulness to them (cf. T. Job 4.6) (verse 16).

In the last temptation, the purchase of a burial place for Sarah from the children of Heth near Hebron in spite of God's promise that He would give the land to him, Abraham likewise shows himself the true convert. See 19.3–4:

> And we [the angels of the presence] were testing him whether he would exercise self-control [K. Berger, *Jubiläen*: 'ob sein Geist geduldig sei']. And he was not impatient [Berger: 'unwillig' (resentful, angry), Lat: pusillanimus, cf. ὀλιγοψυχία in Ps. Sol. 16.11] with the words of his mouth and he was found self-controlled in this also and he was not filled with anxiety [Berger: 'und wurde nicht verwirrt'] because with the self-control of his spirit he spoke with the

> sons of Heth so that they might give him a place in which
> to bury his dead.

See also verses 8, 9:

> This [is] the tenth trial with which Abraham was tried. And
> he was found faithful, controlled of spirit [Berger:
> 'geduldigen Geistes']. And he did not say a word concerning
> the rumour which was in the land that the LORD said
> [Berger: 'Und er sagte kein Wort über die Rede von dem
> Land, von dem der Herr gesagt hatte'] he would give it to
> him and to his seed after him, but begged a place there so
> that he might bury his dead because he was found faithful
> and he was recorded as a friend of the LORD in the heavenly
> tablets.

Just like Job Abraham is patient and self-controlled; he shows this
by not speaking sinful words: though the Lord has promised him the
land, Abraham politely asks the children of Heth for a place in which
to bury his dead (verse 4) and pays forty silver pieces for it (verse 5),
though they were willing to give it to him free (verse 6), and there is
no impatient or angry word in his mouth.

So neither the convert Abraham nor the convert Job sins with his
lips. In T. Job the sinful words are addressed to God, here to men
(the children of Heth). In fact, however, the two reactions amount
to the same thing: both Job and Abraham show their trust in and
adherence to God in temptation in this way.

After having thus demonstrated his faith and patience, and
consequently the genuineness of his conversion, Abraham is recorded
as a 'friend of the Lord' in the heavenly tablets (verse 9). Likewise
the convert Job, after having persevered and been patient in all the
things he has gone through, is called by God his 'servant' (T. Job
42.5).

In T. Job 26.6 simplicity, the complete devotion to the Lord, is
the virtue that preserves Job from abandoning God to which Satan
tries to provoke him, and that gives him strength to persevere in
suffering. See for that also:

(1) Past. Herm. Vis. II.3.1–2: in a letter from heaven that Hermas
receives it is written that he has come to great afflictions of his own
because of the transgressions of his family, but that he will not perish

by it, for 'not having broken away [ἀποστῆναι] from the living
God saves you and your simplicity [plus: and great temperance].
These things have saved you [already], if you remain in them
and save all who ... walk in innocence and simplicity.' Here as
in T. Job simplicity is the power that enables one to be steadfast in trouble and suffering and preserves one from abandoning
God.

(2) If simplicity gives power to persevere, it is understandable
that the opposite attitude, that of being double-minded (διψυχέω,
cf. Sir. 2.12), encumbers it. See 2 Clem. 11.5, where double-minded-
ness is found as the opposite of perseverance: 'Therefore, my
brothers, let us not be double-minded, but let us be persevering'
(ὑπομείνωμεν). See also Past. Herm. Vis. II.2.7, where not being
double-minded is the same as remaining steadfast (ὑπομένω),
and Sim. IX.21.3, speaking about the double-minded who, when
they hear of affliction, become idolaters (a sign of apostasy) through
their cowardice and are ashamed of the name of their Lord. In
Jas 1.8, in a context of temptation, the double-minded man is
said to be unsteady in all his ways and consequently he has no
power to persevere.

The provenance of these conceptions

This investigation shows that the term 'perseverance' in T. Job
with its three aspects of standing firm, stubbornness or toughness,
and patience or enduring patiently, and the ideas of suffering
of the believer connected with it agree with or are closely affiliated
to Hellenistic-Jewish concepts, found in contexts describing the
suffering of the believers, on occasion especially the convert as
in T. Job (Jos. As. 12.9,10; Jub. 17.15–19.9) or someone with
a comparable status (Sir. 2.1–6). Here too suffering is not in-
frequently caused by the devil, either directly or indirectly. As
in T. Job it is either for God's sake (it can even end in death
as a martyr, cf. 4 Maccabees), or it is meant as temptation and
trial.

These concepts were adopted in Christian literature, especially
in martyria and other passages about the suffering of believers,
but in this investigation no elements have come out that are to
be considered as typically Christian. It confirms the opinion that

T. Job 'is essentially Jewish in character'.[85] There are no traces of
a special connection with a specific movement in contemporary
Judaism (Essenes or Therapeutae).[86]

It must be noted, however, that for the vision of Job in 3.1–
5.2a, in so far as it is a vision that prepares Job for his coming
suffering, I could as yet find parallels only in Christian martyria.
There it is the heavenly Lord Jesus, who appears to his apostles
and announces to them their coming suffering and here also death.
Like Job, they show their willingness to suffer, here by heading for
martyrdom, not fleeing away when they are arrested or abandoning
the preaching of the gospel that will be the cause of their coming
death. See:

(1) Mart. Petri 6 (I, 88, 5–12): Jesus appears to Peter, who is
     leaving Rome in order to escape his death by martyrdom.
     At this meeting Jesus makes clear to him that he must do
     his will and die for his sake in Rome. After that, Peter
     returns to the city joyful and glorifying the Lord.

(2) Mart. Andr. prius 8 (II.1, 50, 18–24): Jesus appears to
     Andrew and tells him to take up his cross and to follow
     him, for he who will throw him out of the world is hurrying.
     He waits for the outcome of this word of Jesus.

(3) Mart. Matt. (II.1, 217–62): Jesus appears to Matthew as a
     youth and speaks with him. At the end of ch. 4 (221, 9–11)
     he says to him: 'Hurry then, Matthew, and go away from
     here, for the departure of your body through fire is near
     and the crown of perseverance.' After that Matthew goes
     quickly to the town where he will meet his death (ch. 5). Cf.
     T. Job 4.10.

(4) Act. Petri et Andr. 2 (II.1, 117, 18–118, 8): Jesus Christ

[85] So Spittler, *Testament of Job*, 833. See also the opinion of Rahnenführer,
'Testament des Hiob', 77: 'Auch unsere Schrift entstammt dem hellenistischen
Judentum'; Kee, 'Satan', 55: 'thus it is highly probable that Test. Job was written
in Greek-speaking Jewish circles ...', Schaller, *Testament Hiobs*, 309: 'An der
jüdischen Herkunft des Testaments Hiobs kann daher kaum Zweifel bestehen.'

[86] See K. Kohler, 'The Testament of Job: An Essene Midrash on the Book of Job
Reedited and Translated with Introductory and Exegetical Notes', in *Semitic
Studies in Memory of A. Kohut*, ed. G. A. Kohut (Berlin, 1898); and M. Philonenko,
'Le Testament de Job et les Thérapeutes', *Semitica* 8 (1958), 41–53. See also
his *Testament de Job*, 15–16.

appears to both apostles in the figure of a youth and predicts to them that they will endure much hardship and oppression, after which they start with their work. A martyrdom is not immediately in sight here.

(5) The combination of the announcement of the coming suffering and death with a sealing of the martyr is found in the martyrdom of the saint and all-praiseworthy apostle Thomas (II.2, 290): the Lord appears to Thomas and announces to him his coming suffering and death. After that he seals him (line 9) and returns to heaven. Thomas instructs the people and is captured.

The coming suffering and death can also be announced in a different supernatural fashion. See:

(1) Acts 20.22–4: Paul knows through the Holy Spirit that imprisonment and hardships await him in Jerusalem and declares himself ready to give up his life for the Lord's sake, if need be.

(2) Mart. Pol. 5.2–7.3: Three days before he will be captured, Polycarp falls into a trance and sees his pillow being consumed by fire. Through that he realizes that he is to be burnt to death. He submits himself willingly to his arrest, though he had the chance to flee. See his statement in 7.2: 'May the will of God be done' (cf. Acts 21.14).[87]

---

[87] For the readiness of the martyr to suffer there are many parallels in Jewish and Christian martyria. See 2 Macc. 7.2 (cf. 4 Macc. 9.1), 5.23; Ps-Philo, LAB 6.4.11; Philo, *Leg. Gaj.* 209 and 308; Acts 20.24 and 21.13–14 (cf. 5.41 and Heb. 10.34); Mart. Pol. 7.1 (cf. 11.2); Mart. Lugd. 1.29: the old Photinus has an intense desire for martyrdom.

The readiness to suffer may express itself in assisting in one's own suffering, frequently by offering one's body to the tormentors or executors, or by hurrying to the place of execution. See 2 Macc. 6.19, 7.10 (cf. 4 Macc. 10.19); 4 Macc. 11.3; Mart. Pauli. 5 (I, 115, 16); Mart. Pionii 21.1. Comparable to Job's action in putting back the worms (T. Job 20.9) is that of the martyr Germanicus in Mart. Pol. 3.1, who in the arena drags a beast on top of him as a demonstration of his perseverance.

Sometimes the readiness to suffer goes so far that the execution is no longer waited for. See 4 Macc. 12.19: the last of the seven sons throws himself into the boiling pan that is prepared for him; Mart. Carpi c.s. 44: Agathonice throws herself joyfully upon the stake; Mart. Agape c.s. 7.2: the martyr Irene throws herself upon the pyre, singing and glorifying God.

The existence of only Christian parallels for Job's vision can be explained in two ways: either it points to Christian influence on this part of T. Job, or the vision is a Hellenistic-Jewish parallel to those found in the beginning of Christian martyria. The second assumption is most likely given the overall Jewish character of T. Job.[88]

[88] I wish to thank the Netherlands Organization for the Advancement of Pure Research (ZWO) that made it financially possible to visit the 42nd International Congress of the Studiorum Novi Testamenti Societas at Göttingen (24–8 August 1987).

INDEX OF PASSAGES

Mart. Pauli
  4, 5, 6, 144
  5, 153
Mart. Petr. et Pauli
  61, 140 n
Mart. Petri
  6, 152
Mart. Pionii
  21.1, 153 n
  21.4, 144
Mart. Pol.
  General, 142
  2.4, 140 n
  3.1, 153 n
  2.3, 144
  5.2–7.3, 153
  7.1, 153 n
  11.2, 153 n
  14.2, 144
  17.1, 140 n
  19.2, 143
Mart. Thomas
  General, 153
Pass. Andr.
  2, 119 n, 120 n
  7, 11, 144
Pass. Bart.
  1, 119 n
  7, 120 n
Pass. St Pauli Apost.
  7, 140 n
Past. Herm. Mand.
  II.1 and 7, 133 n
Past. Herm. Sim.
  VI.3.6, 141
  VIII.6.3, 141
  IX.21.3, 151
  IX.19.1, 141
Past. Herm. Vis.
  I.2.4, 133 n
  II.2.2, 141
  II.2.7, 151
  II.3.1–2, 150
  III.8.7, 133 n
Visio Pauli
  General, 8, 27

I Greek and Roman writers

Apuleius
  Met. 7.6.3, 97 n
Aristophanes
  Thesm. 830 f., 97 n
Eusebius
  Hist. eccl. V.17.1–4, 108
  Praep. evang. 9.25.3, 119 n
Gelasian Decree
  5.6.4, 7, 8, 12
  5.8.6, 7
Herodotus
  Hist. VI.96, 119
Homer
  Iliad 4.505, 123 n
  Iliad 6.107, 123 n
  Iliad 22.96, 123 n
Josephus
  Ant. 1.154–6, 119 n
  Ant. 1.157, 121 n
  Ant. 6.183, 141
  Bell. 6.37, 129
Lucian
  Alex. 12–13, 112
  Dial. meretr. 5.3, 97 n
Philo
  Abr. 70, 119 n
  Agric. 152, 126
  Agric. 97, 126 n
  Agric. 105, 126 n
  Cherub. 78, 118 n, 126 n
  Deus Imm. 13, 118 n, 126
  Deus Imm. 98, 142 n
  Leg. Gaj. 209, 153 n
  Leg. Gaj. 308, 153 n
  Omn. Prob. Lib. 24–6, 126, 144
  Omn. Prob. Lib. 24, 118 n
  Post. C. 22, 142
  Sacr. AC 90, 142
  Somn. I.120, 126
  Somn. II.225, 142
  Vit. Mos. I.25, 126 n
  Vit. Mos. I.181–7, 132 n
Tacitus
  Germ. 19, 97 n
Tertullian
  De patientia 14.5, 7, 108
  De patientia 13, 26

INDEX OF AUTHORS AND SUBJECTS